The Business of Charity

Women in American History

Series Editors

Mari Jo Buhle

Nancy A. Hewitt

Anne Firor Scott

Stephanie Shaw

*A list of books in the series
appears at the end
of this book.*

The Business of Charity

The Woman's Exchange Movement, 1832–1900

Kathleen Waters Sander

University of Illinois Press

Urbana and Chicago

© 1998 by the Board of Trustees of the University of Illinois
Manufactured in the United States of America
1 2 3 4 5 C P 5 4 3 2 1

This book is printed on acid-free paper.

Library of Congress Cataloging-in-Publication Data
Sander, Kathleen Waters, 1947–
The business of charity : the woman's exchange movement,
1832–1900 / Kathleen Waters Sander.
p.   cm. — (Women in American history)
Includes bibliographical references (p.   ) and index.
ISBN 0-252-02401-X (acid-free paper). —
ISBN 0-252-06703-7 (pbk. : acid-free paper)
1. Women's exchanges—United States—History.
2. Women—Employment—United States—History.
I. Title. II. Series.
HD6076.S26 1998
381'.1—dc21   97-45249
CIP

For John and Libby,
with love and appreciation

Contents

Acknowledgments ix

Introduction: From Ladies to Working Women 1

Part 1
The Antebellum Exchanges: The Idea Begins

1. "To Win for Themselves That Blessed Independence": Countering the Stigma of Paid Work 11

2. "One of the Most Attractive Shops on the Street": Making Self-Help Fashionable for the Genteel Poor 26

Part 2
The Postbellum Exchanges: A New Era, a New Model

3. "The Time Was Ripe for a Change": Self-Improvement and Economic Security for All Women 41

4. A "Prosperous Existence in Every Town": The Exchange Idea Spreads throughout the Nation 60

Part 3
Postbellum Managers and Consignors:
"To Engage in Some Useful, Creative Occupation"

5. "We Sell Everything Good, from a Pickle to a Portiere": Exchange Managers as Entrepreneurs 79

6. "An Excellent Way to Earn an Income": The Consignors' Alternative to the Industrial Workplace 101

Epilogue: The Exchange Movement Continues   115

Appendixes
A. Tables   121
B. The Woman's Exchange of Cincinnati   127
Notes   131
Index   159

Illustrations follow pages 38 and 100

Acknowledgments

Anyone who has ever shopped or lunched at a Woman's Exchange will more than likely recall with fondness its special magic. I was fortunate enough to learn that many years ago. Growing up in Cincinnati in the 1950s and 1960s, I remember well the elegant Woman's Exchange on Fourth Street, right in the heart of the busy downtown shopping area. For decades, news of the Exchange, its fashionable patrons, and "lady managers" filled the society pages of the Cincinnati newspapers. At a time when mothers still dressed young daughters in white gloves and prim hats for shopping excursions into town, the Exchange was *the* place to lunch on Saturdays. But on my visits, when leaving the Exchange after a tasty meal, I always wondered why such a stylish restaurant also displayed cases of clothing and other eye-catching items. Thirty years later and a scholarly journey away, I was to discover the answer. Delving into the records of the Cincinnati Exchange, and many others as well, gave me a special opportunity to once again connect with my hometown and many fond memories.

Bringing to life the story of the Woman's Exchanges—a movement that has not only a grand history but also is alive and thriving—would not have been possible without the enthusiastic support of many friends and colleagues. This research began as a doctoral dissertation, completed in 1994, at the University of Maryland College Park under the expert guidance of Hasia R. Diner, friend and mentor, who never failed to smooth the rough spots so familiar to any student first venturing into historical research. She was immensely supportive of the project from the start and always on hand with an encouraging word to dig just a little deeper to find that elusive but essential bit of information needed to tie the study together. Of great help on the dissertation committee were Robert F. Carbone, R. Gordon Kelly, Robyn Muncy, and Jo Paoletti, who each provided knowledge unique to his or her specialization in the study of American cultural history.

I am grateful to the fine editorial staff of the University of Illinois Press, who patiently and generously helped transform the dissertation into a book. Karen

Hewitt, senior editor, greeted the project with warmth and enthusiasm and provided much-needed cheerfulness, comfort, and expertise. Anne Firor Scott and Mari Jo Buhle were each enormously helpful and greatly enriched the study with their scholarly input and suggestions. I greatly appreciate their confidence in my research. My gratitude also goes to Mary Giles, a skilled and thoughtful copy editor, who carefully tied together many loose ends and helped to bring the manuscript to its final form.

I thank the many current Exchange managers and officers for their tireless efforts in keeping the Exchange movement prospering after more than a century through a network of nearly thirty Exchanges nationwide and in providing valuable firsthand assistance throughout this project. It has been a great honor to write about a subject that holds such a special place in the hearts of so many. My thanks go to Anne Owen, president of the Federation of Woman's Exchanges, and Ann Uhlhorn and Kris Sammons, past presidents of the Federation, who over the years offered their resources and institutional knowledge of the Exchange movement. I extend appreciation as well to other women currently working in the Exchanges who helped to uncover hard to find information not readily available through conventional sources: Manie Van Doren, president, and Catherine Dinehardt, former executive director, of the New York Exchange; Jacque Thieme, manager, and Julia Lawnin Gordon, grandaughter of the founder, of the St. Louis Exchange; and Rita Knox, former manager, Diane H. Coleman, executive director, and the late Irene Kirby, former president, of the Baltimore Exchange.

As any historical researcher knows, reference librarians are a special breed of humanity. My great appreciation goes to the many librarians and archivists in various cities who made long-distance research a little easier, particularly, Anne Shepherd of the Cincinnati Historical Society, and those librarians of the Library Company in Philadelphia, the Valentine Museum in Richmond, Virginia, the Library of Congress, and the Historical Societies of Pennsylvania, Virginia, Milwaukee County, and Western Pennsylvania, among others, who eagerly helped to track down "just one more" tidbit of obscure—but vital—information. My thanks also go to Mary Goljenboom, who was with me from the start, helping to uncover photographs and illustrations to complement the study.

We can all turn to the earlier influences in our lives, those remarkable people who help to turn dreams into reality. My late parents, Nelda Usinger Waters and Edgar W. Waters, instilled the value of perseverance and "stick-to-it-ness," traits not fully appreciated until attempting to complete this decade-long project. To my mother, who graduated from college at the age of sixty-four, I extend special thanks for showing firsthand the importance of life-long learning. I also appreciate the financial support offered through a bequest from my late aunt, Vivian Inez Waters of Pensacola, Florida, whose generosity made possible the full-time research and writing in the early years of this study. As a home economist, Vivian spent her career teaching vocational skills to women in the United States and abroad through her work with the Farm Security Administration and the United Nations Relief and Rehabilitation Administration. I know that she would have approved of supporting a study of women's attempts to gain economic security through their domestic skills and initiatives.

Most important, I extend an enormous debt of gratitude to my life-support system. My husband, John, lived through countless moments of anxiety and elation, eagerly shared with me long-lost ledger sheets and records of nineteenth-century Exchanges, and enthusiastically supported my research every step of the way. And my daughter, Libby, an insightful student of history at Bryn Mawr College, is already learning the great contributions women have made to American culture and how much of their story remains to be told.

Introduction:
From Ladies to Working Women

Looking back on her unrelenting crusade to help women gain financial security through their domestic and artistic skills, Candace Wheeler, co-founder of the New York Exchange for Woman's Work in 1878, recounted one moment that captured the essence of her labors. At a luncheon attended by women who were arts entrepreneurs, philanthropists, and writers and others who had joined her efforts over the years, Elizabeth (Libbie) Custer, widow of the "Boy General," George Armstrong Custer, looked around the room and earnestly exclaimed, "Why, we are all working women, not a lady among us!"[1]

Custer's enthusiastic comment might have startled the founders of the first Woman's Exchange, Elizabeth Stott, a wealthy Philadelphian, and her sixteen "benevolent associates" who started the Philadelphia Ladies' Depository Association in 1832 to help formerly wealthy women support themselves in times of financial stringency. Far from openly celebrating a woman's working status, as Custer would do a half-century later, the founders' objective was to discreetly help gentlewomen avoid public disapproval. These "ladies," as they would have described themselves, had the idea of helping other ladies use their skills in embroidery, sewing, and fancy work as a means of earning money. Drawing on the long tradition of American women's voluntary benevolence, and based on a particular charitable model of self-help borrowed from Europe, they set up a shop to accept women's consigned items to sell to other women who could afford some household luxuries. In the decades before the Civil War, the beneficiaries, or consignors, of the Depository were exclusively the "genteel poor" who needed to earn income but felt uncertain or inadequate about jobs in business or industry. Well-to-do women were, in theory, to be supported by fathers, husbands, or sons; it was not quite respectable to "go out" to work. Producing needlework at home and stealthily selling it at the Depository could be seen as appropriate behavior and a way to save face while making money.

For their first four decades the Exchanges—known in the antebellum years as Depositories—remained static and class-bound. But the alluring decorative arts displays at the 1876 Philadelphia Centennial Exhibition proved to be a watershed. Soon after the Exhibition, Candace Wheeler and Mary Choate, a New York socialite, hoping to combine women's traditional work in decorative and domestic arts with practical, marketable employment skills, established the New York Exchange for Woman's Work.

The newer, postbellum Exchange model was immediately successful and moved swiftly across the country in the last two decades of the nineteenth century; the idea of self-help had been adapted to assist *all* women—rich or poor—to reach the goal of financial security. Women in more than seventy cities as culturally and geographically diverse as San Diego, Detroit, Little Rock, Topeka, and New Orleans quickly spread the idea through a well-connected national network of voluntary organizations, essentially forming franchises to replicate marketplaces to sell merchandise at a reasonable profit. In postbellum Exchanges, not only "decayed gentlewomen" in need of income but also working- and middle-class women could earn money, learn a vocational skill, and, above all, as the managers of the Cincinnati Woman's Exchange emphasized, "keep what is dear to every true woman, her self-respect."[2]

By the closing decades of the nineteenth century, Exchanges were both popular shops and gathering spots for wealthy patrons in cities across the country. But Exchanges served a valuable purpose beyond providing copy for the society pages of local newspapers. They created employment opportunities and helped thousands of women earn the income that often meant the difference between poverty and a respectable livelihood. For consignors—sometimes as many as sixteen thousand a year nationwide—Exchanges offered alternative economic employment to those who needed income but chose not to work in the commercial workplace. Consignors could become entrepreneurial by producing and marketing handmade merchandise through an Exchange and often branching out on their own as self-employed businesswomen. From 1878 through 1891 the nine largest of the country's Exchanges paid nearly $1.2 million in commissions to consignors.[3] Exchanges had become such an economic force that Lucy Salmon, a Vassar College historian, noted that the movement "has already had an appreciable effect on economic conditions" and "thus assumes a not unimportant place in the history of women's occupations."[4]

Consignors profited by selling their merchandise at an Exchange, and well-to-do women—the managers who organized and ran Exchanges—also benefited. The Exchange, a variation on ancient practices of benevolence, was a visible way of doing good, and operating one allowed managers to exercise administrative and entrepreneurial skills in a commercial venture, something that as women of the upper class they might be reluctant to try on their own. Managers learned successful commercial techniques by trial and error and became good at running their shops. Exchanges provided quasi-careers in entrepreneurial philanthropy, offering managers a sense of personal fulfillment and leadership as well as visible public roles as business executives. Their work allowed them to break free of cultural limitations and subtly mock propriety. They undertook creative approaches in running their enterprises and staying competitive in the rags-to-riches world of Gilded Age consumerism, constantly adapting to cultural and economic changes to keep the enterprises viable. They also raised public consciousness about working conditions and the exploitation of wage-earning women as well as the need for all women to have vocational skills and a source of income.

Exchanges blurred the lines between the commercial and voluntary sectors and allowed the women involved to participate freely in business activities that otherwise would have been limited. All proudly became "working women," either as consignors earning income or as managers running fashionable shops in their communities.

Woman's Exchanges represent one of the oldest continuously operating, voluntary movements in the United States. Many of the seventy-two or more Exchanges formed in the nineteenth century are still flourishing, including those in Baltimore, Boston, St. Augustine, New York City, New Orleans, Philadelphia, St. Louis, West Hartford, and Brooklyn. That Exchange managers and consignors would find a sense of social and economic empowerment through philanthropy is not surprising. The myriad voluntary organizations that women formed throughout the nineteenth century were perhaps the greatest tool they could employ to wield power and push beyond limited societal boundaries.

Women's voluntarism was not a marginal contribution to America's cultural history but was an integral component of that history. Since the beginning of the Republic, American women created strong, separatist voluntary associations to advance political and social opportunities for themselves and to address unmet needs for the less fortunate in their communities. By the time the Exchange movement started in the 1830s, women's voluntarism already had effected important social and political changes, such as ameliorating poverty and homelessness and initiating schools, libraries, and orphanages in communities across the fledgling nation. The Woman's Exchange idea, as it accelerated during the course of the nineteenth century, provided still another important tool—an economic one—to gain self-control and counter forces that worked to women's economic disadvantage. Exchanges, which combined such seemingly diametrically opposed elements as charity, commerce, domestic and decorative arts, and cooperation, operated within a separate economic system, the voluntary sector, and provided a source of economic and social empower-ment to all classes of women involved.

Examining the Exchange movement makes it possible to question—and an-swer—many aspects of nineteenth-century women's lives. Why, for example, did well-to-do women, who seemingly had the greatest stake in society and enjoyed the most financial security, form vast networks of like-minded peers across the country to create organizations like Woman's Exchanges that countered domi-nant economic institutions? Close study of the development and the history of Exchanges illuminates the cultural and economic factors that converged to make women respond to such negative forces. Those who occupied the upper eche-lons of society—the founders and managers of Exchanges—did not feel unequiv-ocally secure. They, too, felt legally, economically, and politically marginalized by society. The elite founders of the first Exchange, the Philadelphia Ladies' Depository, were acutely aware of how quickly the erratic antebellum economy could place them into poverty. "Who can say, in these difficult times," they wrote as the Panic of 1837 lingered well into 1840, "when poverty follows so rapidly in the footsteps of wealth, that a similar lot will not be their own?"[5] There is no rea-son to believe that well-to-do women did not feel financially vulnerable in the uncertain economy of the nineteenth century and take steps to rectify their own situation and that of other women. Women's involvement in controversial move-ments such as temperance and abolition, and later the settlement house move-ment, proved how aggressively they could attack what they perceived as social injustices. Woman's Exchanges also offer evidence of an eagerness to mitigate if not correct economic disadvantages.

Although women who managed Exchanges used a conservative approach to financial security by promoting domestic vocations and homework for con-signors—work traditionally considered to reinforce women's circumscribed sphere—they increasingly masculinized their voluntarism by emulating the commercial world. Such efforts might be interpreted as a bold foray into the public sphere of the male-dominated business world. Despite their compro-mising approach to solving the dilemma of women's financial independence by encouraging domestic arts, they changed the lines of gender identification by using masculine entrepreneurial methods within the context of feminine charitable activities. Exchange managers, steeped in the tradition of benevo-lence, combined entrepreneurial skill with philanthropic ideologies of self-help to form commercial enterprises. Although critics such as Lucy Salmon fault-ed the Exchange for not being a true "business house," managers made every effort to emulate many of the merchandising practices of the commercial gi-ants around them and to build a parallel employment system by giving cred-ibility to their organizations as business enterprises. They worked diligently to convince not only the public but also, and more important, the consignors of the Exchanges' value as reputable and viable businesses. "It is the desire of the managers that the consignors should not look upon the Exchange as a *charity,* but as a business medium," the Cincinnati Exchange managers emphasized in 1889.[6]

Until the era of women's studies, women's lives were usually described by others' documentation and descriptions, through popular literature, from religious sermons, in medical journals, and in occasional references in prominent men's journals. But such documents have not revealed the full richness of women's lives; in fact, such sources have for too long relied on stereotypes and minimized the contributions women made. Contemporary scholars, however, have sought new methodologies to examine the everyday lives of nineteenth-century women—how they perceived and implemented their roles in society, how they reacted to the forces around them, how they developed relationships to each other and within their communities, and how they influenced and shaped American culture.

The history of the Exchange movement is meant to be such a story of how everyday women were motivated to take action against economic and cultural conditions that thwarted them. Exchange records contain a wealth of information about nineteenth-century women and American culture, particularly about how women created counter economic solutions outside of mainstream capitalism to achieve financial goals and change their lives. The records describe women's attempts to turn societal limitations to their economic advantage and to question passive acquiescence to unjust economic and social forces. The records also reveal the disparity between popular rhetoric and the reality of women's lives—the image of a well-protected, contented woman, as opposed to the all-too-sudden reality of joblessness, poverty, and, for the wealthy, idleness and boredom. Exchange records bring to life some of the hopes and despairs of women across the country in the nineteenth century.

There is little doubt that Exchange founders and managers wanted to leave their mark in historical archives. They left behind abundant documentation: beautifully published annual reports, meticulous treasurers' accounts, sales catalogs, and carefully crafted meeting minutes. Happily, newspapers aided their cause through copious stories about local Exchanges and their quaint merchandise, successful consignors, and fashionable managers and patrons. All attest to Exchange women's belief in their mission and their seriousness to archive their activities for posterity. The records also show that Exchange women, despite geographical and cultural distances, shared a common goal and determination in their entrepreneurial philanthropies and had far more similarities than differences.

Aside from the rich and detailed documents recorded by Exchange managers, publisher Frank Asa Lincoln of Massachusetts in 1891 compiled the only known compendium and history of the Woman's Exchange movement in the nineteenth century. In his *Directory of Exchanges for Woman's Work: With Methods for Dealing Them,* Lincoln provided a treasure trove of information about the seventy-two Exchanges that existed at the time of publication. Information contained in the *Directory* is accurately corroborated through records of individual Exchanges. Of the *Directory,* Lincoln wrote, "It is the first and only one that has attempted to give women the opportunity of knowing how important and extensive is the work of the Woman's Exchanges."[7] The *Directory,* along with newspapers, periodicals, and commentators' observations, enriches our understanding of the Exchange movement throughout the nineteenth century.

Some of the historical record might not have pleased the managers. Exchanges generated many jokes in the late-nineteenth-century popular press; the very term *Woman's Exchange* in itself inspired numerous puns. Ruth McEnery Stuart's 1893 parody of the Exchange movement tells of an old farmer who came into the Simpkinsville Exchange hoping to "exchange" his wife: "I heerd th' was a woman's exchange over here, an' I come to see if I couldn't change off my ol' 'oman."[8] Similarly, the minutes of the Richmond Exchange refer to a newspaper article that related a similar story about a (real-life) farmer who came to town in hope of exchanging his wife. *Life* magazine provided yet another take on the joke in 1899 in a two-page cartoon, "The Husband of a Strong-Minded Woman," that showed a timid-looking man and his formidable wife. The husband, arms folded in disgust, asks: "Where did you say the Woman's Exchange was? I've something I'd like to swap."[9]

But the story of the Woman's Exchange movement, told from the perspective of the founders and managers, is one-sided. The voice of the consignors, who always remained anonymous, is unheard. "Our lips are sealed upon that subject [the identity of the consignors]," the managers of the Philadelphia Ladies' Depository emphasized.[10] The identities of consignors and their satisfaction with being affiliated with Exchanges must be surmised through managers' financial records and rhetoric.

As Lincoln pointed out, "Each Woman's Exchange has a history peculiarly its own and each, if the successes and failures could be read on the pages of recorded history, would unfold a varied experience."[11] This study examines the varied, revealing experiences of several nineteenth-century Exchanges, the evolution of the Woman's Exchange movement during the first and second halves of the nineteenth century, and the impact Exchanges made in the lives of the women involved. It explores how the transformation in the mission of the movement over the century reflected changing attitudes about women's work issues, as well as how women increasingly harnessed the untapped potential of the voluntary sector for employment opportunities.

Part 1 explores the original Exchange founders' vision of their new commercial enterprise and the specific cultural and economic influences that converged during the early years of industrialism before the Civil War to prompt them to find economic alternatives for genteel poor women. It also offers a case study of the first Exchange, the Philadelphia Ladies' Depository, whose trailblazing managers nurtured early entrepreneurial efforts to protect "decayed gentlewomen" from the mainstream workplace and promote financial security for women, an idea not fully acceptable at the time.

Part 2 examines the charitable nature of postbellum Exchanges and the forces of the 1870s and 1880s that fueled their quick expansion through a vast national voluntary network. Well-to-do women across the country, influenced by the decorative arts movement, self-improvement, and self-help, expanded the original Exchange philosophy by helping women of all classes gain financial security by capitalizing on what they produced in their homes.

Part 3 investigates the commercial side of the postbellum Exchanges' dual personality and the ways in which different populations of women, both the wealthy managers and middle- and working-class consignors, found personal and professional fulfillment through being affiliated with Exchanges. Their combined efforts made postbellum Exchanges successful businesses that mirrored the retailing world and were parallel to, yet contingent upon, the mainstream commercial sector.

The following account throws light on the changing self-image of American women and how they responded to rapid social changes in the concept of "woman's sphere." The growth and popularity of the Exchange movement over the course of the nineteenth century testifies to many changes in cultural expectations for women and shows how they used unconventional channels to leverage such expectations—and limitations—to their economic advantage. The Woman's Exchange story is as much about the change in women's lives over the decades as it is about the development of an innovative system of benevolence that offered economic alternatives for those who quested for financial security and self-expression through voluntary associations. It is the story of how the women who made the Exchange movement successful joined Libbie Custer's passionate call to no longer be called ladies but rather working women engaged, as the *New York Evangelist* noted on September 28, 1882, in "some useful, creative occupation."

Part 1

The Antebellum Exchanges: The Idea Begins

I

"To Win for Themselves That Blessed Independence": Countering the Stigma of Paid Work

Although fortified with an indomitable charitable impulse and an unswerving sense of moral purpose, the seventeen wealthy founders of the first Woman's Exchange, the Philadelphia Ladies' Depository, nonetheless felt the need for divine intervention to launch their new commercial venture in February 1832. "Believing it [the Depository] to be founded on the principles in strict accordance with the Divine precepts," they noted, "[we] trust the blessing of Heaven will attend future efforts and crown them with abundant success."[1]

Help from a higher authority might well have been in order, for the founders faced seemingly overwhelming odds when they opened their charitable consignment shop for business. Women who enjoyed the city's greatest wealth and highest social status were venturing into uncharted territory by collectively opening a retail shop based on voluntary principles, an activity that would have been socially off-limits for them to attempt individually in the commercial sphere. They sought to tear down the cultural and economic barriers that prevented "decayed gentlewomen"—their peers who had met with financial misfortune—from earning a livelihood that would save them from abject poverty. Hoping to diminish the sense of shame such women experienced when seeking honest labor in times of financial reversal, they wanted to ease the "unworthy feeling which leads women to look upon their own courageous labors as derogatory to their former positions," although it was more of an "imaginary stigma, which the prejudices of friends and relatives attached to woman's labors, than the actual sting of poverty."[2] Nonetheless, the sudden loss of family income must have been terrifying for women, and the founders envisioned providing a discreet work alternative to protect peers from the "rough and unkind treatment to which they are frequently exposed in their efforts to obtain employment."[3]

The founders did not need to look far beyond their own sheltered enclave in Philadelphia's fashionable Girard Row area to understand just how rough and unkind the treatment could be for any woman suddenly confronted with the loss of family income and forced to earn a living in antebellum America.[4] Formidable cultural restrictions, minimal employment options, and the many workplace perils all made work a menace for formerly wealthy women whose financial plight, Depository founders professed, was "augmented by a natural feeling of delicacy."[5]

The popular press of the day reinforced fears of the consequences of sudden impoverishment and uncertain employment. As Horace Greeley observed:

> Many who dance in jewels one year are shivering in garrets the next. It was but a week ago that a respectable woman, reduced from competence to poverty by sudden calamity, traversed the streets of our city for two or three days in search of some employment by which she could earn bread for herself and her children. Finding homework as a seamstress, she worked for a week and was first given only "credit"; with this she was to return to her desolate, destitute home. Such scenes are occurring daily in our city and all cities; [they are] willing to labor for the humblest fare, yet unable by labor to procure it.[6]

Another New York chronicler of nineteenth-century urban life noted wryly that women in the industrial workplace had far more to fear than humble fare. There were "many men who make it a business to ruin females who are obliged to work for a living. The employers do it; the male employees, the *roués,* the sporting men, the fast men and the accomplished villains. In the upper part of the city there is a large manufactory where many females are employed. They get small pay, as may be naturally assumed, and have to work very hard, which no one will doubt. The proprietor of the factory is a married man. In the course of two years, he has ruined three beautiful and promising young women."[7]

To protect their peers from such possible ruin in the workplace, the founders hoped to create a new kind of charity that offered "safer" work experiences. Most antebellum charities established by the wealthy operated under a sense of noblesse oblige and helped the chronically poor: destitute widows, families of unemployed breadwinners, and the "other" working poor who were born into poverty and by all expectations would maintain that status throughout their lives. Founders of the first Depositories in Philadelphia and New Brunswick in 1856, however, hoped to "reach a class the usual charities could not assist as effectually—the gentlewoman of limited means, a class including thousands who have seen better days."[8] These women had been "reared in delicacy and disqualified for labor in a more public sphere."[9] Consignors, who would make their needlework—sewing and embroidery—at home and sell it at the Exchange, would include women of old wealth who had met with financial hardship and those women whose families had reached the upper echelon of the new antebellum mercantile wealth before becoming financially tenuous as a result of the unpredictable early-industrial economy. The Depository would also serve as a means of support for widows of well-to-do men and wives and daughters of prominent families that had met reversals of fortune. All would be helped in their efforts "to win for themselves that blessed independence."[10]

In charity work, this classification of the poor—those women "who have had means and are suddenly thrown upon their own resources for their own support"—had not been widely recognized.[11] By the 1830s, however, genteel poor women had become increasingly visible in urban areas. Unconstant economic conditions produced a growing but unstable mercantile class, a fact that Depository founders—who became managers—recognized when they wrote, "in a city like Philadelphia, with its vast populations and unnumbered enterprises, reverses of fortunes must frequently occur and by none are they more sadly felt than by amiable hapless females who are suddenly reduced to poverty."[12]

By the early decades of wage-earning industrialism the despair of the "amiable hapless female" left to her own resources to earn a living moved from whispered conversation in parlors to more public debate. Alice Hyneman Rhine recalled that during the antebellum years the "helplessness, the misery, the degradation of womanhood, laboring and starving on beggarly wages in rich and prosperous cities, arrested the attention of the thinking class to woman's needs as it has never been arrested before. How to help woman to better her condition became the burning issue of the day."[13]

But the calls for women's financial independence did not reach the highest levels of industry. The onus of responsibility to improve working conditions or find alternatives to them fell instead on women themselves. In 1830 the Rev. James Gray of the Philadelphia Female Academy implored graduates not to limit their interests to "promoting the polish of social manners that contribute largely to the amount of social pleasures." Instead, he instructed them to "pour balm into the wounds of bleeding humanity, to still the storm of social passions and to impart popularity and confidence to virtue through your example."[14] Similarly, Mathew Carey, a Philadelphia entrepreneur, philanthropist, and social commentator, in 1829 castigated the "influential ladies of our great cities" for "being highly culpable for their neglect" of the plight of the woman forced to earn income. Carey recommended one solution that proved to be particularly prophetic of the Woman's Exchange idea: "Let ladies form associations in order to have some of the poor women, who are half-starved making coarse shirts at 6, 8, and 10 cents each, taught fine needlework, mantua-making, millinery, clean starching, quilting, etc. There is always great want of women in these branches."[15]

There is no way to know whether the founders of the first Woman's Exchange responded directly to the Reverend Gray's or Mathew Carey's recommendations when they initiated the Philadelphia Ladies' Depository in 1832. But as Carey observed, the effort of keeping genteel poor women from charity's doors and offering them a safe, discreet, and acceptable means of earning income at a time when options were few was left to the "influential ladies." The solution fell not under the domain of the captains of industry but rather to women of means, who presumably could use their influence and social standing to establish such an enterprise. "To Crown the whole," Carey pleaded, "let ladies who lead the fashion take up the cause of these poor women. It is a holy cause."[16] It was a cause met—and fulfilled in part—through the voluntary actions of the founders of the Philadelphia Ladies' Depository.

"An Angel's Inspiration"

The founding of the first Exchange, Lincoln observed, represented "an angel's inspiration to save the decayed gentlewoman."[17] In reality, the Exchange idea had far more earthly beginnings in Scotland.[18] Creating a charitable consignment shop exclusively for genteel poor women may have been an untested plan in the United States in 1832, but Americans often fashioned their charities on European ideas of philanthropy, and a well-established charitable self-help template for needy gentlewomen did exist in Europe. Elizabeth Stott had gone to Scotland in 1831 and visited the successful Edinburgh Depository. There she saw for sale the handiwork of poverty-stricken Scottish gentlewomen, once the beneficiaries but now the victims of early-nineteenth-century industrialism. The hybrid charity–retail store initiated by fashionable Scottish benevolent women provided a discreet outlet for the sale of needlework and had likely evolved from the English and Scottish idea of women's bazaars and "Fancy Fairs," popular and fashionable vehicles for charitable fund-raising. Often, a bazaar was a grandiose event lasting for days and netting much-needed income to fill the charity's coffers. By the 1820s benevolent women in Scotland, including the founders of the Edinburgh Depository, had created an interesting variation of the bazaar by establishing permanent retail shops around Great Britain.

One day, a year after her visit to Scotland, Stott witnessed an impoverished gentlewoman trying to sell embroidery to a Philadelphia merchant. Such a practice was common in the early years of industrialism, when women in need of income would quietly wholesale home-produced items to shopkeepers. The "merchant refused to purchase a piece of fine needlework from a woman who asked a ridiculously low figure. [Stott] questioned the woman and learned that she was the widowed mother of four young children, whom she was unwilling to place in an institution. The mother exhibited some hand-embroidered pieces of needlework worth possibly treble the amount she asked of the merchant. [Stott] afterward learned such a sad condition existed to quite an extent." Stott acted immediately. An account of the Depository's founding revealed that "the charitable woman [Stott] assembled some of her friends one day to discuss the matter. She recited to them the incident of the poor woman and suggested that they organize a society along the lines similar to the association [she] had seen in Edinburgh."[19]

For her efforts, Elizabeth Stott was to be remembered as a "kind, generous-minded woman of culture and refinement . . . who labored so earnestly to arouse in the community an interest in the hard and often bitter struggle to which educated and refined women are so frequently exposed when financial reverses compel them to rely upon their own exertions for support."[20]

The sixteen women who responded to Stott's call to action in 1832 represented Philadelphia families that had enjoyed great wealth and status since before the Revolutionary War and had intermarried for generations to secure wealth and social standing. Listed as founders in the first annual report were: Mrs. Joshua Lippincott, Mary Hazlehurst, Mrs. John Sergeant, Mrs. Richard Alsop, Mrs. John Markoe, Mrs. J. Browne Smith, Amelia Davidson, Mrs. Stephen Simmons, Rebecca Chester, Mrs. Dr. Harlan, Mrs. Lewis Clapier, Janet Colquhoun, Mrs. James Coleman, and the Misses Clapier, Keppele, and Montmollin. Many of the women had for several years waged a battle for better working conditions for wage-earning women. On January 13, 1829, six who would eventually found the Depository had joined several other prominent Philadelphia women in petitioning the secretary of war about the exploitive and demeaning working conditions women encountered as outworkers and laborers in the industrial workplace.[21] Among other outrages, the petitioners wrote that "the extreme distress produced by low wages too frequently reduces them [working women] to the degradation of pauperism, from which it is difficult to arise."[22]

By 1832 the six women and Stott had established the Philadelphia Ladies' Depository. There, genteel poor women, instead of selling their handiwork to merchants at a pittance, would profit by selling their goods directly, minus a small commission. Lincoln later wrote that the originators "possessed an intelligent interest in the welfare of a large number of women, when they gave them this new and broad field of opportunity to help themselves."[23] Stott credited her niece, Adelaide Montmollin, who would serve on the board of the Philadelphia Ladies' Depository for fifty-nine years until her death in 1891, with helping to implement the first Exchange, recalling that "to Miss Montmollin is due a share of the merit and of the steps taken."[24]

To generate capital, enthusiasm, membership, and clientele for their new enterprise, Depository founders turned to their friends and neighbors within the Girard Row area and their families' business colleagues around town. Within the first year they had recruited 225 members, or subscribers, which would have made the Depository the third largest of approximately thirty-one charities operating in Philadelphia.[25] The only ones with larger enrollments were the Northern Liberties Society, with 450 subscribers, and the City Infant School, with 320 annual subscribers. The Dorcas Society, a popular women's charity in many cities, ranked as the fourth most popular charity in Philadelphia and had two hundred subscribers.

From the start, the Depository's roster of members (subscribers) and benefactors included the most affluent families in Philadelphia, who shared a common interest in the plight of the genteel poor. Many founding members, individuals who paid annual dues of $1 to $5, represented families such as the Biddles, Whartons, Wistars, Copes, Walns, Rushes, Wetherills, and Cadwaladers, which had amassed vast fortunes in shipping, commerce, insurance, and manufacturing in the eighteenth and early nineteenth centuries. Like the founders, the majority of subscribers also came from the upper reaches of Philadelphia's wealthiest families, with assets estimated between $100,000 and $250,000.[26]

An English visitor, Frances Trollope, came to Philadelphia in 1832 and described the aristocratic women of that city. It is quite likely that she socialized with some of the Depository's founders. Perhaps she had someone specific in mind when she wrote:

> the most important feature in a woman's history is her maternity. This lady shall be the wife of a senator or a lawyer in the highest repute and practice. She has a handsome house, with white marble steps and door-posts, and a delicate silver knocker and door handles. She rises, and her first hour is spent in the scrupulously nice arrangement of her dress; she descends to her parlour neat, stiff, and silent. . . . Her carriage is ordered at eleven; til that hour she is employed in the pastry room. She steps into it, and gives the word, "Drive to the Dorcas Society." She enters the parlour appropriated for the meeting, and she finds seven other ladies, very much like herself, and takes her place among them . . . [presenting] her contribution of broad cloth, her ends of ribbon, her gilt paper and her minikin pins. She then produces her thimble and asks for work and the eight ladies all stitch together for some hours. In the evening . . . the lady receives at tea a young missionary and three members of the Dorcas Society. And so ends her day.[27]

But the seventeen women who gathered to form the first Depository did far more with their days. Despite their families' prosperity and social standing, the women who gathered in 1832 to form the Philadelphia Ladies' Depository

Association, and the subscribers who supported their cause, were well aware of just how swiftly poverty could descend and how desperately elite women might need employment options. In helping their less fortunate peers, Depository founders may very well have been fulfilling altruistic motivations; they hoped to "do to others as she would that they should do to her, could their circumstances be exchanged."[28] Just as likely, they may have been thinking of self-preservation should poverty strike and they, too, need a culturally acceptable means to earn income.

"The Vicissitudes of Fortune"

"In every large city, a numerous class of persons is found, whom the vicissitudes of fortune have reduced from a stage of ease or affluence to the necessity of gaining a subsistence by their own personal exertions," the founders explained.[29]

Their observations countered the advice given by many popular antipecuniary writers of the day. In February 1832, Sarah Josepha Hale, for example, editor of the widely read *Ladies' Magazine* and later, *Godey's Lady's Book,* wrote that "our men are sufficiently money-making, let us keep our women and children free from the contagion as long as possible."[30] Hers was a widely held but inaccurate notion of well-to-do women's financial and emotional security. But Caroline Dall, an antebellum writer, noted that as much as Americans cherished "that old idea, that all men support all women . . . [it was] an absurd fiction, but one with enormous social consequences."[31] Ideally, wealthy women should have been shielded from the harsh realities of earning income and facing the workplace. But the reality was that most lived one man away from poverty—and the possibility of needing to earn money.

As Elizabeth Stott had noted at the time of the founding of the first Exchange, the "sad condition" of a genteel woman's instant poverty and bleak employment prospects "existed to quite an extent" in the early decades of the nineteenth century, not only in Philadelphia but also in all cities undergoing rapid industrialization. In the roller-coaster antebellum economy major economic depressions struck every eighteen to twenty years; minor recessions occurred far more frequently. Poverty could descend with lightening speed upon a family of any class.[32] "These are no fancy sketches," the managers of the Philadelphia Ladies' Depository assured the public in their reports, "but incidents of real life."[33]

During a visit in 1831 and 1832 Alexis de Tocqueville wrote of the financial vulnerability of Americans, observing that "in no country in the world are private fortunes more precarious than in the United States. It is not uncommon for the same man in the course of his life to rise and sink again through all the grades that lead from opulence to poverty.[34] Sidney George Fisher, a wealthy Philadelphia attorney, bon vivant, self-appointed commentator of Philadelphia's upper crust, and charter member of the Philadelphia Ladies' Depository, described his wealthy colleagues' fears for the future. Of the Panic of 1837, he wrote that the "universal topic of conversation is the present distress & melancholy prospects of the commercial community. Some of the largest houses have failed for enormous amounts. . . . greater disasters are expected daily and many fear a universal crash in the moneyed affairs of Europe and of this country."[35] Even the normally gay and opulent holiday parties of the Girard Row area became gloomy and infrequent. As the Panic of 1837 stretched into its fourth year, Fisher noted that "losses of fortune from the disasters of the times have deprived many of the ability to entertain and spread a gloom over the whole city. The suffering of many families formerly rich or comfortable is severe and there seems nothing better in prospect."[36] A year later, conditions worsened, and Fisher wrote, "The streets seem deserted, the largest houses are shut up to rent, there is no business, no confidence, no money."[37]

Many factors could lead to financial misfortune among elite women thought to be sheltered from earning a living in the paid work force. Poverty often came swiftly as a result of the loss of the family business, the abandonment of a husband or father, or the death of a debt-ridden husband. The rapid rise of industrialism, with its increasing dependence on male wages outside the home and the emergence of an elite class vulnerable to the economy's erratic behavior yet adamantly opposed to gentlewomen's paid employment no doubt greatly contributed to the sense of urgency that founders of the first Exchanges must have felt in creating what they thought was a reasonable employment option— consigning needlework—for their colleagues.

A well-to-do girl growing up during the antebellum years learned that no matter what the circumstances, a woman did not seek work in the public sphere. However desperately women needed income, writers of the day stressed the importance of women staying within their proper domain of activities by discreetly selling needlework should financial emergency strike. In 1857 a writer pointed out in *Letters to Young Ladies* that "needlework, in all forms of its use, elegant and ornamental, has ever been the occupation of woman."[38] Editor Hale emphasized that women should never encroach into the male sphere: "Now we do not desire to change the station of the sexes, or give women the work of men. We only want women to become fitted for their own sphere."[39]

Newspaper advertisements of the day testify to genteel poor women's unrelenting search to find acceptable employment within such proscribed limitations. They often advertised themselves as seamstresses, milliners, or makers of gloves or mantuas (cloaks). A gentlewoman might also become a governess, a teacher, a lady's companion, a missionary, or inherit her family's business or shop. In 1832 a Philadelphia woman sought employment by placing the following advertisement on the front page of the September 25 *Daily Chronicle*: "Respectable middle aged woman wants situation as a nurse, seamstress, and has no objection to traveling."

Other options were to remarry, a condition that might offer some financial stability, or look to the extended family for financial help. Often a well-to-do family could easily take in a destitute daughter or daughter-in-law and her children. In 1854, however, Sara Willis, who wrote under the pen name Fanny Fern, dispelled that choice in her novel *Ruth Hall,* which followed the trials of Fern's semiautobiographical heroine after she has been widowed and left penniless and without family assistance. Willis's advice was practical: "When you can, achieve financial independence. Freedom from subjugation may be gotten by the fruits of your own labors, and by your own efforts you can learn to conquer yourselves."[40]

If all such attempts failed, a gentlewoman would become dependent on the community's charitable resources. That public affirmation of her fallen state, however, bore almost as much stigma as seeking work as a prostitute. Succumbing to beggary or prostitution were the greatest threats elite Americans thought would befall gentlewomen. A Dr. Van Rensselar of New York captured the dilemma faced by gentlewomen who might resort to prostitution for lack of other options for survival. There were, he said, "many instances of young and even middle-aged women who have lost their virtue, apparently by no other cause than the lowness of wages and the absolute impossibility of procuring the necessaries of life by honest industry."[41]

"Peculiarly Their Province"

It might have been easy, certainly convenient, for the founders of antebellum Depositories to ignore the plight of their less fortunate peers. But their earnestness in helping genteel poor women earn the "necessaries of life" represented the tidal wave of antebellum voluntarism fueled by the volatile combination of erratic industrialism, urbanization, and the religious and reform fervor of the Second Great Awakening. If the 1830s marked a time of dramatic economic and social change, it was also distinguished as one of the country's greatest eras of reform: the "Age of the Benevolent Empire."[42] Fifty years after the American Revolution, many Americans wanted desperately to right the economic inequities and seeming social disorder that were becoming increasingly apparent. The Exchange idea developed at the height of this formative period, when women's voluntarism became increasingly visible. James Silk Buckingham, an English visitor, was impressed by the number of women's community charities and observed that "there are perhaps ten times the number of women in good society in New York who interest themselves in the support and direction of moral objects and benevolent institutions that could be found in any city of the same population in Europe."[43]

Voluntary organizations benefited both communities and the women involved. Wealthy women could move into civic activities and counter the rigid cultural restrictions imposed upon them in the new industrial order of the early nineteenth century.[44] The Rev. Jonathan Stearns, among many other orators of the day, reaffirmed such activities, pronouncing in a sermon in 1837, "Discourse on Female Influence," that "the cause of benevolence is peculiarly indebted to the agency of woman, [for] she is fitted by nature to cheer the afflicted, elevate the depressed, minister to the wants of the feeble and diseased, and lighten the burden of human misery. God has endowed her with qualities peculiarly adapted to these offices."[45]

Such activity fell within the acceptable boundaries of female behavior; poor relief—particularly for women and children, who usually needed it most—was often not of much interest to men. Efforts by groups such as the Female Moral Reform Society and the Providence Employment Society solidified a strong women's culture, reflected antebellum women's increasing awareness of the plight of working women, and highlighted benevolent women's self-appointed mission to take action to ameliorate those conditions. The first president of the Providence Employment Society noted that although there were some "spheres which ladies ought never to enter. . . . There are subjects with which they are neither called nor qualified to meddle," fighting for better conditions for working women and helping them earn a decent wage was not one of them. "On the contrary, it is peculiarly their province. They, if any, understand what female labor is worth and what female suffering means."[46]

The majority of antebellum women's voluntary groups, such as the Depositories, remained primarily gender-segregated and community-based because women built organizations around religious or humanitarian needs of their cities and towns. The national network that would characterize postbellum women's voluntarism began to take shape during these decades before the Civil War, as women increasingly turned to friends and relatives in distant cities to swap ideas and trade information for the development of voluntary organizations within their own communities. In 1820 Lucretia Mott, then a young bride living in Philadelphia, wrote to her mother-in-law in Nantucket about starting a charity: "A few members of this district have in contemplation to form a society for the relief of the poor [and] . . . have asked me to write thee on the subject. . . . Any information thou mayst judge useful to us will be acceptable . . . and if it is not asking too much, I should like to have a copy of your constitution."[47]

The idea for a second Woman's Exchange was transplanted from Philadelphia to wealthy women in New Brunswick by a relative of one of the charter subscribers of the Philadelphia Ladies' Depository. In 1856 the wife of Dr. Alexander Proudfit of Rutgers College initiated a Depository at the urging of "the Rev. Mr. Proudfit" of Philadelphia, who had subscribed to that city's Depository Association in its founding year.[48] Identical in mission to the Philadelphia group initiated twenty-four years earlier—and borrowing liberally from their predecessor's annual reports—the New Brunswick Depository sought to "enlist in a special manner the earnest sympathy of every woman, as it provides employment to those whose only resource is their needle."[49]

Like many American philanthropists, Elizabeth Stott and her colleagues in Philadelphia, as well as the Proudfits of New Brunswick, drew their charitable plans from European ideas of self-reliance. European philanthropy emphasized the need to provide self-help and training, not alms-giving, to the needy *and* to ameliorate poverty by setting the poor—even genteel poor gentlewomen, whom Depository managers hoped to help—on the road to "blessed independence."

"Alms Are Not Offered"

By the early decades of the century, many Americans viewed self-help as the panacea for poverty, with well-known authors heartily endorsing such efforts. In an essay written in 1841, "Self-Reliance," Ralph Waldo Emerson encouraged self-help for the poor, sharply admonishing the "foolish philanthropist" who gave "alms to sots."[50] That same year, Catharine Beecher advised that "this land is so abundant in supplies, and labor is in such demand, that every healthy person can earn a comfortable support. The primary effort in relieving the poor should be to furnish them the means of earning their own support, and to supply them with those moral influences which are most effectual in securing virtue and industry."[51] Frances Trollope confirmed the strength of the American philanthropic impulse when she wrote in 1832 that the "absence of poor-laws is, without a doubt, a blessing to the country. I suppose there is less alms-giving in America than in any other Christian country on the face of the globe. It is not in the temper of the people either to give or to receive."[52] Confirming the self-help credo, the Philadelphia Depository's founders wrote of their efforts to conform to this philosophy, noting in 1840 that the "Depository could hardly be called a charity, as nothing is given for its equivalent. Alms are not offered, or indeed even thought of . . . [only] work is given."[53]

As a guide for forming their own charity to help the genteel poor, Exchange founders drew upon increasingly popular models of self-help charitable organizations that assisted the very poor: "houses of industry," "fragment societies," or "employment societies." By the 1820s and 1830s philanthropists in most northeastern urban areas could boast of having started such enterprises, which blended charitable and mercantile characteristics. Antebellum houses of industry typically supplied poor women with cloth and thread to make items to sell, compensating them for their work with daily essentials such as food, firewood, clothing, and, occasionally, small amounts of cash. But houses of industry did not improve much upon the exploitive "putting out" or piecework system. Such enterprises, in fact, were modeled directly on the industrial order they hoped to counter. However much the benevolent women managers of houses of industry hoped to create a more hospitable workplace for poor women, the scenario of women doing piecework and depending on a pittance compensation did not differ from the industrial workplace. The amount houses of industry paid would have been no more than the most minimal wage women could gainfully earn in industry. Women in dire straits could depend upon the "wages of charity" about as much as they could depend upon the benevolence of an employer in the industrial workplace.

But the wealthy founders of the first Depositories more than likely found such charities that served the underclasses of Philadelphia undesirable for "decayed gentlewomen," who, like themselves, "desire privacy and retirement to procure an honest support."[54] The founders instead sought a more dignified and discreet solution "for relieving this class of females; to afford them facilities for disposing of useful and ornamental work in a convenient and private manner."[55] To create such an enterprise, they drew from another popular antebellum influence—cooperation—used predominately by industrial wage-earners seeking their own solutions to economic disadvantages.

"In the Interest of the Worker"

Cooperation, a direct countermovement to corporate industrialism, was not generally a philosophy adopted by wealthy women—those believed to benefit most from the fruits of industry's labors. The antebellum Exchanges, however, offer early evidence of some elite women's interest in applying working-class cooperative ideology to form enterprises that would support the sale of products made by women of their own class.[56]

The cooperative movement, influenced by the writings of Robert Owen and Charles Fourier, among others, grew out of increasing dissatisfaction with the new relationship between wage-earners and their employers and called upon individuals to create nontraditional, collective methods to counter the negative forces of a materialistic, capitalistic, and inherently inequitable industrialized society. Cooperatives, specifically cooperative retail stores, became increasingly popular during the antebellum years as workers banded together to produce and sell their own products for their own profit.

Exchange founders might have felt that cooperation fell within the acceptable boundaries of feminine domestic expectations, for it offered a noncompetitive system of work and was antithetical to the "contagion" of money-making capitalism condemned by popular writers such as Sarah Josepha Hale. For women imbued with the ideals of domesticity yet keenly aware of the harsh realities of life performing paid work at home and selling it through a voluntary, cooperative association softened the lines between public and private spheres without encroaching on the male sphere or encouraging gentlewomen to leave their "proper sphere" for income. Such an arrangement could prove beneficial to women with children. Mathew Carey, in *A Plea for the Poor,* found that "not one in fifty of the hundreds of women desperate for work could go into service because they were needed by their families."[57] Elizabeth Stott was especially sympathetic to women who were "unwilling to place [their] children in an institution" and feared that paid work in the commercial sphere would mean that their children would be taken from them.[58]

Stott and her associates were influenced by the cooperative philosophy when they founded the Depository, and Lincoln later observed that "previous to this time, there was no place in this country where the work of woman was gathered together and sold in the interest of the worker."[59] The rhetoric in the annual reports reveals the influence of cooperation on the Exchange idea. The Philadelphia Ladies' Depository sought to provide "a medium through which unhappy women could dispose of their work"; similarly, the New Brunswick managers hoped to serve as a "medium between workers and their employers."[60]

Although the wealthy founders of the first Exchange lived within the sheltered enclave of Girard Row, it is doubtful that they were completely removed from the labor turmoil and worker unrest around them or unaware of wage-earners' attempts to counteract harsh working conditions. The 1830s saw great worker tumult in northeastern industrial cities, and Philadelphia witnessed intense ethnic and labor agitation, particularly in working women's organized efforts. The first federation of working women's organizations was formed in 1835, when women tailoresses, seamstresses, binders, folders, stock markers, milliners, and corset and mantua makers joined together to form the Female Improvement Society.

It is possible that many of the founders of the first Depository met Frances Wright, a feminist and pioneer of the English and Scottish models of cooperation during Wright's visit to Philadelphia. On June 26, 1830, Wright spoke at the Arch Street Theatre, near the locus of the wealthy area of Philadelphia where the founders lived and where the Depository would open two years later. Wright, who sought no less than to transform all of society, incited her audience by asking if the American Revolution had been fought "to crush down the sons and daughters of your country's industry under neglect, poverty, vice, starvation, and disease," questioning "if the new technology was devaluing human labor, by making people appendages to machines, and crippling the minds and bodies of child laborers."[61] Frances Trollope, a long-time friend of Wright's, witnessed the presentation, as did many others. "I immediately determined to hear her [Wright], and did so," she wrote, "though not without some difficulty, from the crowds who went thither with the same intention." Trollope reported that there "was a larger proportion of ladies present than I ever saw on any other occasion in an American theater."[62]

The early Exchanges functioned as quasi-producers' cooperatives by providing a retail outlet for consignors—producers—many of whom, as the managers of the Philadelphia Ladies' Depository noted, "would be wholly at a loss in what manner to dispose of the products of her fingers."[63] Like other cooperative efforts of the time, Depositories sought to offer a fair remuneration to producers "at a much smaller commission than merchants require."[64] The managers explained that "the prices, too, the Board do not hesitate to say, are moderate. They have never professed to have work done at a cheap rate, but on such terms as will afford a reasonable compensation to the depositors. Were it otherwise, the Institution would not answer the purpose for which it was intended."[65]

Like cooperatives, which operated on the one share–one vote principle, the early Exchanges required active financial participation of members and consignors alike. Not only did the charity's members buy a "share" or a subscription in the Exchange, but consignors were also obligated to "buy in." If a consignor could not afford to purchase a subscription (or a consignor's permit), which was often the case, the Exchange offered subscriptions donated by more affluent members. Such an arrangement established both members and consignors as owners—"stock holders"—of the Exchange.

Given the uniqueness of the Exchange concept and its emphasis on helping "decayed gentlewomen," the founders of the Philadelphia Ladies' Depository carefully explained their new mission to the public. Providing a permanent marketplace where genteel poor women could sell their handiwork was an idea not generally accepted. In their first annual report, the managers wrote: "The plan and object of the Ladies' Depository, appearing not to be generally understood, the managers take this opportunity of explaining the nature of the establishment and the cause of its formation. . . . Instances have come to the knowledge of the managers of the most praiseworthy exertions being met by repulsive and almost insulting conduct, which not only wound the feelings, but tended to discourage further effort."[66]

But the founders needed more than the good will of wealthy friends and the written persuasion of annual reports to assure the success of their commercial enterprise. To succeed, they needed to make their store visible to fashionable patrons, credible as a business and helpful to the producers they hoped to rescue from "the rigor of painful adversity."[67] The "Divine precepts" they invoked in their first annual report would prove useful as they set upon the road of entrepreneurial philanthropy at the corner of Chestnut and Seventh streets in downtown Philadelphia.

2

"One of the Most Attractive Shops on the Street": Making Self-Help Fashionable for the Genteel Poor

*E*lizabeth Stott and her sixteen "benevolent associates" set high expectations when they opened a charitable consignment shop for the genteel poor women of Philadelphia. They sought to provide a stable, permanent outlet where consignors could sell handcrafted "useful and decorative" needlework. Inspired by models of self-help and cooperation, the founders hoped "to sustain in [consignors] a spirit of independence which proves a stimulant to further effort."[1] To attain such a lofty goal, they first had to create an attractive, fashionable, and well-managed shop where members of Philadelphia's prosperous classes who could afford the "moderate, not cheap" prices of the merchandise would want to be seen as patrons.[2] Merchandise offered there would have to be of a high enough quality to meet the standards of the increasingly affluent carriage trade.

The founders, in essence, established a competitive retail shop in the most fashionable section of town and stocked it with handmade merchandise—men's and women's clothing accessories and home accouterments produced by genteel poor women who had somewhat marketable but undeveloped sewing skills. As European fashions and mass-produced American goods increasingly tempted the upper classes, undertaking such an enterprise proved a serious challenge. Yet the founders created—in what would become a hallmark of the Exchange movement—a specific niche, drawing upon the nostalgic idea of promoting women's handcrafted items of quality higher than that which mass production offered and evoking the preindustrial era when women's work had status. The founders hoped to appeal to Philadelphia's fashion-conscious philanthropists and combine charity with business by persuading wealthy patrons where to buy merchandise that would attest to their new prosperity and philanthropic sympathies.

In a pattern that postbellum Exchanges would follow several decades later, Depository managers selected the most prosperous area of town for their new enterprise to ensure an elite clientele for the shop. Although Philadelphia's upper class lived in many areas of the city, by the 1830s the majority of pre-Revolutionary War wealth as well as most of the emerging, moneyed classes had gathered in a residential and commercial enclave. The stronghold of native-born Presbyterians, Episcopalians, and Quakers was centered around the stylish Girard Row near Chestnut Street. This "most fashionable" area, with its tree-lined streets, stately homes, and small shops, was coincidentally named after one of the city's leading philanthropists, Stephen Girard.[3] Located near Washington Square and a block from the historic Independence Hall area, Girard Row lay within walking distance of the city's bustling commercial center yet provided the insulated security that Philadelphia's prosperous classes desired. An antebellum guidebook boasted that the Girard Row area, renowned for its spectacular houses, was "unrivaled in any city for architecture, taste and elegance."[4] Many of the houses were valued at $22,000 or more, equivalent to the amount of wages that the average male textile worker would earn after seventy-five years in the factories of Philadelphia.[5]

It is probable that the Depository managers and patrons spent their lives within the confines of the Girard Row area's genteel atmosphere of wealth and elegance.[6] Within an eight-block area, encircled by the Delaware River on the east and the Schuykill River on the west, they would have had little reason to step beyond their insulated and comfortable surroundings of friends, churches, shops, and theaters.

"A Subject of Congratulations"

The Depository opened for business on February, 1, 1832, on Seventh Avenue between Arch and Race streets, three blocks north and two blocks east of Girard Row. That location immediately proved unsatisfactory, however. Within the first month, after "complaints being made that this situation was not sufficiently central," the Depository moved south to the more prestigious corner of Chestnut and Seventh streets, Philadelphia's social and commercial hub at the heart of the wealthy residential, shopping, and theater district.[7] An observer noted that "upon the south side of Chestnut, between Seventh and Eighth, there is more retail life than we have yet seen."[8]

The Exchange likely was housed in a two- or three-story, brick, federalist-style building, popular at the time in the Girard Row area. It must have been far more modest than the elegant, sprawling building that housed the Philadelphia's Merchants' Exchange, not too far from the Depository, where the captains of industry met to trade and confer. That building was described as "an imposing three-story building, constructed of the purist Pennsylvania marble, ornamented by two gigantic lions."[9]

At one point the managers boasted that the front display window made the Depository "one of the most attractive shops on the street," testimony of their eagerness to compete with nearby businesses.[10] Small, elegant shops were becoming increasingly important to the new elite consumerism of the antebellum years. By the 1830s and 1840s the Colonial-era general store, which sold a range of merchandise, was slowly but undeniably overshadowed in wealthy urban areas by shops that specialized in one particular item—umbrellas, shoes, hats, or dresses—or by a group of closely related items, such as women's or men's accessories. By 1820 elite families were buying more clothing and household goods, such as pantaloons, shirts, children's clothes, shawls, and bonnets, from retailers.

Managers of the Philadelphia Ladies' Depository modeled their enterprise on the fashionable boutiques and dry goods shops of Girard Row. Many of the city's finest shops and dressmakers were located within walking distance of the Depository. Within a two-to-three block area of Girard Row, eight dressmakers and eighteen "Parisian" milliners provided sewing services, and Mrs. Field of 210 Walnut Street advertised as the "inventor and teacher of the art of cutting ladies' dresses in a scientific manner by measuring the person."[11]

Although untested as businesswomen, the managers did not hesitate to flaunt their increasing business savvy and the Depository's success. When business slackened, as it did occasionally through the many national economic ups and downs of the antebellum years, they compared the Depository's good fortune to the "embarrassed state of many of the moneyed institutions throughout the country [that] have reduced multitudes who considered themselves wealthy to the necessity of making personal exertions for their maintenance."[12] Banks and major industries, which managers felt caused the misfortune that brought many consignors to the Depository's doorsteps for help, were often targets of special wrath. After one particularly distressing recession, the managers wrote that, compared to other businesses, "it is a subject of congratulations that in this long season of business depression, they [the managers] have met with no losses.[13]

Such bravado might seem misplaced for a fledgling charitable consignment shop, but benevolent women of the nineteenth century were imbued with a sense of superiority of mission and purpose. Contempt for dominant institutions perceived as causing the miseries of the world characterized their charitable and reform efforts. It was, after all, their mission to change such institutions. They firmly believed that their benevolent work grew out of wholly authoritative, moral, and uniquely Christian fervor.

Managing a commercial enterprise such as an Exchange would have required far more business knowledge and volunteer time than participation in traditional charities. Judging by annual reports and steadily increasing business, Depository managers were confident of being able to operate their hybrid charity/store. They became engaged in quasi-careers of some rank and public visibility that would now seem highly managerial and corporate. Setting a standard that their postbellum counterparts would eagerly embrace a half-century later, they used volunteer work as careers that placed them in community leadership positions denied them by more conventional channels. Masked safely under the guise of charity, they could immerse themselves in the corporate world of commerce.

The managers, as did the owners of other businesses on Girard Row, oversaw all phases of their enterprise's operation: making sure coal was delivered on time, locating and advertising the latest fashionable merchandise, hiring personnel, keeping accurate accounts for investors (patrons and members), marketing consignors' goods within a highly competitive retail market, and investing in stock. They became particularly adept at investing in the stock market. By 1859 records indicate a return on their investment of $110.09. In 1864 managers voted to invest $716.12, and in that same year the return on their total investments rose to $347.23.[14]

Managers soon learned the advantages of combining the public's philanthropic impulses with their own commercial entrepreneurship to build sympathy for the "suffering female" and thus keep their shop afloat. It was not just their aptitude for business that brought the carriage trade to the Depository's door. Managers always kept the primary mission of the Depository visible: to help the "decayed gentlewoman." To this end, they relied heavily on the charitable impulses of antebellum Philadelphians and drew upon images of the hapless woman victim—"the lonely, suffering, friendless female" (1837), the "sufferings of females under such circumstances" (1834), and "amiable, helpless females who are suddenly reduced to poverty" (1837)—and provided "employment for many who did not know where to find it for themselves."[15]

"The Generous Support of a Liberal Public"

The managers dealt constantly with competition from all sides. Not only did they need to stay current with the latest fashion trends but they also competed with other local charities. Such divergent competition reflected the dual nature of the Depository as a charity and a commercial enterprise. In one instance the managers specifically attributed a slack period in business to competition from other businesses and charities when they wrote of "various causes—the general depression of business, the large number of imported garments thrown into the market at reduced prices, and the number of [charity] fairs which have been in successful operation during the autumn and winter."[16]

The Depository's sources of annual income underscored its hybrid nature. To maintain the shop as a permanent outlet for women's work, the managers needed constant income. A 6 percent commission from the sale of each special order or consigned item provided the primary source of revenue but never completely defrayed the maintenance of the shop, an added expense that most charities did not have to face. To supplement their income, the managers turned to a tried-and-true source: the "fostering care and generous support of a liberal public," contributions of cash and in-kind gifts.[17] The managers professed their "regret to state that the necessary expenses of carrying on the business still exceed the reliable income of the society and they are obliged from time to time to encroach upon the same capital, composed of legacies and donations, which they hope at some future time may be added to the building fund and invested in the purchase of a store."[18]

Managers were not only volunteer workers but also financial supporters and benefactors. Property laws still restricted married women's ability to control money, but widowed or unmarried gentlewomen would have been able to use their discretion when subscribing annually or making special annual contributions of $5 or $10. The majority of the founders and members appear to have been married or widowed women, many of whom made special contributions beyond the $1 annual membership fee. The first annual report, for example, lists twenty women who gave from $3 to $10 in special contributions. Some of the biggest contributions were made by men—or at least in the names of men—perhaps by wives who might have been reluctant to use their own names. Of sixty-four special contributions the first year, more than one-third, twenty-three, were listed as anonymous gifts.

Depository managers counted on the support of wealthy peers and were not hesitant to ask either men or women for support. Husbands were particularly useful; many of the Depository's male members or husbands of members traveled in elite circles of Philadelphia society. Two years after the founding of the Depository, a group of the wealthiest men in the city started the prestigious Philadelphia Club. Five of the eleven founders were husbands of Depository members, and two were husbands of Depository founders.[19] Membership rolls of two other exclusive men's clubs formed at the same time, the Walking Club and the Philosophical Society, indicate many husbands of members or male members of the Depository.[20]

It took three years, but finally, in 1837, the managers announced to their public that "the benevolent character and usefulness [of the Depository] are so well understood."[21] They could concentrate on helping the needy consignor in her quest for financial self-sufficiency and "reward her for her industry [and] relieve her of her distress."[22]

As women who socialized within the luxurious milieu of Girard Row, the founders were intimately familiar with the tastes and expectations of the men and women who would become their patrons and subscribers: their friends, neighbors, and colleagues. They also knew well the abilities and cultural restrictions placed upon, as the managers wrote, "the suffering and friendless female," the consignor who would provide merchandise for the shop.[23] It was these women, newly fallen from wealth, whom they hoped to rescue from what they feared was the "repulsive and almost insulting" ordeal of wage-earning in the industrial workplace.[24]

"Many Who Have Been Relieved from Difficulties"

Cloaked in heavy veils, consignors would bring needlework to the back door of the Depository at night. Little wonder then that managers felt that rescuing them from the "repulsive and insulting" ordeal of industrial wage-earning required the utmost discretion to ensure anonymity and protection from public scrutiny. A consignor applied for a permit to a manager, "whose duty it is to inform herself, as far as is needful and proper, of the circumstances of the individual [and] in a way that must be most acceptable to a person of delicacy and refinement."[25] Anonymity of consignors was critical because it allowed the Depository to encourage and support women in their quest for financial security and still honor antebellum restrictions against work in the public sphere for elite women. Such anonymity unfortunately also limits full understanding of the consignors. The managers reasoned that many consignors were "influenced by the feelings and opinions of near relatives or friends . . . who might be seriously offended by such exposure."[26]

Managers took pride in what they perceived to be their increasing role in reversing consignors' downward economic spiral and helping them regain some measure of financial standing. In 1840 they wrote that "the continued connection with this institution tends strongly to impress their minds with a deep sense of the untold sufferings and privations which many are called to endure."[27] As friends and associates of the founders, consignors were women in adverse circumstances and willing to improve their unhappy lot through industry and initiative. In the eyes of the founders, that willingness proved them worthy of assistance and exemplary in character.

In annual reports, always from their perspective, managers without fail wrote of "the cheerful countenances and grateful acknowledgements of the many who have been relieved from difficulties."[28] One case seemed to typify the founders' mission: the Depository assisted "a family in independent circumstances and surrounded by all the comfort and many of the luxuries of life . . . reduced almost to poverty by the failure of the banks in which their money was invested, and the daughters are compelled to employ the talent which has heretofore been only a source of gratifications to themselves and friends . . . to obtain support." In another case, "two young ladies, whose mother died during the past winter, were enabled to minister to her wants and provide everything necessary for her comfort."[29] Three years later the Depository assisted when "a father of a large family [who] has been unfortunate in business, [and whose] declining health renders it impossible for him to make the exertion necessary to regain his former standing." That same year, the Depository helped "a widowed mother, who has supported herself and an only child principally by the proceeds of work derived from the Ladies' Depository."[30] The managers, reaffirming their self-help mission, reported that "many families have been entirely supported and when money and wood are offered, the answer has frequently been 'employment is all we wish, not charity.'"[31]

A recurring theme in many annual reports is the managers' acute perception of how quickly poverty could strike their class; they often cited the need to advance "instant aid" to a new consignor who was completely poverty-stricken.[32] Having enough funds on hand to extend emergency cash to consignors continued to be "the one great need and trouble of the managers."[33] Similarly, they frequently reported that "very few [depositors] could afford to invest a sufficient sum of money to purchase fine and handsome materials to be made up, and coarse articles are found to be unacceptable." They solved the problem by initiating a special fund to make "special advances" for consignors in dire need.[34] Indeed, managers made every attempt to scrape together needed funds. "These applicants, some of whom have been generous patrons of the Depository in their more prosperous days, should not be turned away," they reaffirmed in 1840.[35]

The number of consignors increased steadily in the early stages of the Depository's development, nearly doubling from 100 to 183 in the first three years. Over the next decades the number of consignors fluctuated greatly, dipping to 116 permits in 1840, following the protracted Panic of 1837, and then rebounding as the Panic eased. Ironically, at a time when poverty hit the hardest the Depository assisted the fewest consignors. The managers attributed the slack in business to the consignors' inability to purchase materials to produce goods and the need for patrons, feeling the effects of the financial depression, to cut back on purchases. In 1840 they wrote that the "same causes which have obliged some families to seek employment to relieve their necessities have obliged others to economize, and to do as much as possible for themselves, and have thus cut off the regular supply of work, and lessened the amount of sales."[36]

The managers' greatest challenge was not in riding out business fluctuations but rather in honing the consignors' needlework ability and perfecting those skills "heretofore used for their [the consignors'] own amusement only." No matter how many "fancy stitches" consignors may have learned as young girls growing up in wealthy households, managers struggled constantly to keep needlework skills marketable and up-to-date in a competitive retail market. Their efforts apparently proved successful.

"We Can Make Anything That the Needle Can Make"

Depository managers would have kept close tabs on the latest clothing and home fashions, particularly accessories and embellishments they could sell to wealthy patrons and that would be within the sewing abilities of the consignors. By the third decade of the nineteenth century, Philadelphia had emerged as a center of high fashion. *Godey's Lady's Book* was published, beginning in 1830, by Louis Godey on Chestnut Street, near where the Depository would locate two years later. Like similar periodicals of the time, it promoted and interpreted the fashions of Paris and London to an eager, fashion-conscious American audience, and it became an arbiter of good taste and upper-class sensibilities during the nineteenth century.[37]

Before the 1830s, most clothing, particularly for the upper classes, was customized and hand-sewn; mass-produced, machine-made apparel did not appear in quantity until the Civil War. Accessories gained new importance, with ruffles, collars, hats, shawls, ribbons, and bows causing one foreign observer to note, "How the ladies dress . . . with flutterings of ribbons and silk tassels and cloaks."[38]

To keep current and fashionable, women purchased new dresses and accessories seasonally, regularly updating their wardrobes to meet haute couture's latest requirements. To capitalize on those changes, the managers advertised in 1849 that "we can make anything that the needle can make."[39]

Most consigners would have been familiar with executing "fancy" stitches, being of the wealthier classes and having learned needlework from an early age. Young girls embroidered intricate samplers that had verses reflecting expectations for humble, selfless, and obedient lives.[40] The pastime had a didactic function in that it taught the alphabet and the verses; it also allowed young girls to express their artistic skills by making decorative objects for their homes.

Popular magazines of the day such as *Godey's Lady's Book,* the *Ladies' Repository,* and the *Ladies' Garland* encouraged the domestic priorities for young women. *Godey's,* for example, offered a new embroidery design in each issue and regularly prescribed the latest stitch that a fashionable woman would want embellished on her shawl or evening dress. The most popular items that consignors would have learned to sew and embroider were sheets, pillowcases, linen towels, chemises, and fashions for dolls, as well as "modesty pieces," "drawers," "sacks," and "spencers."

The managers handled the delicate problem of occasional inferior merchandise by devising a method to allow each consignor the opportunity to offer a sample of her work on a piece of cloth displayed at the Depository, permitting patrons to choose the desired items. The managers "determined to receive orders at the Depository for plain sewing; and in order to finish specimens of work, a piece of linen was purchased [by the managers for the consigners] and placed in the hands of several depositors to be made up and afterwards kept at the Depository for examination [by patrons]."[41] The system worked. "As fast as the articles [special order] have been made up, the money has been remunerated and much employment has been furnished in this way."[42]

Consignors produced an impressive range of merchandise that "would defy competition with that produced from any other establishment in the country."[43] In the first year, they executed 1,178 pieces; by the next year there were 1,667. Of that number, 334 articles were made from fabrics purchased by the committee. By 1837, special orders had increased to 2,206 items. By the eighth year, the annual report listed the following items that had been made to order:

> 394 shirts, 189 chemises, 108 frocks, 52 aprons, 113 collars, 52 caps, 35 pillow cases, 1 bolster case, 52 capes, 113 capes and collars transferred, 39 petticoats, made and quilted, 16 handkerchiefs, 21 pair cuffs, 19 sheets, 15 articles repaired, 34 night gowns, 11 cushions, 4 sachels, 22 handkerchiefs lace-stitched, 5 infant's blankets embroidered, 6 handkerchiefs hemmed, 69 collars and cuffs hem stitched, 74 infant's shirts, 2 reticules, 2 coats, 15 yards muslin scalloped, 2 handkerchiefs ditto, 5 cloaks, 13 pairs pantalets, 4 collars embroidered, 1 chair cover worked, 45 pairs drawers, 4 dresses embroidered, 9 yards cambric lace-stitched, 12 boy's dresses, 7 shirts bosoms, 6 pairs wristbands, 3 mantillas, 2 spencers, 21 flags, 3 handkerchiefs embroidered, 2 bags ditto, 4 infant's petticoats, 2 ottomans worked, 2 ottomans filled up, 1 pair suspenders worked, 1 coverlet quilted, 470 pieces marked.[44]

The pricing arrangements of the Depository are obscure. Postbellum Exchanges depended on consignors to price their own merchandise, thereby assuring a desired profit if the item was sold. Possibly the managers of the antebellum Depository used this plan, as well. The idea of fixed prices was just catching on in American stores; customers had traditionally bartered for the lowest price or paid individually fixed prices for customized goods.[45]

Because no records or names are available for sales made by individual consignors the amount women could earn by selling handiwork at the Depository is unclear. Monthly sales records for 1840 indicate that the Depository sold a total of $2,502.40 of merchandise that year. The busiest month was December, with $282.45 in sales; the slowest were February and August, with $149.83 and $154.13 in sales. That year, 116 women applied for permits. Assuming that all consignors sold an equal amount (which is unlikely because some items would be more saleable and of higher quality than others), their incomes would average about $22 a year, well below $58.50, the minimal annual wage that out-workers earned in the 1830s. A consignor would have had to produce several items per day to exceed the minimum wage offered in the industrial workplace. It is likely that a few consignors earned a respectable amount and the majority's earnings were below average. Nonetheless, unlike recipients of most charities, a consignor would have been paid in cash and would have had an opportunity to increase sales on her products, depending on their marketability (Table 1, Appendix A).

Like other shopkeepers on Girard Row, the Depository employed agents, also needy women, to "attend to the reception and sale of articles."[46] By the second year, the Depository's agent had proved so valuable that the managers increased her salary from $3 to $4.50 per week, or $234 annually; a male clerk in a retail shop might have earned about $250. By 1837 the Depository enjoyed enough prosperity to hire an assistant agent.

The managers emphasized long-term job opportunities that formerly wealthy women could develop through their early training in executing fancy stitches. Aside from items sold and made to order in the Depository, the managers also considered part of their mission to "direct their attention to other occupations as well as to needlework."[47] To increase women's chances for self-sufficiency and financial security, the Depository encouraged the entrepreneurial talents of consignors by nurturing an atmosphere where ambitious women, through the skills learned as consignors, could strike out on their own as self-employed seamstresses, dressmakers, or milliners. As in Colonial times, when women often specialized in producing a particular item to sustain themselves economically, managers also encouraged consignors to improve their skills so they could work full-time at one particular type of employment, develop a clientele for their merchandise, and perhaps earn enough to live securely. They could independently pursue such tasks as goffering (sewing pleats), clear starching, transcribing, and marking clothing for alterations through contacts with customers at the Depository.

"The Blessing of Heaven Will Attend Future Efforts"

Recognizing the futility of doling out day-to-day palliatives and unable to ignore the plight of their less fortunate peers, the founders of the first Exchanges sought a more fundamental transformation in women's work conditions. Their idea would remain localized in the Northeast during the first half of the century. Through the mid-decades of the century, however, the antebellum image of Lady Bountiful would transform itself into that of an urban foot soldier, and a later generation of Exchange women would push beyond helping only the genteel poor and experiment with the liberating possibilities that voluntary associations held for economically empowering a range of women. By the 1870s, notions of "false pride," women's right to earn income, and the role elite women played in effecting cultural and economic changes on a national level would accelerate dramatically.

The Exchange idea, as it grew from isolated Depositories before the Civil War to a national movement of more than seventy-two Exchanges by the end of the century, would reflect that epic change in attitudes about women's need for gainful employment and vocational training. Both consignors and managers, eager to move beyond the restrictions of ladies to more productive lives as working women, would find their expectations fulfilled.

By the late 1870s the Philadelphia Ladies' Depository and the New Brunswick Ladies' Depository would give way to the modern postbellum Exchange movement that expanded the idea to provide work opportunities through domestic arts to all women, rich or poor. The Exchange idea would continue to build on the age-old philanthropic ideas of self-help and cooperation, but by the closing decades of the century women would become far more aggressive in how they operated Exchanges. Entrepreneurial philanthropy, tested locally in the antebellum years, would flourish nationwide by the closing quarter of the century. Several powerful economic and cultural forces, unique to the period, would reshape and reinvigorate the Exchange idea and elevate it to a national movement by the 1870s and 1880s as women found innovative ways to use the voluntary sector to their economic advantage. They stepped up their efforts to help women "win for themselves that blessed independence which is so precious to every true proud spirit."[48]

Frances Trollope, upon leaving Philadelphia, her favorite city on her American tour, observed—perhaps prophetically—of the women she met there: "Should the women of America ever discover what their power might be, and compare it with what it is, much improvement might be hoped for. While at Philadelphia . . . their comparative influence in society, with that possessed in Europe by females holding the same station, occurred forcibly to my mind."[49]

During the course of the century, Exchange women did discover exactly "what their power might be." As they had hoped from the start that "the blessing of Heaven will attend future efforts," the founders' charitable experiment, begun in downtown Philadelphia in 1832, was indeed "crowned with abundant success."[50] It laid the groundwork for one of the most widespread and popular women's voluntary movements a half-century later.

Mrs. Richard Harlan (left) and Mrs. John Markoe, along with Elizabeth Stott and fourteen other prominent Philadelphia women, in 1832 started the first Woman's Exchange, where women of their own class could discreetly sell their needlework during hard times. (Harlan courtesy of the Historical Society of Pennsylvania; Markoe courtesy of the Library Company of Philadelphia)

Influential editor Sarah Josepha Hale, pictured here in *Godey's Lady's Book* in 1850, encouraged women to avoid the "contagion" of the workplace. (Special Collections, the University Library, University of Illinois at Chicago)

In the erratic economy of the nineteenth century, poverty could quickly descend on even the wealthiest family, as shown in "Ruined," an 1869 woodcut from *Harper's Weekly*. " Who can say, in these difficult times, when poverty follows so rapidly in the footsteps of wealth, that a similar lot will not be their own?" the founders of the first Exchange asked in 1840. (The University of Chicago Library)

WANTED—25 GIRLS, to work in a MATCH FACTORY. Such as will work steady can make from $2 50 to $3 per week. All wages are paid *every Saturday in cash*. Apply either at the FACTORY, No. 412 COATES Street, above Tenth, or at FATMAN BROTHERS & CO., No. 28 BANK Street.

Also, Wanted, a SERVANT GIRL, for doing Housework in a small family. Good recommendations required. Apply as above.   je12-2t*

Genteel poor women had few work options in the antebellum years. Factory work and domestic servitude, as advertised in Philadelphia's *Public Ledger* in 1844, were often perilous and paid low wages. (The Historical Society of Pennsylvania)

Most charities, like the Barnabus House of New York City, helped impoverished women by offering food and shelter. The Exchanges, instead, offered a way for women to earn fair remuneration for their work. (North Wind Pictures Archives)

The block of Seventh and Chestnut streets, the commercial hub of Philadelphia in the antebellum years, was the site of the first Woman's Exchange in 1832. (The Library Company of Philadelphia)

The founders of the first Exchange modeled their enterprise on successful shops, such as the "Philosophical Millinery Store," that catered to wealthy women. From Frances Trollope, *Domestic Manners of the Americans* (1832). (Northwestern University Library)

Frances Trollope, popular lecturer and author, described the aristocratic women of her favorite city, Philadelphia. More than likely, she met and socialized with some of the founders of the Philadelphia Ladies' Depository during her tour of America. From Frances Trollope, Domestic Manners of the Americans (1832).

The displays at the Women's Pavilion at the 1876 Philadelphia Centennial Exhibition showcased women's many achievements in the home and the workplace. One display in particular, that of London's Royal School of Art Needlework, inspired the postbellum Exchange movement. From *The Official Catalog of the United States International Exhibition* (1876). (Northwestern University Library)

Candace Wheeler (above) and Mary
Atwater Choate in 1878 opened the New
York Exchange for Woman's Work, a
fashionable outlet for women from any
socioeconomic background to sell
home-produced merchandise. (Wheeler
from a painting by her daughter, Dora
Wheeler Keith, reprinted in *Development of Embroidery in America* [1921];
Choate courtesy of Choate Rosemary
Hall Archives)

Part 2

The Postbellum Exchanges: A New Era, a New Model

3

"The Time Was Ripe for a Change": Self-Improvement and Economic Security for All Women

"It is the most important sociological phenomenon of the century," Charlotte Perkins Gilman wrote in 1891 of the postbellum surge of women's voluntarism. "The whole country is budding into women's clubs."[1] She was not exaggerating. By the last decades of the nineteenth century, both small hamlets or large urban areas might have too many women's voluntary associations to count. By 1890, for example, Portland, Maine, boasted more than fifty women's clubs.[2] If the antebellum period marked "The Age of the Benevolent Empire," then the closing decades, according to Alice Hyneman Rhine, represented "the philanthropic era for women."[3]

Voluntarism had gained great momentum throughout the mid-nineteenth century as women increased their city-to-city connections to build a strong national network of charitable, religious, and cultural organizations and aggressively accelerated efforts to deal with the inexorable forces of industrialism and urbanization. Following their impressive showing on the U.S. Sanitary Commission and other Civil War relief organizations, women expanded voluntarism from congregations and communities to activism on a national level. The Rev. Henry W. Bellows, chair of the commission, remarked that women's involvement in the cause sparked "an uprising of women in the land" as hundreds of women, North and South, rushed to aid soldiers and war-ravished families and helped solidify women's voluntarism nationally.[4]

The women who formed strong national alliances during and immediately following the war lived in a far different world from antebellum women who labored hard in their communities to establish charitable and reform institutions. Through the middle of the century, women, as Frances Trollope had hoped, had indeed discovered "what their power may be" and transformed community-focused energies into highly effective political, cultural, and social voluntary associations on the national level. Postbellum voluntarism was fueled by a new spirit of philanthropic reform. "The last quarter of the century," one commentator noted, "witnessed a noble outburst of energies to help suffering brethren."[5] The outburst was engendered by changing views of poverty and new ideas about helping the poor as well as applying self-help to empower all women economically through their initiative and training. Unlike antebellum notions of poverty, which largely cited moral failing on the part of the individual as the primary cause of destitution, by the closing decades of the century reformers cited environmental and economic factors as contributing to poverty—in particular to the plight of women in the workplace.

Postbellum voluntary organizations often overlapped in both membership and mission. Women moved freely among various associations, often joining several groups within their communities, hoping to improve not only the lives of the poor but also their own. Women's bonds with their organizations were reinforced by their shared reform crusades and common cultural denominators of interests and backgrounds. A strong woman's culture solidified during the century as women wrote lovingly of the friendships formed from being associated with various groups. Edith Dow Littlehale Cheney, a reformer, writer, abolitionist, and suffragist, commented in 1890 on "our club as a home, and of a tie that binds us together as a family tie. If it be possible to know a more sacred relation, I wish to say a word showing how we have known here a communion of souls, broader, if not closer than the family tie . . . a company bound together by high thought and tender love."[6]

Not only did women form valuable friendships in voluntary organizations, but they also learned practical management and business skills. Entrepreneurship took on a new meaning.[7] Living in the post–Civil War bustle of growth in industry and economic production, women became more businesslike and adopted corporate-style structures and operational methods for voluntary organizations. The final decades of the century witnessed the masculinization of benevolence, as women increasingly tempered feminine rhetoric to include male-oriented values of commercialism and entrepreneurship to their organizations.[8] As Alice Rhine wrote in 1891, "A few decades ago, women's attention was absorbed in organizing small, local, sectarian sewing societies, Sunday School classes and church fairs. After the Civil War, these few circumscribed channels no longer sufficed for women's activity, and an expansion took place that made itself felt in the organization of [many] societies. In their management of these institutions, women displayed an amount of executive ability and enlightened interest in public need that surprised men."[9]

Antebellum Exchange managers successfully combined self-help, cooperation, and entrepreneurship to create quasi-commercial enterprises to assist genteel poor women in averting financial disaster. By late century, these three influences gained great popularity and credibility among benevolent women nationwide and helped catapult the Exchange idea from isolated, community-based efforts in the Northeast to a nationally connected movement that included more than seventy-two groups by the 1890s. Women's voluntarism and the movement grew during the closing decades of the nineteenth century within the fervor to promote not only charitable self-help for the needy but also self-improvement among all women. Self-help expanded to include the notion of encouraging all women, rich and poor alike, to become more stable financially by learning marketable vocational skills.

"Fifty years have witnessed a silent revolution of unprecedented importance in woman's work, lot, and outlook," noted the editor of the American Bible Tract Society's *New York Evangelist,* a conduit for the spread of the Woman's Exchange movement in the 1880s.[10] Nowhere was the change in "woman's work, lot, and outlook" highlighted so brilliantly and brought to national attention so intensely as at the 1876 Centennial Exhibition in Philadelphia. Women representing voluntary groups from coast to coast gathered in the city where the Exchange idea had started four decades earlier to show the strength of their numbers and collective force. The Centennial was a watershed, where women learned not only how to use the voluntary sector to their economic advantage but also how to reinstate home production to the respected social and artistic status it had once enjoyed. The Centennial, with its vibrant displays and electrifying new ideas, became a springboard from which to expand the antebellum Exchange idea nationally.

"Women of all classes had always been dependent upon the wage-earning capacity of men . . . but the time was ripe for a change," Candace Wheeler commented after visiting the Centennial.[11] Two years later she would open the doors of the prototype of the postbellum Exchanges, the New York Exchange for Woman's Work. At the Centennial she learned how traditional ideas of self-help, used successfully in antebellum Exchanges, could combine with new influences of decorative arts and entrepreneurship to advance women's economic opportunities. Wheeler, along with the hundreds of women across the country who would found Exchanges during the next decade, created models of self-help and self-improvement that would help other women's struggle for financial security and personal fulfillment.

An Artistic Awakening

The Philadelphia Centennial Exhibition mesmerized the hundred-year-old nation. As the country faced the inexorable consequences of industrialization and urbanization, the Centennial offered dazzling displays of technology and gadgets hardly imaginable to a largely rural population. Although opened during the third year of one of the country's severest and most prolonged economic depressions, during its six-month run the Centennial drew more than ten million people, a quarter of the nation's population, and featured thirty thousand exhibitors from fifty countries.

To many, the Centennial's exhibitions of women's integral roles in industry, the arts, and the domestic sphere symbolized an increasing sense of liberation from old restrictions and responsibilities and helped solidify women's interests in seeking new ways to contribute to American culture. One visitor, Sarah Orne Jewett, expressed in "The Flight of Betsey Lane" the Centennial's liberating effects and the seemingly limitless worldly possibilities it offered, far removed from the provincial, everyday routines of most women's lives.[12]

The Women's Pavilion in particular testified to how eager benevolent women were to showcase many achievements that had been made in the home and the workplace. Built by financial contributions of women representing local Centennial Committees across the country, the Pavilion, the first of its kind, highlighted women as achievers and contributors to American society.[13] Rather than presenting women as passive and compliant, an image that had dominated much popular literature during earlier decades of the century, Centennial exhibits revealed the important and proactive role of women. They highlighted women's talents, from painting to sculpting, as well as technological inventions, photographs of American institutions established or run by women, and displays of needlework and art by women from other countries.[14] The exhibits conveyed women's collective strength, focusing on similarities rather than differences across class and geographical barriers.

But the Women's Pavilion might have remained just a dream without the quick action and financial backing of the Women's Centennial Executive Committee of Cincinnati. A little less than a year before the opening of the Centennial, Alfred T. Goshorn, the Centennial's chair and a well-known Cincinnati businessman, informed the chairwomen of Centennial Committees in thirty-one states that women who had been promised display space would not be allowed to display with male exhibitors. Instead, they would be required to erect their own building, at an estimated cost of $30,000. Angered into immediate action by Goshorn's last-minute reversal, committees around the country raised more than enough money to construct the needed building. Not surprisingly, Cincinnati women—who would become leaders in the decorative arts and Woman's Exchange movements—contributed the largest percentage, more than $5,000, one-sixth of the amount needed. After all, Goshorn was a fellow Cincinnatian. The women were amply rewarded with a thousand-square-foot space to house the Cincinnati Room in the most advantageous area of the Women's Pavilion.

Given the paradoxes of late-nineteenth-century women's lives, it is not surprising that the Women's Pavilion drew criticism and praise from all sides. To moderate proponents of woman's rights, the building was a starting point for those whose political and social consciousness was just awakening. To more progressive feminists such as Elizabeth Cady Stanton and Susan B. Anthony, the building fell far short of the cause of woman suffrage. To make a stronger statement for women's place in society, Anthony and others boldly stormed the main platform of the fair and later held their own event by reading the Woman's Declaration of Independence on the other side of Philadelphia.

Although the displays in the Women's Pavilion celebrated women's important contributions to nineteenth-century American culture, one exhibit—not American—provided impetus for the proliferation of the Woman's Exchange movement in the last quarter of the nineteenth century: the popular and greatly admired embroideries of London's Royal School of Art Needlework. That exhibit, one of the Centennial's most visited, had been personally dispatched by Queen Victoria, who reigned as the Gilded Age's symbol of women's power and was a patron of the school.

Already in its fourth year of operation by 1876, the Royal School demonstrated how such seemingly odd bedfellows as philanthropy, art, entrepreneurship, and self-help could be integrated to provide economic opportunities for women. Developed as part of the larger aesthetic movement, popular in Europe earlier in the nineteenth century as a response to mass production and industrialism, the Royal School, or the South Kensington School as it was often called, had revived the craftsmanship and needlework of the medieval period. It taught embroidery that required intricate stitching and used original, highly embellished, medieval-inspired designs and softly hued woolen thread. The unique decorative art form caught on quickly among elite London women.

It is likely that London's Royal School of Art Needlework grew from the same early-nineteenth-century idea of European charitable self-help to assist the genteel poor that had inspired the Edinburgh Depository. Supported by wealthy English gentlewomen, the Royal School was a workplace and consignment shop that provided training for London's genteel poor women. To fashion-conscious and philanthropic Victorians, the South Kensington School served a purpose beyond providing wealthy Englishwomen with more accouterments for their homes. It, like the Philadelphia Ladies' Depository, targeted women of some social standing who were required to earn a livelihood but restricted by custom to hide their need to work. *Art Amateur* in 1884 noted that the Royal School "was designed exclusively for the benefit of ladies, in the English sense of the word, who are forced to earn their incomes wholly or in part. And it is so ordered that this may be done without exposing their needs or in any way wounding the feelings which are kept keenly susceptible by the particular construction of English society."[15]

The Royal School's mission was to restore "ornamental needlework to the exalted high place it once held among the decorative arts." And, not least, according to one observer, women's efforts would be "real work, to be faithfully performed and duly paid for."[16] By encouraging poverty-stricken gentlewomen to learn and execute the new embroidery styles of the Royal School, wealthy patrons found an avenue that would enable the genteel poor to earn income. At the same time, women's traditional home production became elevated to its former well-regarded status.

The Centennial solidified the link between women, philanthropy, industry, and the arts as women realized how the revitalization of home productions executed according to higher, more artistic standards of the Royal School could economically empower them. Much as the Edinburgh Depository had inspired Elizabeth Stott to initiate the Philadelphia Ladies' Depository in 1832, so would the other successful template of European self-help influence wealthy American women four decades later. At the Centennial, many women who over the next two decades would become Exchange founders and later managers learned to combine traditional interests in self-help and charity with interests in craftsmanship and entrepreneurship, allowing them to create business and professional opportunities for women within the voluntary sector.

"The Idea of Earning Had Entered into the Minds of Women"

The Royal School's exhibit caught the eye of many American women visitors, particularly New York arts patron and entrepreneur Candace Thurber Wheeler. "It was the year of the first 'World's Fair,' held in Philadelphia in 1876," she would later write, "and among other things of interest I came across the exhibit of needlework of the newly founded 'Kensington School of Art Needlework (London).'"[17] Compared with the exhibit, American decorative art seemed dismal. Although the United States had outpaced Europe industrially and economically after the Civil War, it lagged far behind culturally. By the time of the Centennial, England was well ahead in refining and promoting the decorative arts and setting aesthetic standards. American women reacted enthusiastically to the new decorative art styles. *Scribner's* noted that "the showing America then made in art of any kind was not too flattering to Americans, and in decorative art especially there was a noticeable inferiority which struck forcibly a few ladies of cultivation and public spirit."[18]

The exhibition of refined decorative art, reflecting the highest standards of English taste, came at a propitious moment. Expanding American middle and upper classes, unrelenting in their quest for material acquisition and obsession with conspicuous consumption, lacked the needed refinements of cultivation and art. As *Scribner's* admonished, "Everybody remembers, though it has already become a distinct effort of memory to recall it, the general condition of our household art less than a decade ago. In many houses there was unquestionably a great deal of feminine taste and tact displayed [with] some object of feminine accomplishment, the relic of two or three generations back. But, aside from the crudity of all this . . . to speak heroically, the household art ideal of that day was the notion of neatness allied with industry."[19]

The Centennial provided the conduit to transmit British ideals of artistic quality to the United States. America's elite had at last found a paragon of taste to validate their wealth. The decorative arts would provide a standard by which the wealthy could accumulate and the middle class could emulate. Under the dictates of the new decorative art standards, as prescribed by women's and art periodicals, items such as samplers, quilts, India china, brass skillets, and "tidies" (doilies), all dreary reminders of a more rural, rough-and-tumble past, were laid aside. Household decorations began to reflect the cultivated tastes of prosperous people. *Scribner's* heartily encouraged women to buy embroideries embellished with the intriguing "South Kensington" stitch (created by the Royal School), exquisite handpainted china, silk tapestries, detailed wood carvings, custom designed pottery, "mantel and bracket lambrequins, decorated table and other house linen, panels for cabinet work painted upon wood or leather, paintings upon silk for screens, panels, fans, etc., decorated menus, dinner cards, note paper and articles of a like description."[20]

To Candace Wheeler, the Royal School of Art Needlework represented potential in several areas. As an arts patron, she saw the opportunity to replicate an exciting new art form that could be easily understood by fashion-conscious and materialistic Gilded Age Americans. The Royal School's technique, influenced primarily by medieval and Japanese art, provided an unexplored artistic area for wealthy Americans, and Wheeler sensed the financial potential of endorsing such an entrepreneurial venture. "The 'Kensington School,' as this effort was called," she explained, "was fortunately connected with an impulse toward the revival of many of the medieval arts, which in the past had enriched the life and history of England."[21]

A woman's rights supporter, eager to see women gain status and fair remuneration for their labors, Wheeler felt the Royal School's popularity and widespread acceptability in England would help to elevate American women's traditional but devalued skills in needlework to new, more respectable levels. As she noted, "Embroidery became a means of artistic expression and a thing of value."[22] Although a century earlier society had greatly valued women's skills at needlework, by the late nineteenth century technology and other realities of life had contributed to a decline in craftsmanship. The sewing machine, the increasing availability of ready-made goods, and the association of needlework with low-income wage-labor all diminished the status and popularity of hand-made productions. Needlework "had died, branch and stem and root, vanished as if it had never been."[23] Providing an outlet for American women to sell their artistic creations, Wheeler speculated, would offer "the greatest remedy of a resuscitation of one of the valuable arts of the world, a woman's art, hers by right of inheritance as well as peculiar fitness."[24]

Wheeler saw in the Royal School, with its emphasis on self-help and practical training, a model of charitable good works that would provide a way to market women's products while promoting an acceptable employment option safely within the voluntary sector. She noted that the school "had been established to meet exactly the circumstances which existed among people I knew here in New York. Its primary object was to benefit a class which it called 'decayed gentlewomen.' This phrase, so constantly used in connection with whom the praiseworthy and sympathetic effort was being made in England, was utterly rejected by our more sensitive ears and tastes. We would not use so unsavory an epithet for our friends, but, although I rejected the phrase, I was much taken by the idea."[25]

The idea of self-help moved into the popular vernacular as middle- and upper-class women became more interested in self-improvement and financial survival. "Self-help" in earlier decades had been a concept used primarily in charitable programs, and founders of antebellum Exchanges had employed the idea to help the genteel poor. By the late nineteenth century the idea had taken on a broader meaning as it extended women's traditional role as moral and cultural stewards of their communities. It applied to any woman who sought self-expression and vocational training. Self-education and self-development became major themes of most women's clubs.

Of particular importance in the Royal School model was the possibility of entrepreneurship—a personal application of self-help. Women would help themselves by taking an active role in producing, marketing, and selling products through a retail outlet in the voluntary sector. Decorative arts and industrial application could be linked irrevocably through such a plan, which would lessen women's financial vulnerability in a male-dominated world of corporate industrialism. "I saw that many difficulties of existence were preventable, or at least capable of alleviation," Wheeler explained, "and here came in the benefit of my Puritan childhood experiences, where self-help had been the law."[26]

Wheeler's interest in combining artistic home production with women's earning potential had evolved over many years. Like most Americans raised in a rural environment in the early nineteenth century, Wheeler, born in 1827 on a dairy farm in central New York, witnessed firsthand the importance of women's home industry in contributing to the family's and community's economies. As a young bride, she and her husband had lived on Long Island, where soon-to-be-famous artists of the Hudson River School and the Tenth Street Studio spent hours refining their techniques. Those memories guided her as she became a major force in the decorative arts movement and in devising ways for women to seek financial independence through domestic talents.

Wheeler felt that a quasi-commercial enterprise based on the Royal School model would offer a way to transform attitudes about women—particularly middle- or upper-class women—seeking fair remuneration for their work, a mission first undertaken at the Philadelphia Ladies' Depository. Women's labor, expressed through art, might hold the potential to improve their lives, both personally and economically. "It all interested me," she wrote, "for it meant the conversion of the common and inalienable heritage of feminine skill in the use of the needle into a means of art-expression and pecuniary profit."[27] With the formation of a self-help arts society under the auspices of New York's wealthiest society matrons, women in need of income, training, or self-expression would be able to indulge in paid work acceptable to, and perhaps even lauded by, their friends and colleagues. Happily, to Wheeler, the "idea of *earning* had entered into the minds of women."[28]

The New York Society of Decorative Art: Widespread Enthusiasm for Women's Self-Help

By the end of the nineteenth century, many Americans were ready to share Wheeler's enthusiasm for a separate, cooperative outlet where women could not only sell their work but also enjoy business and professional opportunities. The idea seemed a logical compromise between endorsing women's integration into the mainstream workplace or seeking to confine them to their homes without a vocational safety net should financial disaster strike. "It was still an unwritten law that women should not be wage-earners or salary beneficiaries," Wheeler commented, "but necessity was stronger than the law."[29]

Implementing an organization modeled after the Royal School's charitable goods works appealed to many people for a variety of reasons. Cooperation and charity, tried earlier in the antebellum Exchanges, had gained greater acceptance by the late nineteenth century as wealthy women increasingly endorsed cooperatives within the voluntary sector as an acceptable workplace for women. In an era when many feared that the stability of the American home—indeed, all of American civilization—was being undermined by women leaving their homes for paid jobs, work in the voluntary sector seemed a sensible compromise. Women's artistic impulses should be expressed, but within settings where women would not compete with men or jeopardize domestic responsibilities.

To one individual, Walter Smith, an art educator and critic, the possibility of deflecting women's attention from interests outside the home and back to domestic, artistic skills was essential to the future of the country. In widely published articles he stated that he hoped that women would run off to art studios instead of to suffrage marches: "Give our American women the same art facilities as their European sisters and they will flock to the studios and let the ballot box alone."[30] Alternative employment in the voluntary sector tempered such public outrage; cooperatives could be constructive to women in need of income and spiritually fulfilling to those in need of a creative outlet.

Within a year of her visit to the Philadelphia Centennial Exhibition, Wheeler had enlisted the help of New York society matrons, Louis Comfort Tiffany, and John LaFarge to establish the New York Society of Decorative Art. She explained that "gradually, a plan grew in my mind for the formation of an American 'Kensington School,' which should include all the articles of feminine manufacture, which had been brought together in the great Centennial Exhibition. I wrote out a little circular to explain my project to friends and helpers. I have it now, one of the small and, happily, most effective seeds sown in that day of women's awakening to the duty of self-help."[31]

Wheeler also recruited Elizabeth Custer as a founding member. Not only was Custer well known, but she also typified the needy woman the founders had in mind. Custer was "in New York, looking for some profitable employment, for her government pension is so small that she cannot live on it."[32] Wheeler described their first meeting: "She came, the pathetic figure in widow's weeds, which seemed to hold the shadow of a heart-rending tragedy. So modest in her estimate of herself, so earnest in her desire to do something for our enterprise, and so fixed in her determination to do something practical for her own needs!" Libbie Custer was "engaged at the modest salary we could afford."

Wheeler and her colleagues had in essence transplanted the Royal School model, what she called her "clever English prototype," to New York. She wrote "that there were numberless educated and dependent women to whom a legitimate outlet for their labor would be the greatest boon which society could bestow."[33] With that need as a priority, the founders hoped, as Scribner's noted in 1881, "to restore ornamental needlework to the high place it formerly held among the decorative arts." A parallel goal was to provide a medium for the sale and promotion of products produced by women—artistically acceptable goods—through a national network of chapters. The chapters traded information on artists who were the most skilled and offered tips on orders from commercial manufacturers. The Society of Decorative Art sought to help

> many members of the class of women describable as genteel dependents. If we had here a familiar literature like the second-rate novels produced in such quantities in England, it would doubtless show, as those works do, that owing to certain peculiarities of Anglo-Saxon society, we have a large class of "distressed gentlewomen"... absolutely dependent upon the charity... of relatives and friends and the many others who have just enough to "keep them." [The Society]... gives them... instruction which enables them, if they have any faculty for the work... to supply just the amount necessary to bridge the gulf between dependence and independence.[34]

Like its predecessors, the Philadelphia Ladies' Depository and London's Royal School, the Society of Decorative Art provided an outlet for thwarted artistic talent and also discreet employment for gentlewomen in need of income. "All other activities were closed to women of education and refinement under the penalty of 'losing caste,'" Wheeler observed.[35] *Scribner's* described the Society as an effort to protect "women who might otherwise be obliged to enlist in the large army of 'shop girls,' which, without implying any criticism of its members, as a class may be said to be, in the large cities, at least a peculiarly unfortunate body of working women, owing to their long hours of work, their small pay, the hopelessness of bettering their condition, and other and different considerations."[36]

The Society served as a school. It also sponsored exhibitions and provided a lending library for studying the styles of the Royal School's embroidery, a workroom for executing commissions, and a salesroom for the work of its members. It drew the enthusiastic support of wealthy society matrons and had five hundred subscribers within three years of its founding.[37] The roster of founding members did not include any of the old aristocratic New York names such as "a Vanderbilt nor a Pierpont Morgan," but, Wheeler reasoned, "the aristocracy of brains and wealth changes once in fifty years—the places which knew them once know them no more."[38]

Through Wheeler's leadership and the strong national network of women's voluntary groups, the Society of Decorative Art developed chapters in Boston, Philadelphia, Cincinnati, San Francisco, and Baltimore, as well as in numerous smaller cities. As the technology in communications improved during the closing decades of the nineteenth century, the Society aggressively spread the word of its activities through publications and visiting lecturers. Heightened communications among well-to-do women also encouraged a standard of culture and shared values, particularly in promoting an acceptable kind of decorative art that would aesthetically improve middle- and upper-class American homes.[39] The Society's lending libraries proved especially popular, and women from around the country wrote to chapters to ask for guidance. "We have no opportunities to see anything artistic!" they complained.[40]

Elevating women's needlework skills was challenging. Late-nineteenth-century women fervently read magazines that provided instructions and patterns for making an endless array of decorative treasures such as rag rabbits, wax fruit, Valentine tidies, knitted berries, and toothbrush racks. Desperate to counteract such artistic atrocities, the chapters offered classes in needlework and ceramic painting to improve the skills of producers and brought over instructors from the Royal School to ensure the precise instruction required to execute the more difficult South Kensington stitches. "We soon found that we must educate those whom we are trying to serve," Wheeler observed.[41]

By its third year, the Society of Decorative Art had met with the approval of *Scribner's,* which took pains to enlighten readers on the nuances between acceptable and unacceptable artistic standards, explaining that "drawings and sketches in crayon, pen and ink, oil and water colors (unless applied to decorate some useful article) . . . wax flowers and fruit (heaven be praised!), feather flowers, leather work . . . are not admitted to the showrooms. They are, of course, not art."[42]

Wheeler viewed her efforts as an attempt to promote "the idea of self-help through remunerative labor among women." She mused in her autobiography that "in those early days I found myself constantly devising ways of help in individual dilemmas, the disposing of small pictures, embroidery and handwork of various sorts for friends or friends of friends who were cramped by untoward circumstances."[43]

It did not take Wheeler long to grow disenchanted with promoting only the decorative art of wealthy women. She was also concerned with a wider range of needier women whose lack of artistic ability restricted them from earning much-needed income from the Society. Fearing that eventually the Society would be "forced to choose between charitable and aesthetic priorities," Wheeler found that it "was constantly importuned to receive things which did not belong in the category of art. . . . Philanthropy and art are not natural sisters," she concluded.[44] Bearing in mind the large numbers of widows left destitute after the Civil War and the families thrown into poverty during the protracted Panic of 1873, after a year Wheeler broke from the Society, causing consternation among her colleagues. "Everyone disapproved of me," she recalled. "I remember the stony glare of Mrs. John Jacob Astor when I tried to explain my defection."[45]

Wheeler, fifty-one, saw a need to expand the concept of entrepreneurship through philanthropy to more women by establishing a new model of self-help: the New York Exchange for Woman's Work. This enterprise was the creation of a woman who did much to endorse the idea of self-help and the acceptance of paid work for women from a range of classes, helping women to shed the restrictive connotation of "lady." The New York Exchange, a hybrid of charity, commercial entrepreneurship, and cooperation tested a half-century earlier in Philadelphia and reinvigorated through the influence of the Royal School and the concept of self-improvement, would become the new organizational and ideological template for the formation of dozens of Exchanges nationwide during the last two decades of the nineteenth century.

The New York Exchange for Woman's Work, 1878: "Art versus Utility"

Wheeler's attempts to establish the New York Exchange for Woman's Work met with far less enthusiasm than had her efforts to initiate the Society for Decorative Art a year before. She had invited Mary Atwater Choate to join her in initiating the new organization.[46] Choate, a well-known society matron, was, as Wheeler later observed, a woman "whose name is written in the hearts of thousands of women whom she has saved from utter despondency and failure."[47] In 1890 Choate, along with Caroline Ruutz-Rees, a gifted young English scholar, would found Rosemary Hall for Girls on the Atwater estate in Wallingford, Connecticut. Her husband, the famed New York jurist William G. Choate, would establish the Choate School for Boys nearby in 1896.[48]

Candace Wheeler and Mary Choate envisioned a new organization that would reach out to a broader base of women "to touch the whole round of woman's needs" not just the artistic, as Wheeler noted.[49] No longer would less artistic women be excluded from selling handmade creations; rather, the Exchange would be a "society where a woman can send a pie, if she can make a good one, even though she cannot paint a good picture; or a basket of eggs if she cannot decorate china." The Exchange would move beyond the confines of selling only art and encourage women to use other domestic skills, solving the vexing problem of "art versus utility" faced by the Society of Decorative Art.[50] At the Exchange, Wheeler explained, "a woman of brains, industry, and opportunity might make and sell whatever she could do best, and yet not lose her place. So the bars which had kept clever but timid souls in bondage were taken away; women [would] work profitably and [find] in it the joy of self-help, of doing, and finally of help for the world. It [is] the seed of progress, sown in a fruitful and waiting soil."[51]

Pleased with Wheeler's expanded vision of offering a means for self-help to women, Choate eagerly accepted her invitation. "I can see no other way than to found another society which shall accept whatever a woman can do well and help her dispose of it," Wheeler remarked of their break from the Society of Decorative Art. "We will let this one go on its art path without us."[52]

Like Elizabeth Stott, her pioneering counterpart in Philadelphia a half-century earlier, Choate, too, had once witnessed a poverty-stricken woman denied a fair price for her handiwork. Choate's eagerness to co-found a charitable consignment shop for women had been "brought to a focus by the experience of a timid but talented woman who sought a market for some dinner cards she had made. When this woman received only $2.50, while the cards were sold for $12 by the shop that bought them, Mrs. Choate realized that guidance in business for educated but untrained women was sorely needed and that a market for their work should also be supplied."[53]

Wheeler confessed that in starting the Exchange, "I felt as if I had really found my child. Up to this point I had been nursing a changeling."[54] According to the minutes of the founding meeting, on Saturday, February 28, 1878, Choate and Wheeler gathered six New York society matrons "to discuss a plan of opening to ladies in need of such an opportunity a market for the sale of any wares they would have in their power to offer and which [neither] the stores nor any existing benevolent societies now furnish them the means of selling advantageously."[55]

The plan apparently met with scant approval; guests departed without pursuing the idea or taking steps to organize such a society. Perhaps concerned about promoting merchandise not equal to the discerning artistic standards of the Society of Decorative Art, some members of the group expressed concern about "the propriety of renting rooms for the sale of such articles."[56] Choate adjourned the meeting after participants promised to return the next time with a least one friend who would support the initiative.

Within a week, on March 6, Choate reconvened the group at the home of Mrs. H. H. Anderson, this time with the addition of "forty other ladies."[57] The minutes do not reveal who the "other ladies" were, or how and why they reversed the dynamics of the first group's reluctance about starting an Exchange. The meeting's minutes indicate that "a partial organization was effected," however.[58] The group elected officers. Choate became the president; vice presidents were Mrs. Lucius Tuckerman, Mrs. William E. Dodge, Mrs. F. N. Otis, Mrs. H. H. Anderson, and Mrs. Jacob Wandall; recording and assistant secretaries were Mrs. C. R. Agnew and her daughter, Eleanor; corresponding secretary was

Mrs. F. B. Thurber; and the treasurer was Mrs. E. A. Packer. Conveniently, the husbands of the executive board were named to the advisory board, and thirty-three women friends and associates, including Candace Wheeler, were elected to the board of managers.[59]

Choate later recalled that "soon the meetings were so large and enthusiasm grew in spite of the doubting Thomases." Some of those in attendance wanted to initiate the Exchange immediately; others urged waiting until "Decoration Day" or still later, autumn. It was agreed by all that "knowledge should accompany zeal . . . [and] a house committee was appointed" to find an appropriate and convenient salesroom.[60] A friend of one of the founders, Henry Hilton, made the first charitable contribution, $500, to set up the shop.[61]

Choate later remembered the hesitancy expressed by some of the founders at moving ahead so quickly. "A small lady in slow, measured words and impressive manner said: 'Are you sure, Mrs. Chairman, that the society will succeed?'" Choate responded, "'No madam, but if all the shopkeepers in town today had waited to be assured of success, where could you do your shopping in this big city?'" Suddenly, "an attractive woman . . . stood up and, raising her hands high in the air, clapped them and said 'Good!' and the whole floor crowded with women echoed that little word and the vote was carried: the Exchange for Woman's Work became a reality!"[62]

Choate and Wheeler opened the New York Exchange in March 1878, with thirty consigned items spread out on a table in Choate's parlor at 108 East Thirty-first Street. On Monday, March 25, the following announcement appeared in the *New York Daily Tribune:* "A large number of ladies prominent in charitable enterprises have started a society called the 'New York Exchange for Woman's Work,' having for its object the assistance of capable women in straitened circumstances by establishing in some convenient locality permanent salesrooms where articles of handiwork can be disposed of on favorable terms."[63]

Far from resembling the works of art displayed by the Society of Decorative Art, the Exchange featured such woeful items as "a tea cosey, not aesthetic, 'God Bless Our Home' and 'Home Sweet Home' on cardboard, worsted things in every impossible form, carving on bits of wood telling plainly of no knowledge and poor tools, pin cushions never intended to be pricked by a pin and picture pot boilers painful to remember made an array we shall not forget." Among such creations, "one lovely thing—a well made white worsted shawl"—appeared; it was "a ray of hope." Soon, "a lady entered, attracted by the sign and kindly purchased the shawl. That was the first sale."[64]

Over the next few weeks the founders raised $700 from friends and colleagues, much-needed capital that enabled them to move the Exchange in April to rented rooms, at $1,000 annually, at 4 East Twentieth Street, the former showrooms of the Society of Decorative Art, which had moved on to 34 East Nineteenth Street. To encourage customers to become members (subscribers) or to purchase a consignor's ticket for a needy woman who wanted to sell her goods at the shop but was unable to buy a ticket, the managers "kept open the subscription book at all times" near the front door of the new shop.[65] Like the antebellum Exchanges, the cooperative model of the New York Exchange required each consignor to purchase a ticket if she could or to receive a donated one.

By May of its first year the fledgling enterprise enjoyed so much business that the managers hired two saleswomen, a Mrs. Birdsley and her daughter, who shared part-time duties at $200 a year in salary. Within eight months of the founding meeting, on November 23, 1878, the Exchange incorporated under the laws of benevolent, charitable, and scientific societies of New York State. Its charter of incorporation stated that "the particular business and objects of said society are to aid women who are reduced in their circumstances to help themselves in any proper manner and . . . maintaining in the city of New York a permanent place for the sale of their handicraft." Like antebellum Exchanges, the founders of the New York Exchange emphasized providing a permanent outlet where women could sell their work.

The existence of both the New York chapter of the Society of Decorative Art and its offspring, the Exchange for Woman's Work, must have caused more than a little confusion among their patrons and customers. Exchange managers took steps to set the record straight and to separate their new enterprise from the Society of Decorative Art. "It is still so often asked by visitors if we are connected with the Decorative Art Society [and] it seems proper that we should state here our plan of work and our purpose," the managers explained in their first annual report.[66]

At one of the first organizational meetings, founders of the Exchange invited a guest from the Society of Decorative Art to make a presentation.[67] The speaker stressed the different goals of the two organizations and explained that the Exchange would be "benevolent" in nature, whereas the Society of Decorative Art was "educational," adding that the Exchange would probably prove to be self-supporting in a short time.[68] The "two societies are entirely independent of each other in their work," the New York managers asserted in their first annual report. But they were determined to achieve high standards for the merchandise sold at the Exchange.

Aside from its intent to stress benevolence, the Exchange prided itself on the decision to consign a variety of handmade articles. As the *New York Daily Tribune* noted, "It [the Exchange] is not designed to receive such articles of positive artistic merit as meet the standards of excellence demanded by the Society of Decorative Art in articles admitted to its salesrooms."[69] Although the Exchange sought to ennoble and elevate woman's work, it would not lower its standards and be "one more avenue for the distribution of bric-a-brac."[70] The publicly announced differentiation of "standards of excellence" between it and the Society of Decorative Art caused chronic and continuing problems for the Exchange, which tried to balance maintaining its commitment to help a range of women in need with providing quality merchandise for stylish patrons. *Scribner's* attempted in 1881 to provide a definitive aesthetic difference between the two organizations, and the Exchange did not fare well in the assessment: "To make of the [Society of Decorative Art] a curiosity shop, or rather let us say a commonplace shop, receiving and attempting the sale of all sorts of women's handiwork, good, bad, and indifferent, would manifestly be for the Society to enter into the business of brokerage. Such a place is in itself desirable, no doubt, and such a place, the 'Woman's Exchange,' in Twentieth Street, is."[71]

Exchange managers seemingly overcame such stuffy comparisons and focused instead on their more utilitarian mission. As Lucy Salmon, a Vassar College historian, wrote in 1892, the Exchange met the challenge by offering quality merchandise and valuable services: "It simplifies many housekeeping problems in families where there is more work than can be performed by one domestic employee and not enough for two. It also enables them [the patrons] to purchase articles for use which have been made under the most favorable conditions."[72]

To maintain such "favorable conditions" and ensure quality merchandise, the managers of the New York Exchange appointed a committee to screen undesirable work, much as the antebellum Exchanges had done. The managers explained in the 1879 annual report that "all work is received subject to the approval of the managers, who have decided that wax and feather flowers, hair and leather work, spatter and splinter work, and card board, are too perishable and unsalable to be accepted. We take anything useful and ornamental which a lady can make, urging always the manufacture of useful things, which should, if possible, be made ornamental." Holding out hope that in time all merchandise could be brought up to the discerning tastes of their up-scale customers, the managers added that "a competent committee, appointed to make suggestions, will in time do much to improve the character of articles already salable, and to make sightly many things long considered of necessity ugly."[73]

With its benevolent mission of self-help, the New York Exchange immediately attracted a broader scope of consignors than envisioned by the Society of Decorative Art or the antebellum Exchanges. No longer did only women of the wealthier classes apply; as Choate later recalled, "As far as I could see were sad-hearted women made happy by a new hope within them." Among the many consignors she remembered was "an old lady over eighty years of age who supported herself by the sale of small pies. Again, a young girl less than eighteen who supported her invalid mother and younger sister by her fine artistic work. Another woman, well on in years [who] was very limited in circumstances."[74]

Recognizing, as Lincoln did in the *Directory*, that "a woman of ingenuity has almost unbounded opportunity in the way of producing articles so useful, pretty and rare that they sell quickly," the founding managers of the New York Exchange focused on offering a range of needlework and artwork.[75] Many items were suitable for small gifts that wealthy customers could present as they went about town calling on friends. Plain or fancy needlework included stuffed animals and rag pigs, dogs, and dolls, baskets, boxes, caps, watch and traveling cases, children's clothing, frames, jackets, knee warmers, leggins, mittens, pen wipers, beaded purses, sachets crocheted to look like radishes, driving reins, shawls, socks, sunbonnets, embroidered towels, and knitted undershirts.[76] Reflecting the new decorative arts influence, Lincoln suggested that more artistically inclined consignors, "ingenious and skillful in producing novel and rare bits of art work," might offer "bonbon boxes, hand-painted china bureau sets, holiday cards, book covers, doylies, etchings on linen, paper flowers, glass pictures, lamp shades, oil and water color paintings, photograph frames, pin trays, table scarfs, portieres, folding fire screens, painted tapestries, telegram pads, and jewelry cases."[77]

By the end of its first year, the managers of the New York Exchange boasted that their enterprise "no longer was an experiment."[78] They had broadened the scope of the Exchange idea by giving "impetus to the thought of independent support among dependent women," which in turn established the standard for "stimulating the capabilities of others."[79] Starting with only thirty consigned articles in Mary Choate's parlor, within a year the New York Exchange had paid nearly $14,000 in commissions to consignors and recorded 17,566 consigned (not necessarily sold) items in its ledger. By the next year the Exchange occupied a multi-story building. By 1880 the Exchange would count 1,800 consignors. Such immediate commercial success, assistance to a range of consignors, and support from fashionable society would make the Exchange the prototype and inspiration for dozens of other Exchanges around the country.

Within the next fifteen years the Exchange idea would spread quickly through a conduit of women's voluntary associations, primarily those firmly grounded in cross-class efforts at promoting social, political, and economic opportunities: the Women's Christian Temperance Union, the Women's Christian Association, and the Women's Educational and Industrial Union, as well as numerous cultural arts groups. As Mary Choate mused at the founding of the New York Exchange, "The question of how to make the rich take care of the poor is one that interests all thoughtful people."[80] Just as antebellum Exchanges had made self-help a fashionable way to aid the genteel poor, so, too, did postbellum managers hope to expand the idea to all women interested in economic well-being. Borrowing from a well-tested European template of self-help that had proven successful for their wealthy peers a half-century before in Philadelphia, Exchange managers of the late nineteenth century created a network of employment opportunities that expanded the idea of self-help for women from a range of socioeconomic backgrounds.

4

A "Prosperous Existence in Every Town": The Exchange Idea Spreads throughout the Nation

"There is hardly a city of any considerable size without its Woman's Exchange," F. A. Lincoln observed in the *Directory of Exchanges for Woman's Work* in 1891, thirteen years after the founding of the New York Exchange. News of the New York Exchange spread quickly around the country among wealthy women interested in forming similar enterprises in their own communities. Lincoln, caught up with the overnight popularity of the movement, noted that "as soon as the success of the New York Exchange began to be known outside of that city, others were established in large centers."[1] The *Directory* was intended to guide in the development of future Exchanges and provide a plan of organization and uniformity. Lincoln explained that "within the last few years, constant inquiry has been made, in various quarters, for detailed and reliable information regarding the work of these Exchanges, and the manner of doing business with them."[2]

Yet by 1891, before the nationally published directory was available, women across the country already had established at least seventy-two Exchanges. Lucy Salmon counted even more, finding in 1892 that "there are now in operation about seventy-five Exchanges scattered throughout twenty-three states and the District of Columbia" (Table 2, Appendix A).[3] Not only did the number of new Exchanges show the popularity of the idea, but the money consignors earned also testified to its success. From 1878 to 1891 the nine largest Exchanges paid nearly $1.2 million to consignors (Table 3, Appendix A). The Cincinnati Exchange, for example, in its first decade, paid out nearly a quarter of a million dollars (Table 4, Appendix A).

Candace Wheeler noted years later of the Exchange movement that "its continued and prosperous existence in every town in America, and in Canada and Sweden, tells its own story."[4] Other late-nineteenth-century commentators shared Lincoln's and Wheeler's enthusiasm. Observing the rapid spread of the idea, Alice Hyneman Rhine concurred about the "phenomenal growth" of the Exchange idea. She reported that several dozen Exchanges "have come into existence during the last decade, all of which are operating under the same general plan."[5] Such widespread uniformity in "operating under the same general plan" testified to the intricate communication network among wealthy women and their eagerness to replicate the Exchange idea.[6] Their voluntary organizations provided a conduit to spread a shared cultural gospel and, not least, a common economic mission.

"We Have Modeled Our Own Exchange on New York"

Exchange founders tapped into a strong network of city-to-city voluntary organizations representing literary clubs, decorative arts societies, the Women's Christian Temperance Union, the Women's Educational and Industrial Union, and the Women's Christian Association, among myriad local voluntary associations that encouraged self-help and self-improvement for all women. In some towns, well-to-do women's cultural, religious, charitable, and secular organizations were undeniably bound, and the new emphasis on the decorative arts often provided a common denominator. By the end of the century, most women's groups had initiated programs in arts and crafts. The idea of applying new decorative arts standards, as exemplified at the Centennial, to traditional self-help applications seemed a winning combination as benevolent women tried to help other women learn marketable skills.

As the Exchange idea spread, the influence of the decorative arts movement, which had prompted the formation of the New York Exchange, was an unquestionable influence on the founding of many new Exchanges. Martha Louise Rayne had noted that fact in 1893 when she observed that "in the past few years there has grown out of the aesthetic atmosphere a new and important industry for women in the organization of societies for promoting the use and sale of fancy and decorative work. These are sent to what is known as an 'Exchange for Woman's Work,' numbers of which have grown up around the country."[7] Founders often chose names that inextricably linked their Exchanges with the decorative arts: the Woman's Work Exchange and Decorative Art Society of Brooklyn (1878), the Rochester (New York) Art Exchange (1880), the Woman's Work and Art Exchange of Morristown, New Jersey (1885), which assuredly claimed that it sold "perfect work in every department," and the Art Exchange of Harrisburg, Pennsylvania (for which no founding date is available).[8]

Reflecting the interplay between women's charitable, religious, and cultural organizations of the postbellum years, the Exchange idea also spread within the vast national network of religious and secular reform organizations that had been established at mid-century. Because of increased communications— easier travel, newspapers, and the growth of magazines and publications directed at women, particularly those such as the *New York Evangelist*, which was aimed specifically at Protestants—women of the last quarter of the century connected more easily than had their counterparts a half-century before.

The Woman's Christian Association (WCA) provided a natural spring-board that helped democratize the Exchange and the decorative arts movements, as they spread from more elite northeastern areas to cities across the country.[9] The WCA, later to become the Young Women's Christian Association, had likely begun in England during the 1850s when concerned Protestant women prayed for "our princesses and all who are in the glitter of fashionable life . . . daughters at home of the middle classes . . . young wives and mothers . . . governesses . . . shop women . . . domestic servants . . . factory girls . . . the criminal and fallen . . . and those who are enchained by Judaism, Popery and Heathenism."[10]

Within a few years after the Civil War, Protestant women across the United States had initiated local WCA chapters, but their mission had moved beyond praying for "young women who are dependent on their own exertions for support" to initiating programs to help them.[11] Far removed from the intense evangelical proselytizing of many charity groups a half-century before, the WCA faced the reality of working women's lives in the last quarter of the nineteenth century. The New York City WCA chapter noted that "we must take human nature as we find it, adapting our work to its needs. The hard-working person seldom desires to be instructed . . . but seeks to be amused."[12] The WCA sought to "endeavor to bring them [working women] under moral and religious influences . . . so that amidst the manifold temptations of a large city none might fall from want of a steady occupation."[13] Its activities centered around providing boardinghouses at reasonable rates, employment bureaus, libraries, lectures, and restaurants. Providing young women wage-earners with steady and "acceptable" work was in itself a full-time job for benevolent women.[14]

The Exchange idea spread rapidly through many local WCA chapters, and members may have perceived the potential of adding a charitable consignment shop to their array of services. Within the first six months of 1883, for example, Protestant benevolent women in Cincinnati, Richmond, and St. Louis gathered in their respective cities to discuss a plan already implemented in thirteen other cities that had initiated Exchanges.[15] Cincinnati WCA members were moved to begin a Woman's Exchange after reading a first-page article in the January 19, 1882, *New York Evangelist*, which found that:

> The New York Exchange for Woman's Work, having its headquarters at 4 East Twentieth Street, is now doing, as for several years past, a most excellent office for women who need assistance in the delicate and encouraging way which the Ex-

change contemplates. Having enlarged its accommodations, the society is enabled to extend help correspondingly by receiving a greater variety of work than heretofore. And, contrary to common mercantile experience, the lady managers find that there is a sale "for almost every well made article that the human mind can devise." We need not say that not a few of the best ladies of our city are giving much time and effort to the success of this worthy enterprise.

The twenty-one founders of the Exchange for Woman's Work in Richmond, Virginia, "represented the five Presbyterian churches" in Richmond in 1883.[16] The women had been inspired to start an Exchange after receiving a letter from a manager of the New York Exchange. At their first meeting on February 2, 1883, a month to the day after women in Cincinnati had organized an Exchange, the founders of the Richmond Exchange noted in their minutes that "a letter was read by Mrs. Agnew of the New York Exchange; also quotations from the reports of similar societies in Newark and Brooklyn, explaining their object and the plan which led them to success." They explained in their first annual report in 1884 that "we have modeled our own Exchange on New York."[17] Stressing the charitable self-help philosophy of the day, they wrote of their enterprise, "Surely such a charity will bear scrutiny and criticism even at this day, when people have learned to distinguish so accurately between the benevolence that helps and that which only harms the recipient."[18] The founders organized the Richmond Exchange as a joint-stock company, raising initial capital sold in $25 shares.[19]

The WCA also provided the organizational structure for the New Orleans Christian Woman's Exchange (CWE). One of that city's leading society women, Mrs. H. W. Bartlett, visited the New York Exchange, obtained a copy of its constitution, and immediately set out to duplicate the enterprise in New Orleans, the first Exchange to open in the Deep South. Bartlett took the helm of the CWE for its first year."[20] To recruit members, she ran an advertisement in the *New Orleans Picayune* on March 27, 1881, asking who "in these difficult and troubled times . . . ought any longer to sit with folded hands in luxurious idleness?" Wealthy women were called "to rally at once and step to the front," and forty answered.[21] Starting with a $100 contribution on April 1, 1881, from Paul Tulane, a philanthropist and merchant, the local chapter of the WCA (or the Ladies' Christian Association, as the advertisement stated) initiated a charitable consignment shop. Lincoln described its mission as being for the "relief of their sisters dwelling in poverty."[22]

A few weeks later, the Christian Woman's Exchange opened for business in four adjoining rooms at 41–43 Bourbon Street, with the telephone company installing a telephone free of charge and the gas company waiving its initial fee. In May the organization incorporated and became "the first association organized and chartered in the City of New Orleans by women, for women." Obtaining a charter in Louisiana during the 1880s was not complicated, although the state did require the founders to secure the "signed authorization of their husbands" to undertake such a venture.[23]

The New Orleans Christian Woman's Exchange was an immediate success, and its "growth was rapid and steady."[24] But within two weeks of its founding, it faced stinging criticism from "A Church Member" in a letter published in the *Picayune*. The writer questioned the "policy of making our Woman's Exchange a religious work instead of one of noble philanthropy, based upon the broad, free principles of sweet charity. . . . Why call only upon Christian women!" the critic asked. "Our Jewish women are noble workers, generous donors and staunch supporters of every worthy charity in which their sympathies are enlisted. And, as regretfully as it may be said, it is well known that there are hundreds of good women in every community who are not Christians."[25]

The managers attributed the criticism to a disgruntled participant at the founding meeting who had faulted the Exchange's exclusion of non-Christian women. Undaunted, they set about creating a successful business enterprise that would inspire women in other southern cities to replicate the idea.[26] One of their first orders of business was to make Mrs. Thomas "Stonewall" Jackson, in town for the dedication of a monument in her husband's memory, an honorary member of the Exchange.

News of the CWE's success spread so rapidly that within two years members began receiving requests from women in Memphis, Vicksburg, and Jackson for information about starting Exchanges there. The CWE became so popular in New Orleans that the Southern Art Union, a popular decorative arts organization in the city, formally requested merging with CWE. Because many of the Union's members were also involved with CWE, the proposal "provoked a warm discussion." The proposal was eventually rejected, however, in the tradition of the New York Exchange's separation from the Society of Decorative Art, because the CWE's managers thought it best not to "change the platform on which the Exchange is now working."[27]

The CWE also elicited interest in 1885 from Queen Olga of Greece, who wanted to start a similar enterprise for the women in her country. Similarly, in 1896 Countess di Brazza of Italy, formerly Cora Slocum of New Orleans, who had reigned as Queen of Mardi Gras in 1881, replicated the idea of the New Orleans Exchange when she established a lace-making school for needy Italian women.[28]

Soon other Protestant women's associations around the nation opened Exchanges, among them the Troy, New York, Exchange, begun by women appointed by the YMCA, and the Worcester, Massachusetts, Exchange, where managers were "selected from all the churches."[29]

In addition to the WCA, the Women's Christian Temperance Union (WCTU) served as a conduit for the spread of the Exchange idea, particularly in the western states. By 1878, when the New York Exchange opened, the WCTU already was a force to be reckoned with. Eight years later, in December 1886, members of the Denver Central WCTU opened the Woman's Exchange on Stout Street. By its fourth year the Exchange had 163 consignors and had paid out $8,500 in commissions.[30] Similarly, members of the Santa Barbara WCTU formed the Woman's Industrial Exchange on State Street in 1890. Within the first year, the venture, which specialized in "Mexican drawn art," had paid its eighty-three consignors $3,500.[31]

By the 1880s the WCTU was the largest women's voluntary organization in the country, with more than 150,000 members, and women across the country eagerly joined President Frances Willard's "Do Everything!" campaign. In a strong separatist statement typical of women's late-nineteenth-century voluntarism and Exchange managers' interests as well, the WCTU banned men from leadership roles. Perhaps more than any other group, the WCTU set the ideological stage for women's postbellum activism by insisting on separatism and focusing on domesticity to exalt and protect all aspects of the home. The WCTU sought to transform American society and women's role in it, establishing a broad cultural framework from which other national women's associations operated or drew strength. Affiliation with the WCTU gave thousands of otherwise politically inexperienced women the opportunity to become involved in politics and to effect community change. As Willard summarized the organization's accomplishments in 1891, "the most significant outcome of this movement was the knowledge of their own power gained by the conservative women of the churches. They had never seen a 'woman's rights convention,' and had been held aloof from the 'suffragists,' by fears as to their orthodoxy; but now there were women, prominent in all church cares and duties, eager to clasp hands for more aggressive work than such women had ever dreamed of undertaking."[32]

In addition to the WCTU and WCA, other popular national women's voluntary groups also provided the organizational structure and network for the initiation of new Exchanges. In Boston, the Women's Educational and Industrial Union (WEIU) opened a shop for consigned baked goods within a year of its founding in 1877. The handiwork department opened later and, capitalizing on the revival of crewel and canvas work popularized by the Royal School of Art Needlework at the Centennial Exhibition, offered a large line of crewel patterns adapted from Jacobean and Colonial designs. The WEIU's shop "sold on commissions the fruits of woman's work; [and] opened a lunchroom where women could have varied bills of fare at moderate prices, or where they could sit and eat luncheons brought from home."[33]

The WEIU was begun in Boston in 1877 by several activist women, including Harriet Clisby, one of the country's first female physicians; Julia Ward Howe, the writer of the "Battle Hymn of the Republic"; Abby Morton Diaz of Brook Farm; and Louisa May Alcott, author of *Little Women*. Alcott knew firsthand the perils working women encountered and wrote of her own struggle with economic vulnerability in *Work: A Story of Experience* (1873).[34] The WEIU focused its programs on women's and family issues, citing as its objectives, according to Josephine Shaw Lowell, to "increase fellowship among women in order to promote the best practical method for securing their educational, industrial and social environment."[35] Alice Rhine noted that the WEIU "invites all women to its readings room and parlor. It provides lectures, and classes, entertainments. Some of the classes are industrial. It has 'Mother's Meetings' and 'Talks with Young Girls' from women with high reputation. It befriends the friendless. It is a tower of strength for the helpless. The effective work is to enabl[e] the individual to stand upright of himself, instead of being held in position by charities, reforms, or penalties."[36]

In Hartford, the founders had just such a goal in mind when they established the United Workers, with the Woman's Exchange developing as an outgrowth of that organization's Industrial Committee in 1888. Like the WEIU, the group's purpose was to "give the young women working in the factories and sweatshops club rooms and educational advantages."[37] Within the first year, "500 girls used and enjoyed the library of 950 volumes, and the cheery club room." The Exchange also offered classes in dressmaking, fancy work, and gymnastics. Within the first year the shop counted 217 consignors, logging in its books more than "1,000 fancy articles, 218 dozen doughnuts, 400 loaves of bread, 803 loaves of cake, [and] 832 pies."[38] Four years later the Exchange was so successful that it separated from the United Workers and incorporated on its own.

Some Exchanges more than likely formed without the backing of a national organization. They sprang instead from local social or cultural organizations such as literary, social, and cultural clubs, church groups, and sewing circles that had one common mission: to help women through self-improvement and self-help programs. The St. Augustine, Florida, Exchange, for example, formed in 1892, claimed no connections with the WCA, WCTU, or WEIU. It was initiated by two winter residents, both members of the city's elite King's Daughters Society, who saw a need to "do welfare in the city."[39] An early historian of the St. Augustine Exchange wrote in 1912 of the founding that:

Looking back, try to imagine yourself present at the meeting of the King's Daughters Circle, held at the home of the president, Mrs. Josiah James. One would see articles of Spanish handwork sent in by women of the town anxious to dispose of their handiwork and in that way make for themselves a support, meager in many instances, meaning more to them than we can appreciate. The Circle had been in existence but two years, and from the first there were constant appeals made to help dispose of women's work, and since its institution had done what it could do to help women. When the King's Daughters first opened the shop it was officially called the "King's Daughters Industrial Exchange" and this is the one and only time the name was ever mentioned in the minutes.[40]

To raise money for their new enterprise, "a gala was held on the fort green in August of 1892 and $120.10 was raised for the project."[41] But problems arose. Within the first six months, members of the St. Augustine Exchange questioned who should be in charge of the fledgling organization. The new president, a co-founder, suggested that the Exchange be made independent and add new members outside of the King's Daughters. The other co-founder took exception to that suggestion and insisted that the Exchange could not survive without the financial and organizational backing of the King's Daughters. The controversy raged until "Mrs. S. C. Stanbury, wife of the local minister and a King's Daughter, mediated the difference and on January 3, 1893, the King's Daughters officially voted to withdraw and make the Exchange independent and self-supporting."[42]

"A Queen Whose Throne Was Philanthropy"

The success of an Exchange often depended upon the force of a strong personality during its formative years. Caroline Gratia Williams Walmsley, second president of the Christian Woman's Exchange of New Orleans, was described as "a queen whose throne was philanthropy and whose scepter, benevolence."[43] Elected president of the Exchange a year after its founding, Walmsley served for the next twenty-four years, until her sudden death in 1905, a longevity of service that would characterize those of officers of many Exchanges. Five years into her presidency, Walmsley negotiated two major gifts of cash for the purchase of the Exchange's first building. The first, $20,000, was made by Mrs. Charles T. Howard; the second, $10,000, was from Mrs. M. L. Whitney.[44] The gifts were two of the largest given to charitable organizations by women in their own names during the late nineteenth century. The New Orleans managers eventually decided to purchase the Edwards House, a twenty-six-room mansion facing Lafayette Square. The asking price was $30,000, and the managers offered and settled on $28,500, which they paid in cash.[45]

The Baltimore Industrial Exchange grew under the patronage of a wealthy Baltimorean in 1880. Mrs. G. Harmon Brown, like Mary Choate in New York, first opened the Exchange in the parlor of her home on Saratoga Street, a few blocks north of Baltimore's thriving commercial harbor. There, in the "bleak years following the Civil War," Mrs. Brown "put up for sale handsewn articles of clothing, quilts, fine needlework, baked goods and preserves."[46] She expressed concern about "women unable to make financial ends meet and without access to the business and professional world through requisite training to enter it."[47] Nellie Fisher, an early historian of the Baltimore Industrial Exchange, noted in the *Baltimore American* in 1896 that Mrs. Brown had been inspired to initiate the Exchange to help women who preferred not to seek work in industry. "So much has been done to dignify women's work," Fisher wrote, "and there are so many who prefer to earn money by their own efforts rather than 'eat the bread of dependence,' but until the Exchange was established there was no way open for the accomplishment of this end. By these means women find a way to support themselves from the publicity from which a sensitive nature shrinks."[48]

In St. Louis, Ariadne Lawnin became the driving force behind the founding of that city's Exchange in 1883. Like many of her wealthy counterparts in other cities, Lawnin hoped to see a better life for working women and sought to help them obtain financial security by providing a retail outlet for the sale of their handiwork. When she opened the Exchange, Lawnin coined a motto, "Helping Women to Help Themselves."[49] Her interest in initiating an Exchange had evolved from her earlier work in the St. Louis WCA, which had opened an industrial sewing school and boardinghouse for young women, and a small depository in 1879.[50] Lawnin took such a personal interest in the needy women who became Exchange consignors that she routinely "buried them in her husband's cemetery lot at Bellefontaine, forcing him to buy another for his own family."[51]

Similarly, the Richmond Exchange owed its prominence and success to Mrs. S. H. Hawes, who first convened Richmond's prominent Presbyterian women at her house in 1883 to start the Exchange. Her death stirred an outpouring of grief in the city, and she was eulogized as a woman of "wise administration and catholic spirit. It would be difficult to estimate the good that has been communicated in all directions from this [the Exchange] great work which had so small a beginning."[52]

In some cases, Exchanges evolved from local depositories or similar enterprises established within a decade of the Civil War. In Pittsburgh, a Ladies' Depository, designed to serve only the genteel poor, was initiated on March 6, 1873 ("Thursday morning," as dutifully noted in the minutes), when a "number of ladies met in the parlor of the YWCA to organize a 'Ladies Depository and Employment Office,' which would function as a branch of the 'Woman's Christian Association' of Pittsburgh." The founders modeled their organization on the Philadelphia Ladies' Depository after noting a report "of a similar organization in Philadelphia."[53] Renting rooms in the former office of Dr. James Speer, physician-husband of one of the founders, the new managers set the annual membership dues at $5, which entitled the subscriber to "deposit work for herself or for a friend." The Depository charged 6 percent commission on items sold, which included "any item ornamental and useful."[54]

The Pittsburgh Depository remained small and had difficulty recruiting enough consignors to sell goods and execute special orders. Over the course of the first four months in business, the treasurer listed the number of items deposited and the number of consignors: "April, 2 pieces, one depositor; May, 81 pieces, 12 depositors, June, 28 pieces, 10 depositors, and July, 38 pieces, and 11 depositors."[55] Six months into its first year, the managers wrote that the year had been "a dull one," but they remained encouraged by the steady patronage of "old friends."[56]

The Depository, its philosophy outdated by the postbellum interest to help *all* women attain "that blessed independence," closed its doors in 1879 after only six years. In 1886, however, a new Exchange, modeled on the postbellum Exchange idea, appeared in Pittsburgh. Working from the template provided by the New York Exchange and new philanthropic methods to provide self-help to a range of women in need, the Pittsburgh Women's Industrial Exchange opened its doors on Pennsylvania Avenue to any woman to sell her "art and art needlework, embroidery, knitting, etc.; plain sewing a speciality."[57] It was a markedly different approach from that of the antebellum Exchanges. The new postbellum Exchange model sought above all else "to promote mutual cooperation among women, to help the rich and poor alike to stand upon equality."[58]

Making Class Distinctions Obsolete

The contrast between the old and new Exchange mission was also dramatically highlighted in Philadelphia. In 1894 the managers of the Philadelphia Exchange for Woman's Work, formed in 1888, merged their charitable consignment shop into a "co-partnership" with the original Woman's Exchange, the Philadelphia Ladies' Depository, founded in 1832. The managers reasoned that "the old institution [the Depository] was staggering under a load of antiquated traditions which impeded its speed in the race, and its efficiency."[59] The "antiquated traditions" so outdated by 1894 represented the very factors that had contributed to the rise of the Exchange idea in the antebellum years: to provide a discreet, anonymous means for poverty-stricken gentlewomen, who faced formidable cultural restrictions against seeking paid work, to earn income through the sale of their needlework in the voluntary sector. By 1894, however, the managers found that mission "so limited in its sphere of action [that it] did not supply the entire need." The idea of women being ashamed of paid work seemed passé when managers recalled that the first Exchange had developed when "the prejudices of an ancient regime had full sway [and it] was regarded as *infra dig* for a 'lady' to work for a living; many a proud ancestress of ours preferred to suffer privations to having it known that she sold the results of her work."[60]

The Philadelphia Exchange for Woman's Work reflected a new age of wealthy women's voluntarism and changing attitudes about women's right to seek financial security. Their new institution, the managers asserted, with its "liberal rules and business like methods," encouraged all women, not just "decayed gentlewomen," to boldly seek the financial security so long denied to them. "Women in reduced circumstances no longer feel humiliated, but proud at the thought of being independent and self-supporting," they stated. The managers added that "sociology upon philanthropy, which revolutionized relief work, [makes] class distinctions in such work obsolete."[61] Lucy Salmon confirmed that thought, noting of the new Exchange idea that "its aim and its management show the influence of the present generation and its study of philanthropy as social and economic questions."[62]

Reflecting the new, inclusive Exchange philosophy, postbellum managers across the country extended help to two populations of consignors: wealthy women who needed a channel of self-expression and working- or middle-class women in need of income and who could not (or chose not to) work in the commercial sector. It was the latter group that the managers most wanted to help. Wealthy Exchange managers crossed class lines as they recognized the financial vulnerability and second-class working status of all women.

Exchanges needed "the combined efforts of all the classes" in order to be successful, and managers hoped to demonstrate "that women can work in harmony, thus disproving the old notion that they could not; for in these very struggles together, mutual forbearance and mutual helpfulness have been developed, displacing, in some degree, petty animosities and jealousies."[63] Embracing the wider base of women that poured into the postbellum workplace became imperative. "Only a small number of the Exchanges are so favorably located," Lincoln noted, "that they can fully carry out the original idea of receiving work only from 'gentlewomen reduced in circumstances'; the privileges [of consigning] are extended to many women."[64]

By late in the nineteenth century, working women were no longer seen as inferior. As the *New York Evangelist* noted on the first page of its November 23, 1882, issue, they were deemed honorable, a part of "that large class of worthy, intelligent young women who are dependent upon their own exertions for support, and who are nobly striving to become wholly self-supporting." During the closing decades of the century most benevolent women turned their attention to helping wage-earning women of the working- and middle-classes. The Hartford managers reaffirmed this thought when they noted in their 1888 annual report that they hoped "to dignify labor; to remove any wrong conception of the incompatibility of work and culture."[65]

The Christian Woman's Exchange of New Orleans adopted an egalitarian mission to serve "as a depot or salesroom where any woman from the richest lady in the land to the poorest can place the work of her fingers and offer it for sale." That, according to the *Picayune,* meant anything "from a pot of jelly up to a tapestry embroidery."[66] The Richmond Exchange accepted consignments from "needy women at large."[67] The Milwaukee Woman's Industrial Exchange managers likewise boasted of providing "a place where woman's work of every kind that is purchasable may be deposited for sale, and where orders for such work are taken," adding that the shop operated for the benefit "only of needy women."[68] Similarly, the Richmond managers prided themselves on helping women such as a "young woman, not homeless, but absolutely penniless, with no qualifications of a 'situation' of any kind, [who] has clothed herself comfortably by the proceeds of her own handiwork."[69]

The managers of the St. Louis Exchange targeted working-class women, "the deserving poor," as the beneficiaries of their endeavor. The hope was that the Exchange would serve "as a bridge between capital and labor, this at a time when labor unrest was a source of much concern to society."[70] St. Louis managers insisted that it is "not those who come to our doors in tattered clothing that we hope to assist, as they are an improvident class who have no appreciation of our motto 'Help Those Who Try to Help Themselves.' Nor is it for the sale of that woman's wares whose sphere in life, financially, will allow her to compete with capitalists, but for those who daily walk beside us silently, unmurmuringly, their patient faces not disclosing the warfare they wage with life's misfortune."[71]

Within a few years of their founding, many Exchanges expanded their missions beyond offering retail outlets for women to sell merchandise. Much in keeping with postbellum benevolent women's interest in providing "homes away from home" for working women, and perhaps also borrowing from the model started by department store owners who established residence hotels for unmarried sales clerks and other workers, many larger Exchanges initiated boardinghouses. The managers of the Baltimore Industrial Exchange in 1887 purchased a building on North Charles Street to accommodate such efforts. The four-story brick building had been erected in 1815 as a private home, but by 1860 a new owner had added a five-story rear addition and turned the structure into a rooming house.[72] By the time the Exchange purchased it, the building had five boarding units, which the managers rented to working women.

Similarly, the managers of the Christian Woman's Exchange in New Orleans noted in 1888 that "the possession of a home enables us to greatly enlarge the scope of our work, and increase the number of women benefited."[73] They prided themselves on the rooms the Exchange rented to single working women in a large building on Lafayette Square at the corner of South and Camp streets and noted that many were housed and fed free of charge there. An advertisement for the CWE boasted of the building's desirable location: "Rooms for ladies (en suite or single) with access to Drawing Room. All the comforts, refinements and protection of homelife at reasonable rates. Free circulating library attached. Accessible to Churches, Public Buildings, Art and Shopping Centers, fronting a handsome park and commanding a view of the Carnival Pageants and other processions. Telephone in building."[74]

The Richmond Exchange in 1887 moved to the old YMCA building, which could accommodate both the consignment shop and a low-cost boardinghouse for working women, and the New York managers, by their second year in business, also risked moving into a much larger building at an annual rent of $3,000 so "that we can extend our boarders as fast as circumstances will allow."[75]

Other efforts to reach across class lines focused on providing services that encouraged self-help and self-sufficiency. The New York Exchange, like many others, offered an employment bureau and a "register [that] is kept open for the names of ladies with good references, who desire positions as housekeepers, dressmakers, governesses, drawing and music teachers, and who are willing to do shopping for ladies."[76] And, in 1892, "a desk in the back room had been rented to a woman whose work was painting and developing photography."[77] The Decatur, Illinois, Exchange, managed under the auspices of the Industrial and Charitable Union of that city, offered a "labor directory," where women workers could look for employment.

Managers could offer still other services: "In addition to the aid the Exchange gives women by disposing of their handiwork and other productions, many maintain one or more of the following practical departments, according to the needs of the locality: Bureau of Information and Employment, Registry (references being required), Cooking School, Lunch Counter or Dining-Room (furnished with home-made viands), Library and Reading Room (supplemented with lectures and educational classes), etc."[78] The St. Louis Exchange, for example, offered discounted 4-cent lunches for working-class women, and the New Orleans Exchange was among the first Exchanges to offer a "creche," or nursery. The day care, a "novelty," was supervised by a separate board "consisting of young ladies." "To this nursery," Lincoln observed, "poor women, obliged to work outside their homes, bring their little children, from one to seven years of age, where they are cared for while their mother is at work."[79] Appendix B provides an in-depth case study of the Woman's Exchange of Cincinnati and describes how several elements—the decorative arts movement, the local chapter of the Woman's Christian Association, a short-lived Ladies' Depository, a strong leader, and the new self-help philosophy—combined to create a highly successful venture.

"The Divinely Directed Instrument"

As they expanded their vision to help working-class women, Exchange managers increasingly became economic and social reformers of women's work issues. Lincoln underscored this effort. Referring to himself as "an ardent friend and promoter of this grand nineteenth century [Exchange] movement," he explained of the wealthy women who initiated the Exchanges that "it is more blessed to have been the divinely directed instrument in a work like this, so immeasurable in its benefits, than to sit upon thrones."[80] It is possible that Exchange managers, in their zealotry for their mission, did perceive themselves as divinely directed instruments to help other women. Their work provided a national social reform platform as they created what they felt were reasonable work alternatives for women who needed income and useful lives.

The managers joined a larger national reform effort in the closing decades of the century to address the question of how women's paid employment could be transformed to keep home and family central to women's lives while still offering them financial security. Much had changed since the antebellum Exchanges began, and many openly voiced concern about the disparity between women's financial vulnerability and the consequences on society if they abandoned family responsibilities for the paid work force. By the last third of the nineteenth century, when marriage or career—but never both—became the two choices available for women, home and family responsibilities became lightening rods for arguments concerning a woman's place in society, particularly in the paid work force. Many were concerned over the possibility of family disintegration as increasing numbers of American women, disenchanted with the confinement of marriage, opted for lives without marriage (or divorce) and for financial independence through wider employment opportunities. Given the perception of women's culpability for the breakdown in society, the postbellum issue of women's right to financial independence involved explosive and complex elements.

The debate divided participants into three camps. Conservative opponents such as Charles Elliot asserted in the *New York Evangelist* on September 28, 1882, that women's paid work outside the home made them "unfit to be the helper and companion of man." Worse yet, Elliot charged, competing for men's wages threatened the core of American society; women's rightful place was within the home as wives and mothers. Work outside the home was antithetical to woman's delicate nature and might imperil not only their health but also their integrity.

Opposing forces debunked such ideas, citing instead the health problems created by too many pregnancies, too much housework, and too few creative outlets. Catharine Beecher, alarmed at the numbers of "feeble" and "delicate" American women, conducted a survey of women in two hundred towns. She concluded that no more than 2 percent of those she studied were healthy. Of her own family of nine sisters and sisters-in-law and fourteen female cousins, Beecher found all but two were either "delicate" or invalids.[81] Rather than increasing women's role within the home, this group of feminists heartily endorsed liberation from the drudgery of housework, which would allow more time and freedom to engage in useful and productive occupations. Charlotte Perkins Gilman and others encouraged women to get out of the house and seek more stimulating opportunities: "The homebound woman is clogging the whole world," she wrote.[82]

But ideas such as Gilman proposed were too radical and foreign for the majority of Americans, who continued to see the home as an integral cultural institution in desperate need of bolstering and support. Most Americans remained firmly committed to keeping home and family intact and were not ready to endorse proposals to integrate women fully into traditional male spheres of work. Fearing irreparable harm to family and society, other writers urged women to temper their impulse to run into the commercial workplace. "Only harm can result if efforts are made to induce the women to leave her home daily for work," Josephine Lowell advised.[83]

By the closing decades of the century, a growing, connected group of woman's rights advocates, exemplified by women who initiated and managed Woman's Exchanges, sought to preserve the home and family as the highest priority for women and yet encourage feminist experimental work options that would benefit women's quest for financial security and personal fulfillment. They hoped to homogenize women's private and public lives, enabling them to find sources of income outside of mainstream industry without compromising family obligations.

Like many other Americans of the period, women who managed Exchanges might have been influenced by such writings as Edward Bellamy's *Looking Backward,* a diatribe against the industrialism that many thought was robbing humankind of its morality. The managers had likely begun to think in terms of alternative ideologies, hoping to build new social and economic arrangements that integrated women's public and private spheres without threatening their traditional roles. Woman's rights advocates agreed that women who worked within a nonthreatening, protective cooperative world could more easily integrate their roles as wives, mothers, and breadwinners. By the 1880s many wealthy, benevolent women, including those who would promote such movements as the Society of Decorative Art and Woman's Exchanges, viewed the cooperative, voluntary sector as a compromise.[84] Individual competition, as fostered by industrial capitalism, would be tempered within the cooperative system. Cooperative ideology became an important part of the postbellum Exchange mission as women actively developed economic strategies within the voluntary sector and devised a systematized, economically advantageous escape from the wage system.

It was upon this ideological middle ground that the Woman's Exchange movement took firm root and spread rapidly among women in voluntary associations nationwide. Of particular importance was that the Exchange idea offered the advantages of cooperation and operated at a safe distance from the industrial sector. Exchange managers sought ways to keep women safely removed from the public workplace—preferably at home or in single-sex work rooms—while still offering them opportunities to earn fair remuneration for their labor. As the September 28, 1882, *New York Evangelist* observed in an inspired article, women needed a fighting chance at financial independence: "If so many causes combine to lessen the chances of marriage, certainly women ought to be encouraged to work and to depend on themselves. We have never known of an instance in which her ability to support herself lessened a woman's chance of marriage, but we have known of scores of instances in which it increased the desirability and attractiveness for marriage."

Like Mathew Carey a half-century before, postbellum woman's rights writers such as Antoinette Blackwell encouraged wealthy, benevolent women to take up the cause of improving women's work. "It is not simply exceptional women who feel impelled to put their women's shoulders to some of the lagging wheels of social revolution. There are multitudes who cannot shake off the burden of responsibility," Blackwell stated in 1875. That "burden of responsibility" fell to affluent women, such as Exchange managers, those of the "most graceful and the brightest of polite society," to help in women's quest for financial independence. "Will the matrons who have the leisure or can make leisure for themselves, consent to go on aimlessly frittering away their best energies?" Blackwell challenged. "The busiest of them are taking up these new cooperative enterprises; and those who have the leisure are fast learning how to use it in line with the inquiring spirit of the times."[85]

Annie Roelker, who led the Woman's Exchange of Cincinnati for fifty-five years, was one of many of the "brightest of polite society" who answered the call to action. For nearly six decades she remained committed to the Cincinnati Exchange's efforts to help all women achieve "that which is so dear to the hearts of all womanhood, an honorable independence."[86] Privately, Roelker confidently wrote of the idea that she, and so many of her wealthy peers, had been instrumental in spreading nationwide: "Has the world ever known of a revolution that was started by the moneyed classes comfortably entrenched behind privileges which their gold has purchased?"[87]

It is possible that Roelker and many of her counterparts—Candace Wheeler, Mary Choate, Mrs. S. H. Hawes, Mrs. G. Harmon Brown, Ariadne Lawnin, and Mrs. H. W. Bartlett—felt that the Exchange idea was a revolution, started by the wealthy classes, that provided employment options for working women and an appropriate channel for wealthy women to seek the self-expression too long denied them. Through their efforts, Roelker and others sought to "open up the avenues of usefulness and industry and to make it possible for all, poor and rich alike, to stand upon the same equality of proud independence."[88]

The new wave of postbellum Exchange officers attempted to break down class barriers and offer assistance to any woman who needed an outlet for her merchandise or artistic reflection. They became crusaders in attempting to reform women's working conditions, and from New York to San Francisco their economic reform efforts showed how the Exchange philosophy had changed over the century, adapting to new needs of women and the late-nineteenth-century workplace. "Thank progress!" Lincoln noted of the significant victories won by Exchange officers' hard-fought battles during the "silent revolution" of the nineteenth century. As Libbie Custer had declared the satisfaction of attaining the status of working woman, Lincoln also reiterated the Exchange's mission: "A woman with a noble purpose and ambition is so much more of a true woman; it puts so much more of beauty and happiness into the life to cultivate a resolute heart in honest toil."[89]

Part 3

Postbellum Managers and Consignors:
"To Engage in Some Useful, Creative Occupation"

5

"We Sell Everything Good, from a Pickle to a Portiere":
Exchange Managers as Entrepreneurs

"Few persons whose attention is attracted by the modest sign of the Woman's Exchange, now found in nearly all our large cities," Lucy Salmon observed in 1892, "realize that a new competitor has appeared in the industrial workplace." Salmon watched carefully as these quickly growing phenomena, hybrid enterprises that drew strength from seemingly divergent worlds of commerce, cooperation, and charity, gained quick acceptance in cities across the country. Seeing both fault and value in the Exchange idea, Salmon was particularly interested in its commercial nature, finding, paradoxically, that despite its "unpretentious rooms and unconcern as to economic questions, the Woman's Exchange has already had an appreciable effect on economic conditions and must in the future play a still more important part." She noted that in the previous year, 1891, sixty-six Exchanges had paid nearly $400,000 to consignors.[1]

Combining the decorative arts with practical industrial application and remuneration and seeking to help all women, as the New Orleans managers noted, "from the richest in the land to the poorest," postbellum Exchanges hoped to set women on the path to financial independence by learning a skill and selling handmade items in the voluntary sector.[2] They eagerly provided employment options and vocational training to a new generation of women beyond the scope originally envisioned by the founders of the antebellum Exchanges.

Just as Exchanges were both charities and businesses, they also served dual roles for those involved, allowing each to become working women on their own terms and according to their specific needs. The two primary populations of women engaged with Exchanges—the wealthy managers and the middle- and working-class consignors—used the voluntary sector for work experiences in two entirely different ways, and entrepreneurship and self-help took on disparate meanings for each group, as did Salmon's description of the Exchange as "an industrial competitor."

For the wealthy managers restricted by social convention and, perhaps, fears of working directly in the public sphere, association with a quasi-commercial enterprise provided visible and often prestigious social and economic roles as penny capitalist entrepreneurs. While some affluent women—the "new women" of the late nineteenth century—might have pursued paid careers in journalism, social work, law, or medicine, women who managed Exchanges, like Jane Addams and her colleagues of the settlement house movement or the leaders of the WCTU or WEIU movements, pursued careers within the context of voluntarism. They created nonmonetary employment opportunities for themselves through the most readily available conduit—the strong, well-established system of women's national voluntarism that enabled them to connect with hundreds of like-minded women across the country.

As managers eagerly kept pace with rapidly changing economic conditions and strove to compete with the increasingly important retail trade around them, they became astute business executives, participating in highly entrepreneurial, commercial ventures safely within the culturally acceptable world of philanthropy. As Lincoln reported in 1891, New York Exchange co-founder Mary Choate had "devoted a great deal of time to the development of the successful Exchange, into which she brought business methods and departments of work in keeping with the general progressive spirit of the times."[3] No less important were the managers' self-appointed roles as social reformers and providers of work opportunities. "If we have to shut our business, we will throw two hundred women out of work," the Richmond managers observed.[4]

Wittingly or unwittingly, managers taunted stuffy Gilded Age conventions and propriety and became successful businesswomen—and, as they perceived themselves, businesswomen with a mission. "We *know* that this Exchange is a boon, a blessing, to so many who would suffer and faint by the way rather than give any sign of asking assistance," the Richmond managers wrote in 1889, reiterating that "we *know* their [the consignors'] burdens have been lightened, comforts secured for the aged and the invalid, and rough, hard places smoothed."[5]

As Exchange managers used their voluntary associations to create a national, alternative network of retail outlets for women's home-produced merchandise, their organizational and business savvy became critical to the survival of their enterprises. Lincoln reinforced the importance of the business aspects of the Exchange when he noted that "a regularly organized Exchange is not a private money-making scheme, but is, on the contrary, a business enterprise, instituted and conducted almost exclusively in the interest of needy, unfortunate women."[6] The "fact that [the Exchange] enters the business field as a competitor with other enterprises," Salmon concluded in 1892, "makes it inevitable that it be judged as a business house and not as a charitable organization."[7] It was a professional standard that no doubt the managers as business executives and social reformers, and the consignors as entrepreneurs and producers of quality merchandise, found challenging and flattering.

The Exchange movement saw its greatest growth during the 1880s—the golden age of American retailing—when sixty-three of seventy-two Exchanges were founded. Although they worked within the charitable sector, managers of Exchanges took great pains to borrow entrepreneurial ideas from the commercial world. In the glamorous and highly competitive world of Gilded Age commerce, they emulated successful retailers and increasingly viewed the "business houses" around them as competitors rather than the other charities of the period.[8] In 1899, after noting decreasing profits in one department, Cincinnati managers concluded that "the cause for this appalling deficit is competition alone. Every dry goods house in the city now carries a supply of stamped linens, silks etc., and is able to undersell smaller establishments. The managers realized that their efforts are powerless to compete."[9]

But they were not completely powerless. To promote their economic agenda, managers drew upon organizational models of three significant late-nineteenth-century commercial and cultural trends: the behemoth department stores that gained enormous popularity in the closing decades of the century, small retail shops and home enterprises run by women, and the cooperative ideology that had inspired antebellum Exchange founders.

"How Does the Exchange Compare to Other Shops?"

Despite how "unpretentious" Lucy Salmon thought the Exchanges were, it would be hard to imagine that managers were "unconcerned with economic questions." Cincinnati managers frequently asked, "How does the Exchange compare to other shops?"[10] Their commercial competition—as well as their models for merchandising success—came from all sides.

Like the more modest Exchanges of a half-century earlier, the grand emporiums that dominated American consumerism by the 1870s had begun in one-room shops or street pushcarts a generation or two before. Macy's, Gimbel's, Wanamaker's, Marshall Field, and many other giant retailers could all trace their origins to humble beginnings between 1830 and 1850. The new era of retailing was characterized by huge, multistoried department stores that often covered an entire city block and frequently resembled popular urban exhibitions or circuses. More than a thousand department stores dotted urban landscapes, with annual sales that ranged from $7 to $15 million each. Some of the larger enterprises were visited by more than a hundred thousand shoppers a day.[11]

The stores offered an infinite variety of customer services and a range of attractive—hopefully irresistible—merchandise sold at fixed prices that were controlled by central bookkeeping and management systems. As hubs of consumerism and materialism they encouraged buying through flamboyant, theatrical presentations of fashion shows, parades, music, drama, and circuses that rivaled any theater in town. In 1876, the year of the Philadelphia Centennial Exhibition and two years before the New York Exchange opened, Wanamaker's in Philadelphia opened its Grand Depot, the largest retail sales space in the world. The 129 counters stretched two-thirds of a mile, and 1,400 stools were strategically stationed in front of dazzling displays of merchandise.[12]

But the merchandise seemed almost secondary to the theatrics of the great merchants. Mimicking the popularity of world's fairs and other public attractions, department stores offered an endless array of entertainment, from premiers of symphonies to displays of miniature zoos. In 1896 Wanamaker's provided a life-size replica of the Rue de la Paix as a consolation for Americans who had missed a grand tour to Europe that year.[13] Catering to the whims of customers, particularly women who had expendable income, leisure, and insatiable appetites for new material goods, became the speciality of the big stores. Their owners provided conveniences and luxuries to make certain that customers felt pampered and special: lounges, nurseries, post offices, ticket agencies, elegant tea rooms, and reading rooms.

The Exchange idea accelerated during the 1880s as shopping and consumerism became almost exclusively female domains and, for many, almost full-time careers propagated through the home economics movement, business schools, and popular culture. "The housekeeper of today," one late-nineteenth-century advisor noted, "must become a trained consumer and an effective purchasing agent."[14] Shopping was as healthy for a customer's soul as for a merchant's bank account; it was touted as the cure-all for the almost-endemic neurasthenia that gripped women of the era. One writer observed the "immense factors in bringing brightness and change to many who at other times pass their days in the dull monotony to live [providing] something to think of and talk over, even if the gorgeous and beautiful trappings seen in the stores are not within the possibility of possession."[15]

The role of women shifted during the course of the century from producer to consumer, and owners of grand emporiums drew on the strength of women's increased buying power and tailored their establishments to fit feminine needs and tastes. Their efforts were conveniently aided by articles with such titles as "Shopping as a Fine Art," which regularly appeared in women's magazines.[16] Leading feminists also promoted the cause. Elizabeth Cady Stanton, among others, extolled the virtues of the power of shopping and a wife's right to control the family finances. She often repeated her favorite story of the wife of a member of Congress, who had a faulty stove and a frugal husband. "Go out and buy a new stove! Buy what you need! Buy while he's in Washington! I tell this to you women. GO OUT AND BUY!"[17]

The new department stores benefited Exchanges by drawing huge crowds of daily shoppers into town and provided Exchange managers with innovative merchandising ideas. Many Exchanges offered departments featuring dozens of varieties of merchandise for sale or special order, mail order catalogs, home delivery, advertising, and, often, chic tearooms or restaurants where the city's elite would gather. In comparison to the earlier one-room shops, managers of some of the largest Exchanges created highly organized, departmentalized, entrepreneurial organizations charged with attracting and keeping patrons and meeting the economic needs of consignors. They vied for the spending dollars of up-scale customers who would become the mainstay of Exchanges from Manhattan to San Diego.

The New York Exchange, in its range of merchandise and marketing of goods, was in every sense a small department store. Although not netting the $1.6 million in sales recorded by the massive Macy's in 1877, the New York Exchange in its first year recorded a respectable $20,169.37 in sales and income and paid consignors $13,412.55 in commissions.[18] A visitor to the New York Exchange, which already occupied a multistoried building, observed the complexity of the enterprise in 1891:

> a walk through the rooms of the parent institution, now established in a handsome building at 329 Fifth Avenue, shows the number and variety of workers who avail themselves of its privileges. In the salesrooms, hand-painted and embroidered tapestries hang on the walls; artistic screens, painted or embroidered on all conceivable materials, stand in every nook and corner; elaborately decorated china for ornament or table use lies piled on the shelves; while textile fabrics of all kinds, made up into articles for wall decorations, bed and table use, or personal wear, are tastefully arranged on counters or within glass cases. On the upper floors of the building, women are kept constantly at work inspecting, marking and ticketing goods sent in by the consignees. In the basement are the storehouse and restaurant for receiving and selling cakes, pickles, preserves, and other edibles sent to be disposed of for the benefit of the makers.[19]

Mirroring the dynamic retailing world around them—and eager to open their new enterprise to coincide with up-scale customers coming to town for the opera season—managers of the Cincinnati Exchange launched their commercial enterprise with eleven committees to represent each department and major activity of the venture: house, lunch, edible, purchasing, nomination, auditing, employment, publication, fancy, advertising, and consignors.[20] Special departments highlighted the consignors' goods: infants, men's and women's accessories, household goods, and edibles, among others. And, like the grand Cincinnati emporiums—Pogue's, Shillito's, and McAlpin's—the Exchange employed "supervisors," or agents, to manage the sales staff, which varied from two to four women. By its second year, 1884, when the Cincinnati Exchange, flush with its initial success, had moved to a spacious two-room shop, showrooms were expanded to provide space for not only the display of consignors' "plain sewing, delicate embroidery, and pretty, dainty things fashioned by pencil, brush or the deft fingers of women" but also for "laces, shawls, and objects of art sold for persons obliged to part with the same."[21]

Exchange managers across the country also emulated another important merchant model of the period: the entrepreneurial, self-employed woman shopkeeper. By combining the flamboyant and theatrical merchandising techniques of the grand emporiums with the intimacy and hominess of small, customer-oriented, female-run shops, the managers created hybrid retail endeavors.

Unlike the elite women who founded Exchanges, the majority of women merchants of the nineteenth century tended to come from the working or middle class.[22] Operating a successful shop or home business allowed them to engage in a variety of independent occupations, such as dressmaking and millinery or running boardinghouses and restaurants. Self-employment, or entrepreneurship, particularly with regard to domestic skills, opened the way to economic independence for women and provided a higher degree of status and respectability than working in factories. By late in the century, large urban areas contained virtually thousands of self-employed women, and newspaper society columns frequently mentioned self-employed women shopkeepers positively.

Whether in rural or urban areas, women shopkeepers worked in a male-dominated world of commerce but focused on skills that were extensions of women's domestic activities, particularly dressmaking and millinery. The fashion styles of the day demanded the expertise of trained dressmakers and milliners who knew the precise combinations of feathers, ruffles, and lace that would produce the right look for a lady about town.

Women-owned shops catered almost exclusively to a female clientele, extending women's sex-segregated private lives to their public roles as merchants. Exchanges also capitalized almost exclusively on selling domestic goods and catered primarily to women, drawing heavily upon support from the community, particularly from friends or family business colleagues. And, like female shopkeepers, Exchange managers attained status within their communities. By its second year, after the Richmond Exchange became incorporated, its managers boasted that they "had attained a recognized position in our community."[23] Four years later, they extended gratitude to the supportive newspapers, adding at the end of their annual report that "we do not forget to thank most heartily the daily papers of our city for the kindly paragraphs they have given us again and again."[24]

Exchanges, as did commercial enterprises run by women, remained relatively small and personalized, recalling nostalgic aspects of pre–Civil War life when women could meet daily at their favorite shops. Managers hoped to make their shops homes away from home, downtown clubs where customers could socialize and pass time. As in the antebellum Exchanges, patrons generally hailed from the carriage trade, and most were likely known to the managers, who built a loyal clientele base that would survive for decades. Newspaper clippings from Exchange archives and records around the country are replete with testimonials by customers and consignors alike, and such loyalty lasted for several generations.[25] Typical was a woman who commented that on her annual trek to her New England summer retreat, "Going from Washington D.C. to the Berkshires, we had to change trains at New York City, and if we arrived in Stockbridge without cookies from the Exchange, we were not welcome!"[26] Similarly, Milwaukee managers noted in 1888 that unlike regular customers, who could place special orders in good faith, "a stranger who placed a special order had to leave a 20 percent deposit."[27]

Aside from capitalizing on traditional female skills and relationships, most women's shops employed only a few paid staff—often relatives and friends— and were run on relatively low amounts of capital. Similarly, managers were an Exchange's most valuable work force and always pitched in to help and keep overhead expenses to a minimum.

The intimacy and hominess of Exchanges also demonstrated another similarity with female-run enterprises: The homogeneity between producers and sellers, owners and customers, became blurred in a cooperative environment. Elizabeth Stott and her philanthropic colleagues in Philadelphia in 1832 had recognized the value of modeling their charity as a cooperative retail store. Managers late in the century sought the same goal: to provide consignors an opportunity to become their own employers—entrepreneurs—without forfeiting the profits on their work to a corporation. The women borrowed liberally from the cooperative ideology and "the principle of combination as against that of competition."[28]

In 1891 Alice Rhine noted the influence of cooperation on the Exchange idea, finding that "another phase of work initiated by women . . . carried out on the broad and liberal lines of national cooperation [that has] become a power for universal good . . . the Exchanges or stores [are] instituted for the purpose of selling hand-made articles of women's manufacture and which gives the maker the full price, minus ten percent commission."[29] Rhine explained that one of the primary purposes of Exchanges was to serve as a cooperative agent for producers:

> At the time the . . . Exchange was planned in New York some ten years ago, thousands of women, graduates from the various art schools, were at work in stores and factories, decorating china, painting household adornments, such as portieres, screens, wall hangings, and doing all kinds of fancy work at prices but little, if any, beyond the wages of the average worker on men's and women's clothing. To direct this work into a channel, where the maker and not the employer would receive the profit, was what the originator of the exchange proposed to do for women pressed by poverty into the ranks of the breadwinners.[30]

Exchange managers saw their role as being "friendly middle men between the public and the consignors."[31] Echoing their counterparts of a half-century before, postbellum Exchange managers became active agents between the buyer and seller, "a benefactor to stand between the producer and consumer," as Lincoln explained.[32] Martha Rayne noted in 1893 that Exchanges "sold [merchandise] for the benefit of the manufacturer or artist, with a small commission, which goes to the Exchange."[33] The "judicious way of carrying on the business [of the Exchange] prevents loss to either party," she added.

As cooperative retail stores, Exchanges assured that producers, the consignors, would receive the greatest share of the value for their products. Postbellum Exchanges charged 10 percent commission for each item sold (up from the 6 percent charged by the antebellum Exchanges), with the consignor keeping the balance of the sale. Rhine found that "[the Exchanges] demonstrate how thoroughly practical the scheme is of sending hand-made articles to special magazines to be disposed of for the makers' benefit. The woman who, by sending her work to the exchange, earned $35 for what she, as a wage earner, had received $2.50 from the manufacturer, got the profit that had previously gone to swell the bank account of the manufacturer, middle men and retail dealers. By employing their own labor they accumulated the premiums which, under the old factory and store system, inured to the benefit of their employers."[34]

Exchanges also provided a gentle buffer between producers and employers, a trait often missing in larger commercial enterprises. Increasingly, large retailers of the day had become hierarchical, and managers and owners were generally distanced from their sales staffs and customers. Employees were viewed as easily replaced. Many Exchanges, however, took pride in the longevity of their paid staffs. They filled their ranks of paid workers—sales agents, showroom supervisors, and waitresses—with familiar faces who were known to customers and often enjoyed life-long employment.

For business models, Exchange managers combined the successful merchandising techniques of both large stores and small shops with a humanistic, cooperative ideology. But the title "friendly middle men," as the Richmond managers referred to themselves, belied the aggressiveness and determination with which managers ran Exchanges during the highly competitive Gilded Age. As they created what they felt was a more humanistic countermovement to the industrial workplace, competition—for both managers and consignors—became inevitable.

"Brave Hearts There Were"

The decision to open a retail enterprise of this new sort did not always come easily, as Candace Wheeler and Mary Choate had discovered at the New York Exchange's founding meeting in March 1878. The founders needed first to assess whether their cities could sustain such a commercial activity. Lincoln suggested that they should judge the situation in much the same way as other shop owners, asking if "there exist circumstances in the city and its adjacent towns that decidedly indicate a demand for the services of an organization of this kind?"[35] Founders had to determine whether there were "a sufficient number of women dependent on their own resources for a livelihood, who would become constant contributors of saleable articles, and what is equally important, there must be assured an adequate patronage of the buying public to constantly create a market for such goods." Lincoln recommended that a "personal canvass of the place [city or town] would soon settle these questions."[36]

It is unlikely that the founders of most Exchanges undertook such a formal assessment. More than likely, they enthusiastically jumped at the chance to try the popular new idea and decided quickly to open an Exchange when they learned of the successes of Exchanges in other cities. Once the decision was made, all managers faced similar challenges. As had been the case a half-century earlier, postbellum managers on a shoestring budget faced the daunting task of renting stores in the heart of the most fashionable shopping districts. They knew the importance of taking advantage of the increasing numbers of women who came downtown for daily shopping excursions and lunch with friends, eagerly enticed by merchants' sumptuous displays of merchandise. Lincoln recommended that the managers "secure as good and centrally located salesroom as the immediate prospects for business will warrant, make the display of goods as attractive as possible, advertise judiciously, solicit patronage by personal visitation, and a gratifying degree of success will be pretty sure to follow in due time."[37]

And success usually did follow quickly. Within the theatrical milieu of late-nineteenth-century feminine consumerism, the entrepreneurial managers learned how to compete for business. In Cincinnati, managers were eager from the start to make their commercial enterprise a success, and they risked all to make their shop competitive. By the end of its first year, 1883, the Exchange faced a dilemma that any fledgling enterprise would envy. Its financial success mandated larger quarters. For several months managers had considered a large, airy, two-room corner store under construction directly across the street from their cramped, one-room store. Although offering a far more advantageous shopping location, the $125 monthly rent for the new store would more than triple the $40 they were paying. The managers had already met with their board of advisors, a group of well-known businessmen who were also their husbands, who strongly advised against such a move, calling it too risky for such a new enterprise. According to the minutes of the January 2, 1884, decision-making meeting, "the President again called upon the members individually for expressing an opinion. Brave hearts there were, who strongly and unhesitatingly advocated the move, feeling no lingering doubts, haunted by no fear of failure."[38]

Brave hearts prevailed in other cities as well. The managers of the St. Louis Exchange, for example, also struggled to find the most advantageous commercial location with the lowest rental when they opened their shop in 1883. Within the first year, spurred on by their initial success, they had purchased a building for $15,000 by raising money through donations and fund-raising events.[39]

In the world of highly competitive, late-century retailing, store location alone was not sufficient to guarantee visibility. Display windows had become a primary tool for enticing customers into a store, an idea many managers noted. Among the other attractions that the new Cincinnati location offered in 1894 was "a large show window for the display of the tempting viands."[40] Not all Exchange managers were so eager to dive into such aggressive business tactics, however. One in New York wondered if renting a store with a large window would be seemly. She "feared the society might not be thoroughly genteel" by using such a bold display of their commercial intent.[41] Apparently, she and her colleagues eventually overcame such trepidations, however. By 1892, hoping to profit $1,500 from the venture, they were renting their Fifth Avenue window to patrons eager to watch holiday parades on the famed boulevard.[42]

Once the question of store location was solved, Exchange managers wasted no time in moving ahead with their mission. New York managers immediately made their business strategy known: "Our motto is to keep out of debt, waste nothing and spare nothing which shall contribute to our success as a benevolent enterprise."[43]

Like their antebellum counterparts, postbellum managers were not shy about their accomplishments as business executives. They mirrored successful commercial retailing techniques by searching out markets for consignors' merchandise, advertising to attract patrons, supplying capital to run their enterprises, and setting a standardized measure of merchandise quality for consumers. Their entrepreneurship kept their organizations viable and, generally, solvent. "By the application to the philanthropic efforts of a business principle, which is now recognized as valuable by the modern business world," the Philadelphia managers boasted, "the Philadelphia Exchange for Woman's Work has set an example that might be followed with profit by many rival institutions."[44] Or, as the New York managers less pretentiously described their business savvy, "We sell everything good, from a pickle to a portiere!"[45]

As wealthy women, managers had firsthand knowledge of customers' expectations, and they patterned the shops after the finest retail establishments that they, as customers, frequented. Gaining firsthand knowledge about the machinations of retailing would also have been easy for many, because they frequently were related to well-known retailing executives, often by marriage. In Pittsburgh, Mrs. Joseph A. Horne, wife of the owner of one of the largest department stores, served as corresponding secretary of the Pittsburgh Women's Industrial Exchange. Similarly, Mrs. John A. Shillito, Mrs. Murray Shipley, and Mrs. George McAlpin, wives of successful Cincinnati department store owners and wholesalers, were Exchange managers.

"Pen Wipers, Shaving Balls, and Tidies"

Influenced by the decorative arts movement after the 1876 Philadelphia Centennial, managers insisted that inferior, dowdy merchandise had no place in an Exchange. They worked hard to ensure that their shops were stocked with fashionable, high-quality merchandise that their customers required. The Richmond managers emphasized the need for quality craftsmanship and the dire consequences for failing to provide top merchandise: "Have every article the very best of its kind. Perfectly satisfactory and beautiful work rarely long awaits a purchaser. There is absolutely no market for poor work. If, in any emergency, an inferior article is sold, the inevitable result is to materially injure that worker's future success."[46]

Exchange showrooms highlighted consignors' home-produced needlework and edible items, often displayed on glass-covered counters, another critical merchandising tool. "Our cases contain fine work in crocheting and knitted goods, toilet sets, fancy work of every description, both useful and ornamental, hand-made laces and painting," the Milwaukee managers wrote in 1888.[47]

When space allowed, managers of the larger Exchanges followed the example of department store entrepreneurs by offering departments that featured different types of merchandise, such as needlework, edibles, and special orders. Wealthy women could purchase items to take on their afternoon calling rounds, and some would "purchase a large part of their Christmas as well as other goods, at the Exchange."[48]

The range of merchandise was impressive. As Lincoln reported, Exchanges consigned "all salable or useful goods made by women."[49] Lucy Salmon observed of the offerings that in "the department of needle-work nearly one hundred different articles are enumerated by the different Exchanges, and the number is practically without limit, since it includes every form of plain and fancy sewing."[50] Lincoln compiled a five-page list of "some acceptable items" a consignor could sell at an Exchange, including such Gilded Age accessories as "telegraph trays," bridal trousseaus, rag cats and pigs, embroidered doilies, knee caps (warmers), pen wipers, shaving balls, tidies, and wristlets.

To promote their up-to-date merchandise, eager managers employed what was quickly becoming an essential promotional device for late-nineteenth-century retailers: the merchandise catalog. By the 1880s, with Montgomery Ward leading the way, catalogs had become valuable marketing tools, and in 1894 the New York Exchange initiated its first "Catalogue of Homemade Goods." While Bloomingdale Brothers published a copious 150-page catalog, the New York Exchange followed suit with a 15-page listing. The Richmond and Cincinnati managers likewise recognized the sales catalog's marketing effectiveness and soon began to publish regularly.

Although counting on the patronage of their peers, the carriage trade of the city, Exchange managers did not overlook the business of off-the-street customers. "Orders can be placed for *anything* which any person may desire to have made," New York managers assured.[51] Customers paid top dollar; the handmade goods were generally more costly than those sold down the block at nearby shops and department stores. That allowed consignors to earn the maximum profit on their merchandise, underscoring the charitable mission of the Exchange. Defending their higher prices, the managers of the New York Exchange argued that "it is hardly in keeping with the spirit of the society to gauge these salaries upon the lowest scales paid for similar employment."[52] By shopping at an Exchange, customers could be assured that they were not only purchasing quality, hand-produced items but also helping a needy consignor "to win that which is so dear to the hearts of all true womanhood, an honorable independence."[53] The New York Exchange's catalog listing of children's wear, always a popular item at Exchanges, offered items comparable to—but more costly than—infants' items featured in Bloomingdale Brothers' catalog (Table 5, Appendix A).

Other factors accounted for the differential between Exchange prices and those at other stores. Most items sold at Exchanges were handmade. Only occasionally did managers allow machine-made merchandise; infant slips were one example. The difference would have been indicated in the catalog. Although department stores still sold hand-produced items, increasingly most items sold at larger stores were machine-produced. Mass-produced clothing had become widely used during the Civil War, when the production of uniforms required that sizing be standardized. After the war, ready-to-wear clothing began to dominate the markets. Lucy Salmon also noted that higher prices at Exchanges were a result of "consignors [who] are obliged to purchase their own materials in small quantities in retail markets, and therefore set a higher price on their articles than would be the case could the material be purchased through a central office."[54]

Customers and critics alike responded favorably to the merchandise offered. The Richmond managers in 1888 wrote that "we flatter ourselves that customers begin to find the Woman's Exchange an indispensable convenience, and we respectfully request them to tell their friends of the good home-made dishes and delicacies, the useful household articles in needlework and the pretty souvenirs always to be found on sale."[55] In 1893 Martha Rayne noted of the goods that "everything that can be used in the household is for sale at these places. As the work is nearly all the result of private enterprise, it is much better than the class of goods found in stores; and there is such a general assortment that almost anything in manufactured goods can be found there."[56]

Ironically, managers waged a constant battle to assure patrons that hand-produced merchandise was of equal quality to mass-produced merchandise. As large assortments of machine-made goods became available—and irresistible—department store owners increasingly asserted that the quality was superior to hand-produced items. Yet handcrafted items still held great emotional value, recalling a simpler, better time in American life. Competing against mass production proved challenging, however, and managers focused on the unique aspect of their shops: They sold hand-produced merchandise that represented the talents of needy women producers and quality homemade products that evoked a sense of nostalgia and family-centered values. An Exchange, Lincoln noted, "furnishes the buying public the opportunity of obtaining home-made goods—productions so often sought after in vain."[57] Salmon concurred that Exchanges "raised the standard of decorative and artistic needlework by incorporating into its rules a refusal to accept calico patchwork, wax, leather, hair, feather, rice, spatter, splinter, and cardboard work." She found that customers were able "to purchase articles ready for use that have been made under the most favorable conditions," adding that the "greatest perfection results when articles are handled in small quantities."[58]

Screening out leather, hair, and cardboard work was the least of the managers' problems. Of greater concern was keeping their enterprises financially afloat through creative, if not always conventional, merchandising techniques.

"No Stone Should Be Left Unturned"

Approaching their mission with passion and fervor, Exchange managers across the country shared a common economic crusade: to improve women's work options. They also shared the day-to-day challenge of keeping their enterprises financially solvent, and any scheme or merchandising technique seemed worthy of experiment if it had the potential to bring in much-needed income. "No stone should be left unturned that could further in any way the interest of those dependent upon it, and ensure for it a permanent existence," the Cincinnati managers professed in 1888.[59]

Aside from the 10 percent commission charged to consignors from the sale of each item, other Exchange revenue came from interest in investments, annual subscriptions, and various cash and in-kind donations from the largess of the community and friends. These sources seldom defrayed all of the expenses of running a retail store, however, and managers turned to more creative techniques for income.

Several Exchanges provided a brokerage service for women who needed to discreetly dispose of family treasures for quick cash. By selling their families' valuables at Exchanges, they benefited from obtaining a higher price for the sale than they would have achieved at a pawnbrokers'. Martha Rayne noted that "there is also the modern supply of bric-a-brac, old china, fine needlework, rare cases and often articles of ancient value that used to find their way into pawnbrokers hands to raise money for immediate necessity, [that] are disposed of in these places at something like approximate value, the class of people who patronize them being connoisseurs in art."[60]

A department at the New York Exchange handled the jewelry and other family valuables that a woman might need to sell quickly. The managers noted in 1879 that "we also take, through the influence of an officer, valuable articles which ladies are obliged to part with, and would call attention to a fine portrait of Rembrandt, one of Montesquieu, several handsome vases, and rare pieces of old china, beautiful old laces, crape, camel's hair and lace shawls, evening dresses and jewelry."[61] In the antique department, the New York managers sold a collection of three hundred pieces of jewelry and gems, "intaglios, cameos, and lockets" and unset stones contributed by an anonymous gentleman donor, and also provided an old furniture department, where antiques, including an "old oak Danish chest carved in 1787," were available.[62] In a slight variation, the Exchange in Mount Vernon, New York, maintained a registry for "ladies desiring to exchange goods."[63]

The Baltimore Industrial Exchange also served as an outlet for the sale of family valuables. As the *Baltimore American* noted on February 28, 1896, the Exchange provided for gentlewomen to "discreetly sell their possessions to others who could afford to buy them." That may have been the Exchange's primary purpose in the beginning. After the Civil War, "unable to make financial ends meet and without access to the business and professional world, a number of gentlewomen decided to sell some of their most cherished possessions. In addition to their treasures, the needy consignors also made and sold fine needlework, hand-painted articles, bread, cake and cookies."[64] The Richmond managers noted in their 1899 catalog that "many valuable and beautiful things are entrusted to us for sale—articles which are often relics of beautiful and prosperous homes, and nowhere else in the city would the owners dispose of them to so good advantage as here."[65] The Cincinnati Exchange also frequently listed the sale of old furniture among its yearly income. It is not known how the managers acquired the furniture. More than likely it was either donated, with the proceeds going to the support of the Exchange, or put on consignment by families in need of emergency income.

Managers sought other innovative ways to make the Exchanges more visible and provide work opportunities for consignors and other women. Lincoln suggested providing catering for dinner parties and home food delivery to the sick. Items recommended seemed guaranteed to cure—or kill—the homebound immediately: calf's foot jelly, mutton broth, wine whey, and Iceland moss and cream.[66] In keeping with feminists' calls to relieve well-to-do women from domestic drudgery, many Exchanges offered a variety of catering. By 1891 the Cincinnati managers had already met with some measure of success in their catering department. They noted that "orders for lunches and evening parties, for delicacies for the sick-room, are constantly received and filled to the entire satisfaction of our patrons."[67] "At many of the Exchanges," Lincoln noted, "one may have physicians' prescriptions—diet for the sick and convalescent—faithfully filled; or get lunch-baskets filled for traveling, or for fisherman, picnic or boating parties, or order dishes for luncheons, dinners, suppers or teas, all carried out with the care and painstaking thought of home preparation."[68]

The Cincinnati managers supplemented their Exchange's income by selling cookbooks, presenting lectures, hand-printing wedding and party invitations, selling waste paper, and renting workrooms to women. When business slowed during the summer months, the managers packed up boxes filled with "dainty articles" and sent them to patrons' summer homes in Michigan.[69]

Lucy Salmon observed that "a few [Exchanges] receive scientific and literary work, others arrange for cleaning and mending lace, re-covering furniture, the care of fine *bric-a-brac,* writing and copying, the preparation of lunches for travelers and picnic parties, and a few take orders for shopping."[70] Lincoln added that at some Exchanges "invalids take orders for writing wedding and reception invitations and addressing envelopes. Other women will go to ladies' homes to write for them, or read to children or aged persons, or accompany them on walks or drives."[71]

Fund-raising, which included charity balls, dinner cruises, fashion shows, and the like, became a major occupation for most Exchange managers. Income derived from such sources often meant the difference between paying the rent or not. The New York managers, who recognized the need to supplement other forms of revenue with philanthropic support, began the first year by soliciting membership by distributing circulars in "the best park in the city." To augment their efforts, in 1880 the managers turned to their board of advisors—who were, for the most, their husbands—to help solicit income. Arguing that "the age of experimentation has passed and the society should be placed on a permanent footing," the men collectively signed a fund-raising letter and circulated it among friends. They "hoped to acquaint persons of wealth with the merit of this charity" and encouraged them to "contribute *liberally,* bearing in mind that the two distinctive features of the work are judicious, sympathetic help to those trying to help themselves and it is a business conducted on business principles."[72]

"Our Tables Are Served with the Best Quality of Food"

Exchange managers soon learned to compensate in one area for financial losses in another. A sure income-producer was a tearoom or a lunchroom, which could be one of the most lucrative departments of Exchanges, the "financial guarantee" as Cincinnati managers reported in 1894.[73] The first department store tearoom, which opened in 1876 at Wanamaker's, had the capacity to serve ten thousand diners a day.[74] The idea caught on quickly with Gilded Age shoppers, and many Exchanges, particularly the larger ones, were quick to follow the trend. Finding "that good food is an essential factor in the making up of human happiness," Exchanges did their best to that end.[75] The tearoom soon moved to the top of the list of services offered to customers, becoming an Exchange hallmark and fashionable watering hole for the wealthy in many cities. More often than not, the publicity surrounding an Exchange focused on its tearoom and excellent food, nostalgic atmosphere, and elite clientele.

In Baltimore, the Exchange lunchroom was an immediate success. In 1886 the lunchroom sold five thousand meals, fifteen thousand annually a decade later. Women shoppers, often those from out of town, could count on meeting the right people at an Exchange. The Baltimore Exchange historian noted that "in an extracurricular capacity the Exchange serves as a sort of club for many non-Baltimoreans. Women from Western Maryland, Washington, and the Eastern Shore frequently arrange to meet friends there or arrange to leave their bags there while they shop or transact business downtown."[76] The Baltimore tearoom became so popular with women that a lunchroom was opened in the basement of the building for men only. Dubbed the "Down Under Club," the counter-style restaurant soon became as popular with businessmen as the elegant, white linen tablecloth formal dining room was with women.[77]

The tearoom was also an immediate triumph at the Cincinnati Exchange. Like many other Exchanges, the Cincinnati managers had recognized from the start the difficulty of keeping their Exchange solvent on commissions, subscriptions, and donations. They had begun a tearoom after moving to larger quarters at the beginning of their second year of business to supplement low cash reserves and, more often than not, as they noted in 1885, "to pay the rent."[78] The menu was simple: "Oyster stew, sandwiches, tea, coffee, and bread and butter were served from noon until 3 P.M. only, and the managers divided their time between the shop above and the restaurant below, cutting sandwiches and selling goods."[79] After its first year the lunchroom turned a profit of $1,969.29, allowing the managers to put the windfall aside "for the slack season or rainy day."[80] "Lunch is held in high esteem by the public, and deservedly so," managers boasted in 1887, "and is a great convenience to both ladies and gentlemen, who avail themselves of it, and who constantly encourage us by their presence and their words of commendation." By 1891 the lunchroom employed thirty-one women and provided the Exchange with its primary source of income.[81] In 1894 the lunchroom served 99,027 meals and drew a hearty crowd of businessmen. The managers noted that the "new lunch room with its tasteful furnishings and dainty fittings has now a large patronage. Many men prefer its wholesome fare to the more recherche's menus of the Clubs."[82]

In 1896 the Cincinnati Exchange's lunchroom suffered from the competition of other counter lunchrooms that served an increasing number of workers. Managers had to drop their prices but not their high standards. Although they felt they had become trailblazers in this area, they noted that their "lunch department has suffered in common with other restaurants in the city through competition. Since the successful introduction of counter lunches in Cincinnati, the Committee in charge, to keep pace with their rivals, have been obliged to drop their prices to a minimum. In many cases, the expense of serving in the dainty manner for which the restaurant is noted has entirely eaten up the small profit."[83]

The Richmond managers, who felt their Exchange was too small for such a culinary venture, noted with envy that "in the larger cities the chief source of revenues is the tearoom." Recognizing opportunity when it knocked, in 1894 the Milwaukee managers wrote that the year before they had anticipated great crowds from Chicago's Columbian Exhibition and enlarged the Exchange's kitchen by renting an adjoining room for $26.66 a month. The Milwaukee managers noted that "our tables are served with the best quality of food in the markets, our supplies are purchased invariably from self-supporting women, thereby helping a large number of women to help themselves."[84] As in other departments of the Exchange, needy women were employed as servers and cashiers, and much of the food served had been purchased from needy women who baked and cooked in their own kitchens.

A complement to an Exchange's tearoom was its edible department, which sold many of the popular items offered in the tearoom: breads (Swedish timbals and crumpets); pastries (paté shells and Christmas plum pudding); cakes (harlequin, election, yule babies, and Dolly Vardens); cookies (jumbles and hermits); special desserts (deviled figs and floating islands); and perhaps four or five dozen kinds of the Victorians' favorite, pickles, preserves, and relishes.[85] Perhaps a forerunner to the modern day carryout service, the edible department also allowed customers to choose among a seemingly endless variety of "dainties and substantial viands" to take home as ready-made dinners. If, like Richmond, an Exchange was too small to support a tearoom, an edible department could be a stable money-maker. In 1894, for example, the Milwaukee Exchange augmented its tearoom income by selling thirty-nine thousand loaves of bread, ten thousand cakes, and twenty-five thousand dozen rolls, which amounted to "only part of the food sold" in the edible department. That year, the Milwaukee Exchange sold $29,040.51 in food, $7,000 more than the year before.[86]

Edible departments, like lunchrooms, often carried an Exchange through tenuous financial years. It was not unusual for sales in an edible department to more than triple sales in the plain or fancy needlework departments. In 1891, for example, sales from the edible department and the tearoom of the Cincinnati Exchange totaled $37,918.34, compared to $9,687.53 in sales for the fancy department.

To ensure that food served at Exchanges passed muster, managers used screening committees to sample edibles in much the same way that they screened needlework. "Of course," Alice Rayne noted of quality control in 1893, "the goods offered at the Exchange must pass careful examination or it will not be admitted. The rules which govern the organization are about the same wherever the Exchange exists, and inferior work would soon injure the reputation of the institution."[87]

The Milwaukee Exchange went one step farther. Reflecting the reform fervor of the day, as Americans diligently monitored the conditions under which food was prepared, Milwaukee managers sent a visiting committee to inspect the kitchens in which the food to be sold was prepared. The Milwaukee managers noted in 1897 that "the visiting committee have visited, as often as has been deemed necessary, the homes of consignors; have inspected kitchens, cellars, storerooms, etc., and report without exception, everything clean and in good sanitary condition."[88]

Many Exchanges favored the special-order system for edibles, much as customers would order a needlework item. "The ready sale of our preserved and spiced fruits, pickles, jellies and cake has afforded many ladies a goodly return for their work," managers of the New York Exchange explained in 1879. However, they explained, "we have a standard, and none can bring cake, pickles, or preserves, without first sending us samples of their work."[89]

"We Have Been Able to Keep Out of Debt"

Despite their carriage trade customers and generally enthusiastic community support, Exchange managers, like most retailers, found the job of running a business challenging. Exchanges, like other businesses, were influenced by economic conditions. The Milwaukee managers noted of the Panic of 1893 that "the financial depression has affected us somewhat, particularly since our earnings and savings were held in one of the city's banks that closed during the depression."[90]

The Richmond managers often had trouble with cash flow and occasionally did not pay consignors or monthly creditors on time. In 1889 they realized that their enterprise would likely always hover in the red. "Our resources are limited," they acknowledged, "and our business can never be self-supporting."[91] The New Orleans Exchange, however, which had bought a building within its first few years, enjoyed solvency almost from the start. "The Christian Woman's Exchange," Lincoln emphasized, "differs from most other Woman's Exchanges in that it has been, from the first, self-supporting."[92]

One of the primary reasons for an Exchange's chronic cash-flow problems was turnover—or lack thereof—of merchandise. Department store owners did not let dust accumulate on goods. As one observed, "The dry goods store is for distribution of goods, not for storage."[93] Exchange managers, always mindful of the plight of producers and giving merchandise every opportunity to sell, often kept nonperishable items for up to six months, thereby slowing sales and taking valuable inventory space. The Cincinnati managers wrote of the "pathos" of returning unsold merchandise to a producer: "A few months ago these same embroideries and pretty confections were sent out fresh and dainty—laden with hopes. Now, shop worn and useless, they must go back to make sick the heart of the maker. She is still hoping against hope, and her little venture still awaits a purchaser."[94]

Many Exchanges lacked capital to sustain them through rough times or to make needed improvements in their shops. The New York managers, after one particularly harrowing financial encounter in which they could not pay their rent, were forced to take an emergency loan from a board member. Mary Choate later recognized that the New York Exchange never had more than $1,000 in reserves. Lucy Salmon viewed the lack of capital as a major fault of Exchanges: "The Exchange has no capital. It does simply a commission business, and it is a recipient of whatever goods are sent in which reach a certain standard; its attitude is therefore negative rather than positive."[95]

Despite such near misses with disaster, Exchange managers, like all retail executives, expected growth in their enterprises—a hope that sometimes did not become a reality. In 1894 the Milwaukee managers explained that "improvements were made, salaries raised, additional help secured for the lunchroom and kitchen, and we hopefully awaited results. Our expenses increased, but the expected crowds did not materialize and . . . we found ourselves with an overdrawn bank account, receipts diminishing and our savings held in a closed bank."[96] They were forced to reduce salaries and dismiss nine employees.

But they knew instinctively what to do. "By promptly reducing our expenses accordingly and raising the prices of three articles on our bill of fare," Exchange president Letitia Gray noted, "we have been able to keep out of debt." She added confidently, "It is with much pride and pleasure that I make this statement."[97]

Despite the Exchanges' financial precariousness and the managers' lack of formal business training, managers approached their enterprises with zeal. They measured the success of their enterprises by the amount of money paid to consignors and their steady—if not always increasing—business. After the second year in business, the Milwaukee managers noted confidently that "we have been able to fix upon a system, which not only adds to our income, but redounds to our credit as business women."[98]

"Fully Conscious of Its 'Mission High'"

In 1893 Ruth McEnery Stuart parodied the Exchange movement in a short story, "The Woman's Exchange of Simpkinsville."[99] In the tale, two unmarried, aging sisters, languishing in a life of genteel poverty after the Civil War, decide to earn a little spare cash by opening an Exchange in their tiny hamlet of Simpkinsville, Arkansas. Starting such an enterprise and collecting profits from it will be easy, one sister assures the other: "I seen it tried in the city, an' the magazine is continual tellin' how it works everywhere." There would be no need for money or business experience to start the Exchange, the sister explains, and "that's jest the beauty of it. They get started on nothin'. We just give out thet the Exchange *is started* an' everybody who does any sort of work to sell sends it in, an' we sell it for her an deduc' 10 percent. You see?" The Simpkinsville Exchange limps along, and all the women in town become both consignors and patrons, selling their handiwork—"grateful for whatever it'll fetch"—while eagerly buying their neighbors' goods. In the end, only the sisters benefit, pocketing the meager profits from their friends' labors. "It would have been a hopelessly weary business," they agree, "but for its rich perquisites in opportunities of sympathy and helpfulness."[100]

Throughout the nineteenth century, Exchange managers, like other women reformers, often found their work ridiculed and their mission misunderstood. Yet "the promoters and supporters" were "a noble band of self-sacrificing women, who constantly work and plan for its success, in the face of some discouragements and unkindly criticism, fully conscious of its 'mission high.'"[101] Despite criticism, managers sought to offer women assistance in combating the "weary warfare they daily wage with life."[102] As one observer of the Cincinnati Exchange noted in 1900, its mission represented a "complex system of benevolence."[103]

As it evolved through the nineteenth century, the movement embraced many oppositional forces. It provided financial opportunities to women of both wealth and poverty; combined tenets of self-help, cooperation, and commercialism; bridged domestic arts to industrial application; and merged philanthropy and entrepreneurship. Managers of Exchanges reconciled these dichotomies by adapting to the massive cultural changes of the nineteenth century and to the changing conditions of women's lives and altering their enterprises, both structurally and philosophically, to the evolution in women's place in society and the working world.

The Exchange idea thrived in the last quarter of the nineteenth century as women's voluntary groups became aggressive and corporatelike, eagerly tackling the problems attendant with industrialization and urbanization with aggressive methods and strong rhetoric. Exchanges, as retail enterprises, highlighted this aspect more so than others because managers blurred the lines between charity and commerce and chose to emphasize the business aspect of their enterprises. As managers of the Richmond Exchange boasted of the success and business skills of their counterparts nationwide in 1888, "We may safely say that over one million dollars have gone into the hands of consignors in twelve months."[104]

"Is it any wonder," Cincinnati managers proclaimed, "that giving us as it does, the magic to turn tears to smiles and stone to bread that we have fallen in love with our work?"[105] They had every reason to believe that their economic reform efforts to change attitudes about women's work were of great benefit to more than sixteen thousand consignors nationwide on the annual payroll of Exchanges.

Julia Ward Howe (above left), author of "The Battle Hymn of the Republic," Abby Morton Diaz (right), and Louisa May Alcott joined Dr. Harriet Clisby and other women activists in 1877 to found the Boston Women's Educational and Industrial Union, which soon opened a retail shop for needy women to sell their handiwork. (Howe from Phoebe A. Hanford, *Daughters of America; or, Women of the Century* [1883]; Diaz and Alcott from *A Woman of the Century,* edited by Frances E. Willard and Mary A. Livermore [1893])

Ariadne Lawnin coined the term "helping women to help themselves" when she founded the St. Louis Exchange in 1883. (The Woman's Exchange, St. Louis, Missouri)

In business at the corner of North Charles and Pleasant streets since seven years after its founding in 1880, the Baltimore Woman's Industrial Exchange included salesrooms with a large picture window on the ground floor. A restaurant and boarding rooms were on the upper floors. (Enoch Pratt Free Library)

Annie Roelker, a founder
of the Woman's Exchange
of Cincinnati in 1883,
served as president for
thirty-eight years. She
expressed concern for the
"terrible realities of life
which face the working
woman." (Cincinnati
Historical Society)

Caroline Gratia Williams Walmsley,
a founder and the president of the
New Orleans Christian Woman's
Exchange for twenty-four years,
was described as a "queen whose
throne was philanthropy." (Louisiana Collection, Howard-Tilton
Memorial Library, Tulane University)

The managers made sure the Exchanges were competitive with the best stores in town. Here, the salesroom and "sales agents" of the Woman's Exchange of Cincinnati around 1900. (Cincinnati Historical Society)

As the Exchange idea became popular throughout the country during the last decades of the nineteenth century, the term *Woman's Exchange* attracted much attention in the press, as shown in a cartoon from *Life* (1899) entitled "The Husband of a Strong-Minded Woman." While his resolute wife looks on, a husband asks, "Where did you say the Woman's Exchange was? I've something I'd like to swap." (The University of Chicago Library)

1900   1901

CATALOGUE

OF

THE DEPOSITORY AND

PHILADELPHIA EXCHANGE

FOR

WOMAN'S WORK

N. E. COR. WALNUT and THIRTEENTH STREETS

PHILADELPHIA

Using up-to-date merchandising techniques similar to the grand emporiums, Exchange managers aggressively promoted consignors' goods. The cover of the 1900 sales catalog from the Depository and Philadelphia Exchange depicts the salesrooms on the ground floor of the building, located about six blocks from the Depository's first site sixty years earlier. (The Historical Society of Pennsylvania)

By late century, consignors were producing fashion and home accessories, such as needlework and ceramics, that were favored by well-to-do Gilded Age Americans. Their work often reflected the influence of the decorative arts, exemplified by the abundance of items in the parlor of the Leoni House in New York City. (The Museum of the City of New York, the Byron Collection)

As an option to large, impersonal workplaces such as the A. T. Stewart Department Store sewing room, consignors became self-sufficient and entrepreneurial by producing merchandise at home and selling it for a profit at an Exchange. From *Frank Leslie's Illustrated Newspaper* (April 24, 1875).

6

"An Excellent Way to Earn an Income":
The Consignors' Alternative to the Industrial Workplace

While Exchanges provided careers as merchants and economic reformers to their wealthy managers, they offered another kind of work opportunity to consignors in need of income. They played an important monetary role for women who sold their merchandise at consignment shops. As Lincoln observed, Exchanges could help "a large number of women who cannot labor outside their homes, or would prefer almost anything to the confining employment of the schoolroom, store or office, an excellent opportunity to earn an income."[1] Alice Rhine concurred, noting in 1891 that the goal of Exchanges was "to branch out largely enough in most of the worst paid departments of woman's work so as to force out those employed on such labor."[2] In that year, the fifty Exchanges reporting payments to the *Directory* recorded $370,720 in commissions to consignors (Table 6, Appendix A). Money earned from an Exchange often kept a consignor and her family from poverty's doorstep. Consignors could become entrepreneurial by creating handmade merchandise, marketing their goods, setting prices for their merchandise, and creating a customer following for their specialities. The Exchanges provided, as Lincoln emphasized, "an excellent way to earn an income."[3]

Reflecting the Women's Christian Temperance Union's and the Woman's Christian Association's cross-class efforts to help women in need of income, managers opened the consignment shops to those who could produce quality, saleable merchandise that met the standards of the Exchange. They helped working women, the "deserving poor" who wanted an employment alternative from the office, shop, or factory, as well as middle-class and well-to-do women who needed to vent creative talents and hone vocational skills should misfortune fall.

Keeping alive Candace Wheeler's intent to help less artistically inclined women have an outlet for their merchandise, Lincoln found Exchanges useful to women "unskilled in any particular class of work, who knew not what to do, nor how to do anything well."[4] Postbellum Exchanges, while expanding their mission to help working-class women, never lost sight of their original mission to promote financial independence among wealthy women. As Wheeler had noted upon the implementation of the Society for Decorative Art, "The idea of *earning* had entered the minds of women."[5] That philosophy represented a continuation of efforts started during the antebellum years.

But the primary objective that distinguished late-nineteenth-century Exchanges from their predecessors was not helping well-to-do women. Instead, managers focused their "mission high" on women who needed money but chose not to earn income in the industrial workplace. Lucy Salmon endorsed this mission. "Before the opening of the Exchange," she observed, "as still, indeed, women seeking remunerative employment were forced to go into one of the four great occupations open to women—work in factories, teaching, domestic service, and work in shops. Such women have found through the Exchange a means of support and opportunity for work which they could not find elsewhere."[6] The majority of consignors included the middle- and working-class women whom the WCTU, WCA, and WEIU sought to help. As the Exchange movement swept from the East Coast to the West, so did the decorative arts movement become more democratized and popular, appealing to, and accessible to, women beyond the elite classes.

Seemingly, an unlimited pool of women workers might wish to become home producers and sell goods at an Exchange. In addition to the prolonged Panic of 1873, the ravages of the Civil War were still felt by many families, particularly widows. Alice Rhine observed that "the Civil War began to convert into wage-earners large numbers of women who had been wage-expenders. Delicate women of the South, reared in affluence, were thrown among the breadearners. Thousands of other women, native to the North, like their sisters of the South, were obliged to become producers in the place of being consumers."[7] A historian of the Baltimore Exchange observed that "the Exchange may be traced back to the days following the Civil War, when impoverished old Maryland families made a little extra money by discreetly selling heirlooms, needlework, paintings, and cookies to acquaintances."[8]

The Exchange movement accelerated in the 1880s, when homework was once again promulgated as an attractive option for women who could earn income while still performing domestic duties. As Salmon had found, the Exchange had "pointed out to women a means of support that can be carried on in their homes and is perfectly compatible with other work necessarily performed there."[9] Exchanges existed for those women who preferred to "work in their homes," and they brought "relief and comfort in many cases where want and suffering existed."[10] Women were "learning that society is coming to respect more the woman who supports herself by making good bread, cakes and preserves than the woman who teaches school indifferently, gives poor elocutionary performances, or becomes a mere mechanical contrivance in a shop or factory," Salmon noted. "They are finding that the stamp of approval of ultimately to be put on the way work is done rather than on the occupation itself."[11]

"The Products of Women's Invention"

Consignors could either earn a profit from goods made at home or work at the Exchange if the Exchange offered a single-sex workroom. Lincoln defined the objective of Exchanges as promoting "the sale of the products of women's invention and industry by providing a depository for the reception and exhibition of their articles." He explained that "the God-given force can certainly be as advantageously employed in mixing a loaf of bread, making a tidy or painting a picture, as in copying accounts or writing a book; and of the two, that exercised in the former labors would seem to be the more practical character."[12]

Such home-based work had always held a prominent place in women's economic lives. Self-employed women who worked in their homes proved especially valuable by providing income, and a home-based economy assured that the majority of women would be safe from poverty. Enterprising women learned early to turn their needlework to profit, and fledgling industrialists eagerly sought their skills of spinning and weaving during the transition to a market economy. Unfortunately, women's home-based entrepreneurial efforts declined as producing factory-made goods became more efficient. As Candace Wheeler had noted at the time of the founding of the Society of Decorative Art, women's craftsmanship "had died, branch and stem and root, vanished as if it had never been."[13]

Exchanges hoped to help home producers by countering the dismal working conditions and low wages perpetuated through industrial employment. As Salmon commented in 1892, "Many desire employment but are forced to carry it on in their homes, which gives greater opportunity for the exercise of individual taste and ingenuity. Some women have found through the Exchanges a means of support and opportunity for work which could not be found elsewhere."[14] The idea of Exchanges had "already proven itself to be, and [would] continue more and more successfully so to do, one of the most helpful institutions for those women who must earn by working at home."[15] Managers took pride in encouraging self-sufficiency among consignors. "While the duties and responsibilities have been onerous and wearisome at times—the results have been gratifying in the extreme, and have amply repaid our efforts," the Milwaukee managers wrote in 1897. "Of one thing our friends may be assured, that this Exchange has done much in its quiet way to aid self-sufficient women."[16]

"Not Quite 'Professional'"

As managers sought to promote what they felt were the positive aspects of homework for women, they also needed to counter criticism that emphasized homework's more negative aspects. The Milwaukee managers assured the buying public that the Exchange was "not a money-making scheme for the benefit of the managers and a favored few. The aim is to furnish a place for the sale of any article for which there is a demand, made by self-sustaining women in their homes." And Richmond managers confirmed that thought: "Six years experience prove the practical value, the necessity, indeed, of an organization whose object is to aid reduced women in their efforts for self-support."[17] In 1891 Lincoln, explaining the long-term benefits of seeking work through the Exchange, observed that "there is quite a common fallacy in the mind of not quite a few women that to do work for the Exchange is not quite 'professional' enough; they would prefer operating a typewriter, or engaging in literature. But it is not always the labor one would choose to perform that brings the timeliest reliefs and comforts."[18]

But it was that stance—asking women to continue making sacrifices for home and family while working in separatist, traditionally lower-paid domestic labors—that most provoked the critics of self-help charities. In the closing decades of the nineteenth century, when many leisure- and working-class women united through labor and trade organizations to improve women's conditions in industry, the idea of encouraging a separatist, home-based workplace often seemed to be a backward move. Critics complained that segregating women from the mainstream work force and encouraging home production only perpetuated women's low pay and work status.

Ida M. Van Etten, a labor organizer, charged in 1890 that charities like Exchanges impeded progress and were "one of the direct causes of the wretched industrial condition of working women." She allowed that early charities, which held the singular purpose of "the care and the relief of the sick and those disabled by age or accident," were not the problem. Rather, philanthropy in the late nineteenth century gave working women a "false respect for money and position." Although not naming Exchanges specifically, Van Etten faulted as "a fearful impetus to the causes of the evils" those charities which supplemented women's low wages with services such as boardinghouses.[19] She added:

> Charity has only succeeded in making it easier for the unscrupulous employers of women to exploit them safely and respectably. By the side of the huge factory, whose owner is growing enormously rich upon the spoilation of his women workers, it builds the Lodging House or the Christian Home and this enables the man-

ufacturer to pay low wages below the living point. . . . women workers either must become organized and receive not only equal pay for equal work, but also equal opportunities for working, or they will by degrees, naturally, form an inferior class in every trade in which they enter, a class more poorly paid and who will, in consequence, work longer hours, who will receive less consideration from their employers, and who will be without means of redress, even in those grievances which are most degrading to their womanhood.[20]

Josephine Shaw Lowell concurred in 1896 that too much philanthropic intervention often proved detrimental to wage-earning women and that the benevolent women who ran the charities often accrued far more benefits than the poor women deemed to be the recipients. "It is said," she observed, "that one reason of the low wages of working women in Paris, which makes it impossible for any women to earn a living there by needlework, is the work that is done in institutions for poor women and sold at low rates—that is, those good people who have charge of the institutions for poor women are so possessed with a desire to maintain their institution and to teach the few women they have in them, that they injure thousands of working women."[21]

Salmon, too, faulted the Exchanges' emphasis on charity, finding that such a focus "assumes that work for women is a misfortune, not the birthright inheritance of every individual."[22] If, Alice Rhine agreed, Exchanges could shed their charitable connections, they would provide a more active countermovement to industrial work. "Were they once to become independent of charitable donations," Salmon wrote, "they would branch out largely enough in the worst paid departments of woman's work so as to force out those employed on such labor for the vast retail stores." Her suggestion was to call the enterprises the "Household Exchange," a name that would signify the "character of the goods rather than the nature of the makers."[23]

Perhaps mindful of the criticism, but not deterred by it, Exchange managers made a concerted effort to encourage women's home productions and advance economic reform nationally. To that end, they recruited consignors from cities and hamlets across the country.

"Hundreds of Women from Maine to California"

To ensure that customers had a good selection of fashionable goods and to assist as many needy women as possible, the managers of Exchanges actively sought to increase their national network of consignors. In one year alone, 1891, the ten largest Exchanges paid consignors, who often sent goods from areas far removed from the geographical location of the Exchange, more than

$210,000 in wages (Table 7, Appendix A). Within the first years of their founding, many Exchanges developed a wide network of consignors from urban and rural areas in the United States and from other countries. Doing so not only increased sales but also enhanced the Exchange movement's mission of reaching as many women as possible and creating a national work alternative.

The networking system also encouraged competition among Exchanges, which each vied for the saleable merchandise of talented consignors nationwide. By 1891 the movement was so widespread that Lincoln devoted chapters of his *Directory* to "Packing Goods for Transportation" and "Methods and Expenses of Transportation," adding a comparative list of what it cost to send various items by regular or express mail. As he noted, "A large number of the Exchanges confine their privileges to needy women and any such woman, whether residing in city or country, near by or far from an Exchange."[24]

Richmond managers reported that "a large proportion of the consignors reside in our own city and State; consignments have also been received from the States of Massachusetts, Rhode Island, New York, New Jersey, Pennsylvania, Maryland, West Virginia, North Carolina, South Carolina, Alabama and Florida."[25] The Woman's Exchange of St. Joseph, Missouri, advertised its efforts to "represent consignors from Maine to California," and the Bridgeport, Connecticut, Exchange boasted that it sold "for consignors all over the country."[26] New York managers wrote that consignors from "every state in the union [are] represented in our rooms."[27] By placing her merchandise in several Exchanges, a consignor could greatly increase her annual income, and Salmon found that "hundreds of women from Maine to California are obtaining for themselves and others partial or entire support" by working at Exchanges.[28]

Rural as well as urban women were encouraged to participate in Exchanges. Lincoln found that "women in the country send to the Exchange fresh eggs, butter, cheese, sausages, chicken, turkey, pickles, maple sugar and sirup, jams, preserves, jellies, fresh uncooked fruits, herbs, dried grasses, etc."[29] Salmon observed that in "one village of only five hundred inhabitants one young woman makes and sells daily thirty loaves of bread. In a small Eastern village another bakes and sells daily from thirty to a hundred loaves according to the season."[30]

Lacking the increasingly sophisticated and intricate national distribution networks of large retailers and wholesalers, however, Exchange managers often fell short of their ambitious plan to create a similar national network that could keep pace. They apparently made little attempt to monitor supply and demand of goods systematically. Rhine noted that "an insuperable obstacle to the extension of the exchanges lay in the utter lack of system with which contributors worked," and Salmon agreed that "the passive attitude prevent[s] the Exchange from keeping its finger on the pulse of the market."[31]

Unlike department stores, which sought "to regulate the supply of manufactured goods to meet a possible or expected demand," Exchange consignors had no such guide. Those who made and sent articles for sale had no idea what others were also making and sending. Rhine concluded that: "The result was that women living near or afar, in town or in the country, worked completely in the dark. With no finger on the public pulse in the matter of supply and demand for goods, they were obliged for this haphazard work to purchase their own material in small quantities in the retail markets, while the merchant manufacturers bought theirs in bulk in the cheapest."[32]

Consignors: Incomes and Identities

Although it is possible to garner much information about founders and managers of the Exchanges, wealthy women whose names were most often found on newspaper society pages, the identities of consignors remain a puzzle. Antebellum Exchanges focused solely on providing economic opportunities for the genteel poor, but by the end of the century, as women from a range of classes were included, the precise identities of consignors became more ambiguous.

Their incomes are also unclear, but they varied. Lincoln concluded that "one Exchange had paid over $2,000 in a single year to one consignor of edibles; another in the same time, over $1,000 to one woman for pies alone. One consignor of fine drawn work received over $600 in a single year from one Exchange; another over $1,300 for hand-painted screens."[33]

Managers felt that the onus of entrepreneurship—the responsibility of producing and selling quality work—fell to consignors. "Experience has abundantly proven," managers of the Richmond Exchange explained in 1888, "that it is the truest kindness to the depositor not to encourage the making of anything unsightly or unsalable. We desire to secure the support and patronage of the community by *deserving* it."[34] Alice Rhine also noted the income of the more successful consignors, observing that "one consignee of chicken jelly, etc., got during the year $1,256.89. Of the two consignees in the cake and preserve department, one received $1,019.73, the other $772.42. . . . One consignee received during the spring and fall months $217.35 for articles which she had previously made for manufacturers at $2.50 each and which were sold for $35 each."[35]

Much to the delight of managers, no doubt, it appears that many consignors earned respectable incomes. "It is hardly in keeping with the spirit of this society to gauge these salaries upon the lowest scales paid for similar employment," the New York managers asserted in 1892.[36] In its second year, the Cincinnati Exchange paid its top consignors a total of $4,425.03 out of $15,772,87 paid to all consignors.[37] By comparison to jobs in the commercial workplace, those who were the highest-paid must have been pleased with their annual incomes, although it is doubtful, even unrealistic, to assume that the majority of consignors did so well. It is difficult to ascertain the income of an average consignor because records are misleading. In 1890, for example, the Cincinnati Exchange listed 315 women who sold a total of $26,992. That would indicate that each received an average of $85. It is possible that the Exchange kept a cumulative list of all consignors, whether active or inactive, thereby offering a skewed account of what active consigners earned in any given year (Table 4, Appendix A).

From the amount of commissions—the amount earned on the sale of merchandise—paid to consignors, it appears that some women in dire circumstances could have earned a steady income from the Exchanges. It is more likely that a select number earned an exceptional living. The majority of consignors were perhaps on solid enough financial ground not to depend solely on incomes from Exchanges for a long duration, or perhaps they used such income to supplement their families' income. Exchanges most often were located in areas that would have been inaccessible to the very poor or to immigrant women, who, in any case, could not have afforded to purchase the materials needed to make products. As Rhine observed, "Only women possessed of some means could afford to lay out materials and wait the uncertain chances of its returning to them with a profit. To women of the proletariat, the exchanges were not only unknown mediums by reason of their situation in fashionable thoroughfares, but forbidden factors because of their attendant risks and expenses."[38]

Educated working- and middle-class women—graduates of high schools, industrial schools, and design schools—in need of income were the likely target consignors whom managers hoped to attract. "The Exchanges hoped to solve the ever-perplexing problem of finding remunerative work that women had been taught to do in the various art and industrial schools," Rhine wrote.[39] Records do not reveal with any certainty that the managers reached far beyond "educated," white, middle- and working-class women to embrace those of the immigrant or lower classes, although it might be reasoned that if a woman had a saleable product she would be encouraged to become a consignor. As Lincoln noted, "Any woman who possesses at least one talent and can do one thing *well* and who conforms to the rules of the Exchange, may offer work."[40]

In addition to supporting a payroll of consignors, the managers also hired women to help in showrooms, kitchens, and tearooms. By its second year, for example, the Milwaukee Exchange employed ten sales women whose "aggregate salaries amount to $155 per month."[41] To keep overhead as low as possible, volunteers—members of the board of managers—also helped when necessary.

As in the antebellum years, not all consignors could afford to pay the annual consignor's fee. Richmond managers were typical in finding ways around the issue. Most often, tickets were bought by women who could afford them and then passed along to consignors. In 1886 the Richmond managers initiated a special fund drive for the purchase of tickets: Fifty-five were bought and forty-two were donated to needy consignors.

Exchanges offered guidelines for expectations for consignors. In each annual report, Milwaukee managers issued their nine "Rules for Consignors," which explained the commission given on sold items, the Exchange's responsibility in case of fire or damage, and the length of time an item would be displayed. The managers advised that "consignors are requested to put their own prices on articles, but are earnestly advised to make them moderate, to ensure speedy sale."[42] Lincoln devoted a whole chapter to explaining "Who May Become Consignors," noting that "the Exchange cannot serve the careless worker who will not do her work exactly right every time."[43]

Anonymity was the key to attracting consignors. "Individual cases are not talked about, even among managers," Richmond managers wrote assuredly in 1887.[44] Managers could skirt accusations of favoritism—of promoting one consignor's goods over another—if all articles were accepted and merchandised anonymously and equally. Lucy Salmon found the anonymity requirement to be Exchanges' greatest weakness. The Exchange, she protested, "has required that all its consignors be known by number and not by name, thus allying itself . . . with penal and reformatory institutions." The managers' stand on the issue was nothing short of "moral cowardice," a reaffirmation of old notions that "work for remuneration is honorable for all men; work for remuneration is honorable for women only when necessity compels it."[45] But the managers remained steadfast, reasoning that more consignors would bring merchandise to an Exchange if they knew that their need for work would not be revealed. "What this [anonymity] means it is not difficult to imagine, if one knows anything for the struggle for ordinary comforts, decent support and healthy independence."[46]

But offering a fashionable retail outlet for the sale of consignors' merchandise was only half of an Exchange's mission. As important was the managers' offer of a practical weapon in the battle to win financial independence: vocational training.

"We All Need Much Preparation"

"We all need much preparation," Louisa May Alcott's semiautobiographical heroine Christie muses as she looks back over her struggles to find fair remuneration in the workplace. So, too, did Exchange managers realize the need for women to gain financial security through vocational skills. Consignors needed to be assured that "if adversity comes the work of her hands may save them from want."[47]

Vocational training became the late-nineteenth-century benevolent woman's mantra. "'Tis not enough to help the feeble up, but to support him thereafter," the Milwaukee managers instructed in 1894.[48] Vocational education, women asserted, would not encourage them to leave marriage and flock to the workplace; rather, it would supplement and improve the lives of wives and mothers. A woman who had a vocational skill, Martha Rayne commented, would "be less dependent and more companionable and it is the duty of all who have her interest to unite by word and deed in clearing away all false ideas of the true woman's position in the world."[49]

Women in need of vocational training in the closing decades of the nineteenth century could choose among a wealth of schools and publications. Alice Rhine observed that women long had availed themselves of training opportunities, but it was "not until after the close of the [Civil] war, when conditions made it urgent upon women to work on new lines, did classes increase to any extent."[50] The majority of women who learned vocational skills did so at professional vocational art and industrial schools or through commercial courses taught in public high schools. B. S. Elmes of the Academy of Dress Cutting in Springfield, Massachusetts, for example, offered classes at the local YWCA. The Academy boasted "A GRAND OFFER! A NEW COMPLETE TAILOR SYSTEM of dress cutting, at introduction, school and class price of $5. This is the age of progression and the whole system is so simple that anyone can learn from the illustrated books of instruction in English, German and French."[51]

Similarly, women's magazines of the day were replete with countless advertisements promoting vocational training schools. The J. F. Ingalls Company of Lynn, Massachusetts, claimed to be the "Headquarters for Ladies' Fancy Work": "We have been in the FANCY WORK business for years, and make it a point to keep up with the times! Send your full address and 2-cent stamp for INGALLS' ILLUSTRATED CATALOGUE of Fancy Work, Materials, Stamped Goods, of Lida Clarkson's Art Books, Stamping Outfits, etc."[52]

Women wishing to consign merchandise at an Exchange were guided by magazine editors, who advised on what would sell best. The October 1890 issue of

The Modern Priscilla, in an article aptly entitled "What to Make for Women's Exchanges," provided an up-to-date listing of what was most popular and saleable, as well as the latest techniques in fancy work, knotting, crocheting, and embroidery. The magazine would send the article "free to any address."[53]

The vocational, or industrial, education fervor of the era was part of a continuum. The effort to provide women with vocational training had begun in the middle of the century, when many people "attributed the distress of the factory and needlewoman to the lack of educational training which obliged women to crowd into occupations requiring little, if any, skill." Rhine found that "small, private attempts at industrial schools for the advancement of women had been started by the benevolence of individuals as early as 1856" and were organized and run by charitable institutions.[54] Commercial industrial schools had become serious businesses by the 1870s and 1880s, particularly those available to middle-class or wealthier women whose financial vulnerability had become more publicly acknowledged. The "first serious attempt to give practical shape to the question of higher education for women was undertaken when Peter Cooper made the advantages of the institute founded by him and bearing his name, free in all its departments, to women and to men. The Cooper Institute, opened to the public in 1859, had its free art classes for women, where art was taught in its application to the industries."[55] Of special interest were the industrial and arts schools that catered to "a class that belonged neither to the rich nor to the extremely poor."[56]

Martha Rayne concurred on the need for training and placed the blame for the lack of vocational skill on men, who held responsibility for women's education: "The lower education of women has been shamefully neglected, and the fault is largely due to [men who run schools]." The "working woman of the future will have one great advantage of her prototype of the past—she will have the advantage of thorough training and industrial colleges." Rayne wrote of the relationship between the Society of Decorative Art and vocational training provided by the Exchanges: Consignors "appreciate the [Exchange] as a school and recognized in their own best efforts the teaching of that society and claim that in furnishing a salesroom for the articles rejected, because they are not up to artistic standard, yet in many cases are beautiful and saleable, they are helping those who cannot afford to improve unless efforts give them the means for another trial."[57]

Lincoln reiterated that philosophy when he admonished:

No woman should attempt to assure herself that she can do everything any other can. A woman may become so self-conceited by the flatteries of friends in her school-days, that in later years, as often happens, a crisis comes and she must earn her support, she shall find, with regret, not one of her supposed accomplishments

will enable her to provide the necessities of life. A whole chapter might be fitting-
ly given, were it within the province of this book, urging parents to educate their
daughters, as well as their sons, to careful business habits, and honorable self-
support, so that should fortune play false with them, they may take their places
as successful bread-winners.[58]

To help consignors "take their places as successful bread-winners," Exchanges
offered a range of services in practical training and job placement. Vocational
training proved to be especially important to ensure quality, up-to-date merchandise. The Milwaukee managers recognized that need: "I would suggest the
introducing of some education features into the work of the Exchange," president Letitia Gray wrote in her annual message in 1894, "so that the quality of
goods, especially in the Fancy Department, may be improved."[59]

The managers of the Richmond Exchange noted that "the Exchange is providing a school for the education of workers—developing the artistic instinct,
correcting defects of design and execution, while it fosters a spirit of industry,
energy and independence."[60] To expand its vocational training programs, the
New York Exchange offered a cooking school, lectures, educational classes, and
a "Bureau of Information," more commonly known in philanthropic work as
an employment bureau. In addition, Lincoln reported, "Ladies are taught to
cut and fit by measure, each lady being allowed to make one dress, under the
guidance of an instructor. Four classes, of eight or nine ladies each, are now
studying this useful form."[61]

Vocational training and continued affiliation with an Exchange often meant
that consignors could strike out on their own and be independent businesswomen. Richmond Exchange managers in 1890 noted that they were pleased
to "lend a hand" to self-sustaining women, and that the Exchange had "been
privileged recently to assist several worthy ladies, one of whom conducts a
cooking school, another caters for families and individuals, and a third gives
lessons in embroidery, and all gratefully attribute their success to the fostering care of the Exchange."[62] A number of consignors, after training and selling
merchandise through an Exchange, moved on to self-employment by "becoming florists and gardeners; they are increasing the area of fruit culture; they are
raising poultry; they are painting and firing pottery, carving wood, making
stained glass, decorating houses, carding wool and making silk—in fact—
wherever there is a domestic want, or the possibility of a profit, which has been
overlooked or considered of small account by men, it is taken in hand by some
widowed mother, or some single woman who prefers effort to idleness; and
this new department of energy is largely owing to the Woman's Exchange."[63]

Vocational or industrial education, particularly in the domestic arts, allowed
consignors to become entrepreneurs and, when necessary, self-sufficient.

Managers viewed it as the most practical method to counteract a woman's traditionally low wages and the most viable way to persuade them to work within the parameters of domesticity. As Helen Campbell, a social worker, wrote in 1893, vocational education could "prevent the possibility of another generation owning so many incompetent and untrained workers."[64]

"To Many Struggling Women, This Society Has Become a Necessity"

By 1888 the Exchange movement was so popular and so widespread that managers from around the country gathered for a convention in New York, where the successful postbellum Exchange movement had been launched ten years before. They were sustained in their "mission high" by encouraging words of support from the Rev. Edward Everett Hale, one of the great orators and social reformers of the nineteenth century. His message reinforced the very heart of the managers' mission: "You have therefore organized this Society, of which the ultimate purpose is that every woman who is compelled by adverse fortune to work, shall have a fair chance to dispose of her work on favorable and easy terms and that her work tomorrow shall be better than her work today."[65]

When the Reverend Hale addressed the managers, nearly sixty Exchanges had opened for business since the founding of the New York Exchange in 1878. No doubt his audience shared his enthusiasm for the Exchange mission: "Who are profited by the Woman's Exchange?" the Richmond managers asked in their annual report published later that year. "Could the money annually be given accomplish more good in some other channel? We can truthfully answer that to many struggling women, this society has become a necessity."[66]

In that same year—bringing the Exchange idea full circle—Queen Victoria and her daughter, Princess Beatrice, started an Exchange in London: the Working Woman's Guild. Differing from Victoria's earlier venture of 1872, the Royal School of Art Needlework and its goal to help only the genteel poor, the newer enterprise was based "somewhat on the American Exchange . . . to help women of limited means . . . part of its work being the furnishing of suitable work for the weak hands of invalids."[67]

Through the final decades of the nineteenth century, women of various classes worked together to promote a mutually practical "mission high." Their legacy resulted in the combined efforts of well-to-do women and working- and middle-class women to build and sustain a national network of employment options for those who wanted or needed income or creative outlets but preferred not to enter the industrial or commercial workplace. Throughout the century, the Exchange movement dignified and enhanced woman's work by marketing quality home productions through the fashionable Exchanges and promoting the idea of fair remuneration for consignors' labors. Through their combined efforts, all women connected with Exchanges helped to raise consciousness about working conditions for women and women's need to have some sense of financial security and pride in their work. Within that framework and through their mission and annual reports, those who ran Exchanges also kept public the issues relevant to the exploitation of working women and those that concerned wealthy women who suffered from the boredom and idleness of a restrictive society.

The Cincinnati managers captured the benefits that all classes of women derived from Exchanges. "We have renewed reason to congratulate ourselves upon the fact that our enterprise is conferring upon large numbers of industrious women the highest benefits," they wrote in 1887 after four years in business. "[The Exchange] is exerting wide and beneficent influence in teaching all who fall under its sphere that manual labor is not only useful, but honorable."[68]

By combining entrepreneurial talents with self-help philanthropic ideologies, Exchange managers enlarged not only consignors' spheres but also their own. Exchanges created opportunities to allow consignors to participate in the marketplace and collect a fair remuneration for their labors. They also provided an opportunity for managers to become respected businesswomen and social reformers. Exchanges helped both consignors and managers stretch beyond their homebound duties and become entrepreneurs. They were able to move beyond the circumscribed antebellum role of lady to the more active life of a late-nineteenth-century working woman, who "takes pride in her ability to engage in some useful, creative occupation."

Epilogue:
The Exchange Movement Continues

In March 1934, nearly a half-century after the managers of Exchanges from around the country had met in New York in 1888 to hear the Rev. Edward Everett Hale, and a century after the managers of the Philadelphia Ladies' Depository had published their first annual report, the fourth generation of managers convened at the Woman's City Club in Philadelphia, city of so many milestones in the Exchange movement.[1] They set a different goal this time: to incorporate a national organization representing woman's exchanges. That organization, the Federation of Woman's Exchanges, still continues and meets each spring to bring direction and cohesiveness to a movement that perseveres well into its second century.

The 1934 meeting made clear that during its first century the Exchange movement, like the culture that nurtured it, had radically changed. From the more than seventy-two Exchanges Lincoln recorded in his *Directory* in 1891, the number had dipped to eighteen.[2] Like many business enterprises on which they were modeled—small, female-run dress shops and block-long department stores—several Exchanges had felt the pinch of reversals of fortune and closed their doors.

The number of Exchanges continues to fluctuate, but the entrepreneurship and determination of Exchange managers to keep their enterprises afloat remains constant. Those traits were boldly displayed by the New York managers during the waning days of Prohibition. No sooner had the ink dried on the legislation that signed the Twenty-first Amendment repealing Prohibition into law when the managers quickly opened what became a financial bonanza and a favorite watering hole for New York's carriage trade: the Crinoline Bar. It was named, as the managers noted, for "the hoop skirt fashions of our founders."[3] Although the name evoked the nostalgia of a long-past time of carefree buggy rides and picnics in the country—a marketing technique never lost on Exchange managers—some of the city's more temperance-minded press responded less chivalrously. "One More Blow to Prohibition!" denounced the *New York American.*

The New York Exchange, a successful prototype of the postbellum Exchanges, continues, as it has since 1878, as a firm grounding for the Exchange movement. The shop is stocked with one-of-a-kind items that no doubt would have pleased co-founders Candace Wheeler and Mary Choate. And, always competitive, the Exchange in the summer of 1997 moved, for the ninth time since its founding, to a prime location across the street from one of the stores that had provided inspiration a century earlier—Bloomingdale's.

The St. Louis Exchange followed the lead of the New York Exchange when its managers—after a hotly contested debate—voted to serve liquor in their restaurant in the early 1940s. For many years, Julia Lawnin Gordon, granddaughter of the founder, held sway as one of the Exchange's bartenders. The Exchange remains one of St. Louis's favorite gathering spots—"the place to be seen." Ariadne Lawnin's dream of "Helping Women to Help Themselves," initiated in 1883, is kept alive.

After celebrating its 110th anniversary with great fanfare throughout the city in 1990, the Baltimore Woman's Industrial Exchange continues to capture the enduring complexities and charm of the Exchange movement.[4] Although still housed in its original building on North Charles Street, replete with an unhurried lunchroom reminiscent of another time and a cozy salesroom filled with finely smocked dresses, the Exchange, paradoxically, is well advertised on its own home page on the most modern of communications tools: the Internet.

The Boston Women's Industrial and Educational Union, in its inviting building on Bolyston Street, continues as a popular shopping spot for a fifth generation of New England patrons and boasts one of the country's finest needlework departments, a reminder of the influence on the Exchange movement of the Royal School of Art Needlework in the 1870s.[5] The shop—actually, six shops altogether—specializes in hand-painted, custom-made needlework canvasses and, in keeping with its mission from so long ago, still offers needlework instruction.

The Brooklyn Exchange, which prides itself as being one of Brooklyn's oldest continuously operating enterprises, is housed in one of the borough's historic churches and employs some three hundred consignors a year. Similarly, the St. Augustine and West Hartford Exchanges continue to thrive. Reaching its centennial anniversary in May 1988, West Hartford (which had originated in downtown Hartford) held a grand celebration, inviting all 238 consignors to share the festivities. A West Hartford historian noted that this was "a far cry from the early days when the identity of a consignor was kept secret as it was not quite 'ladylike' to have to earn money."[6] The Exchange still uses the now-famous "Our Lady in Blue" logo—another crinoline-clad, bonneted lady—designed in 1900 by Margaret Lincoln, a graduate of the Pratt Institute and an occasional consignor.

The stronghold of the Exchange movement in the South for many decades, the Christian Woman's Exchange in 1963 shifted its charitable focus. The managers voted to close the consignment shop and concentrate on restoring the Exchange's building to its 1831 elegance, opening the house to the public. The CWE's Hermann-Grima House on St. Louis Street in the French Quarter is a popular tourist attraction, and proceeds earned from tours are directed toward charitable activities. In 1997, returning to its original mission, the CWE reopened its consignment shop.

The Philadelphia Ladies' Depository, originator of the Exchange idea, in 1894 merged with the Philadelphia Exchange for Woman's Work. The new consolidated Exchange, in turn, spawned several other Exchanges in the Philadelphia area over the twentieth century. Not surprisingly, the largest number of Exchanges in the Federation—five—are concentrated in the Greater Philadelphia area. None are located downtown, at the corner of Chestnut and Seventh, but rather are in surrounding suburbs and townships, appropriately near streets with familiar names such as Wistar, Biddle, and Wharton.

But not all nineteenth-century Exchanges have been so fortunate in adapting to change and riding out rough times. Celebrating its seventy-fifth anniversary in 1958, the Cincinnati Exchange's managers—many of them great-granddaughters of the founders—observed the steadfastness of the Exchange mission over the decades and noted that "seventy-five years ago in many circles it was considered 'unladylike' for a woman to work. Few jobs were given to women and few had any business or professional training."[7] By 1958 the Cincinnati Exchange had paid a cumulative $6 million in commissions to consignors since its founding in 1883 and had been especially helpful to Cincinnatians during the Great Depression. The women who ran the Exchange, the *Cincinnati Times Star* noted on December 20, 1931, during difficult times, were "women of the leisure position eager to give assistance and to keep the home fires burning," and they kept "whole families off the bread lines." "Thousands of children," the *Cincinnati Enquirer* concurred on February 5, 1933, "have been brought up on the money earned by their mothers at the Woman's Exchange."

But the Cincinnati Exchange's important place in the lives of that city's women was not to last. In 1985, after 102 years in business, it closed its doors. Like other nineteenth-century Exchanges that closed between the 1950s and the 1980s, it shut down for various reasons: diminishing numbers of downtown shoppers, a decrease in the volunteer help needed to operate the shop and keep overhead low, and the availability of other work and income options for women. On April 21, 1985, the *Cincinnati Enquirer,* which, along with the other local daily newspapers, had enthusiastically reported the Exchange's activities for more than a century, lamented its closing: "Volunteers are now getting older and women prefer paid jobs to volunteering; also, many women who cannot work outside their homes now have social security and welfare." When the Exchange closed its books in 1985, the managers bequeathed more than $100,000 to various women's organizations in the city.

The Richmond Exchange closed in 1955 for similar reasons. After initiating a junior board managers program the year before in the hope of involving a new generation, the Exchange could still not sustain adequate volunteer help. According to the minutes of January 1, 1955, the Richmond managers felt that junior board members "could use their time, efforts and energy more efficiently" in other charitable activities. Before closing, they put consignors directly in touch with customers, enabling them to start their own businesses if possible, a gesture much in keeping with the Exchange philosophy. The Exchange's remaining endowment was given to local women's charities.

A decade later, in 1965, managers of the Milwaukee Exchange also felt compelled to close their enterprise rather than compromise its traditionally high standards of merchandise. As competition with mass-produced merchandise threatened, they took a stand against what they perceived to be an onslaught of shoddy goods. In the 1950s, when nylon became popular, they discontinued the lingerie department rather than abandon their tradition of selling only silk undergarments. Despite aggressive advertising and direct mail campaigns to increase patronage and funding, the managers dissolved the corporation on June 22. The dissolution documents were beautifully hand-scripted, just as the letter of incorporation had been eighty-one years before.

Since 1900, as some older Exchanges have closed others have been founded, begun for the same reasons as were their predecessors: a response to cyclical economic or cultural changes in women's lives. In 1997 nine of the nineteenth-century Exchanges were still in business after more than a century. Three Exchanges were formed during the first decade of the twentieth century; five during the 1930s and the Great Depression; one in the 1940s; six in the 1950s; and eighteen during the 1960s and 1970s, the decades of the largest growth since the closing of the nineteenth century (Table 8, Appendix A). Because of stringent Internal Revenue Service regulations, consignors must now demonstrate financial need, and most Exchanges eagerly accept consignments from men. Much as the Exchange movement in 1888 inspired Queen Victoria and her daughter to open the Working Woman's Guild in London, contemporary Exchanges provide a template for similar enterprises in developing countries, where women are choosing to capitalize on their domestic skills in cooperative, voluntary organizations.

In the 1990s, when entrepreneurship and home industry once again gained importance, the Woman's Exchange movement provided valuable insight into some of the earliest enterprises undertaken collectively by women. Nineteenth-century Woman's Exchanges were early examples of such contemporary retail establishments as shops sponsored by museums, charities, and performing arts organizations that merge the for- and nonprofit sectors.

Contemporary Exchanges face the same business challenges and fluctuations as their counterparts did long ago. No matter what the decade or century, women associated with Exchanges have learned to combine nostalgia, charity, and business acumen successfully. They look to the past for tradition and to the future for innovation. Nora Ephron, director of the 1993 hit film *Sleepless in Seattle,* was inspired to stage a scene in the lunchroom of the Baltimore Woman's Industrial Exchange. One of the waitresses, Miss Marguerite, ninety, who had worked at the Exchange for well over a half-century—which is common in most older Exchanges—had a role in the scene and was later a guest of honor at the movie's premier in Baltimore. After surveying the 113-year-old Exchange, with its novel merchandise and endearing atmosphere reminiscent of a time of gentility and hominess now lost, Ephron exclaimed, "It was out of time"—in other words, a place that cared about its history.[8] Her simple description applies as well to the enduring and revealing Exchange movement, seemingly inviolable since 1832.

Appendix A

Table 1. Philadelphia Ladies' Depository
Commissions Paid to Consignors for
Selected Years, 1834–76

Year	Amount	Change from Previous Years Cited
1834	$ 2,081.60	
1836	3,340.91	60%
1837	3,919.00	17
1840	5,217.96	33
1859	8,931.03	71
1860	9,660.58	8
1869	10,640.52	10
1876	8,744.53	−18

Source: Philadelphia Ladies' Depository, *Annual Reports.*

Table 2. Chronological Listing of Foundings of Woman's Exchanges

1832	The Philadelphia Ladies' Depository
1856	The Woman's Depository and Exchange, New Brunswick, N.J.
1868	The Cincinnati Ladies' Depository
1873	The Pittsburgh Ladies' Depository
1878	The Woman's Work Exchange and Decorative Art Society, Brooklyn, N.Y.
	The Exchange for Woman's Work, New York City (Fifth Avenue)
1879	The Exchange for Woman's Work of Chicago
	The St. Louis Ladies' Depository
1880	The Woman's Industrial Exchange, Baltimore, Md.
	The Woman's Educational and Industrial Union, Boston, Mass.[a]
	The Rochester Art Exchange
1881	The Christian Woman's Exchange, New Orleans, La.
	The Depository of the Union for Good Works, New Bedford, Mass.
	The Exchange for Woman's Work, Newark, N.J.
	The Woman's Exchange, Albany, N.Y.
	The Rhode Island Exchange for Woman's Work, Providence
1882	The Woman's Work Exchange, St. Paul, Minn.

Table 2. (cont.)

	The Woman's Industrial Exchange, Milwaukee, Wis.
1883	The Woman's Exchange, St. Louis, Mo.
	The Woman's Exchange, Cincinnati, Ohio
	The Exchange for Woman's Work, Richmond, Va.
1884	The Woman's Work Exchange, Englewood, N.J.
	The Woman's Work Exchange, Norfolk, Va.
1885	The Woman's Exchange, San Francisco, Calif.
	The Exchange for Woman's Work, Stamford, Conn.
	The Woman's Exchange, Lexington, Ky.
	The Woman's Exchange, Louisville, Ky.
	The Woman's Work and Art Exchange, Morristown, N.J.
	The Woman's Exchange, Columbus, Ohio
	The Woman's Exchange, Lancaster, Pa.
	The Exchange for Woman's Work, Bristol, R.I.
	The Exchange for Woman's Work, Charleston, S.C.
1886	The Woman's Exchange, Denver, Colo.
	The Woman's Exchange, Springfield, Ill.
	The Woman's Exchange, St. Joseph, Mo.
	The Woman's Exchange, Buffalo, N.Y.
	The Madison Avenue Depository and Exchange for Woman's Work, New York City
	The Woman's Industrial Exchange, Pittsburgh, Pa.
1887	The Woman's Exchange, Little Rock, Ark.
	The Woman's Industrial Exchange, Los Angeles, Calif.
	The Woman's Industrial Exchange, San Diego, Calif.
	The Exchange for Woman's Work, Bridgeport, Conn.
	The Woman's Exchange, Elizabeth, N.J.
	The Woman's Exchange, Troy, N.Y.
	The Woman's Exchange, Newport, R.I.
	The Exchange for Woman's Work, Memphis, Tenn.
	The Woman's Exchange, Houston, Tex.
	The Woman's Exchange, Madison, Wis.
1888	United Workers and Woman's Exchange, Hartford, Conn.
	The Woman's Exchange, Augusta, Ga.
	The Woman's Industrial Exchange, Atchison, Kans.
	The Exchange for Woman's Work, Northampton, Mass.
	The Woman's Exchange, Mt. Vernon, N.Y.
	The Harlem Exchange for Woman's Work, New York
	The Woman's Exchange, Utica, N.Y.
	The Exchange for Woman's Work, Philadelphia, Pa.
	The Exchange for Woman's Work, Charlottsville, Va.
1889	The Woman's Exchange, Decatur, Ill.
	The Ladies' Exchange, Topeka, Kans.
	The Woman's Exchange, Wichita, Kans.
	The Exchange for Woman's Work, Detroit, Mich.
	The Exchange for Woman's Work, Duluth, Minn.
	The Woman's Exchange, Plainfield, N.J.
1890	The Woman's Industrial Exchange, Santa Barbara, Calif.
	The Woman's Exchange, Waterbury, Conn.
	The Woman's Exchange, Washington, D.C.
	The Woman's Exchange, Cleveland, Ohio
	The Woman's Work Exchange, San Antonio, Tex.
	The Woman's Exchange, Lynchburg, Va.

The Exchange for Woman's Work, Staunton, Va.

The Woman's Exchange, Oshkosh, Wis.

1891   The Woman's Exchange, Jacksonville, Ill.

Source: Frank Asa Lincoln, *Directory of Exchanges for Woman's Work* (Springfield, Mass.: F. A. Lincoln, 1891).

Note: Exchanges for which a founding date is not indicated include: The Woman's Exchange, Amherst, Mass.; the Woman's Employment Society, Worcester, Mass.; the Art Exchange, Harrisburg, Pa.; and the Tacoma Exchange, Tacoma, Wash.

    a. Although Lincoln lists the founding of the Boston Exchange as 1880, other sources attribute the establishment of the WEIU in that city as 1877, which is used in this study to correspond with the Boston WEIU records.

Table 3. Amounts Paid to Consignors by the Nine Largest Exchanges from their Establishment through 1891

New York Exchange for Woman's Work (1878)	$ 417,435
Cincinnati Woman's Exchange (1883)	175,130
New Orleans Christian Woman's Exchange (1881)	173,233
Boston Woman's Educational and Industrial Union (1877)	148,588
St. Louis Woman's Exchange (1883)	55,000
San Francisco Woman's Exchange (1885)	50,000
Rhode Island (Providence) Exchange for Woman's Work (1881)	48,469
Richmond (Va.) Exchange for Woman's Work (1883)	27,324
St. Joseph (Mo.) Exchange for Woman's Work (1886)	19,223
	$ 1,114,402

Source: Frank Asa Lincoln, *Directory of Exchanges for Woman's Work* (Springfield, Mass.: F. A. Lincoln, 1891).

Table 4. The Woman's Exchange of Cincinnati Commissions Paid to Consignors

Year	Amount	Increase/Decrease
1884	$ 8,491	
1885	15,773	86%
1886	22,002	39
1887	24,087	10
1888	24,782	3
1889	27,654	12
1890	25,228	−9
1891	26,992	7
1892	27,744	3
1893	29,400	6
1894	30,337	3
1895	29,228	−10
1896	30,831	13
1897	27,146	−12
1898	25,597	6
1899	26,051	2
1900	26,084	—
	427,427	
Net increase 1884–1900	207%	

Source: The Woman's Exchange of Cincinnati, *Annual Reports.*

Table 5. Comparison of Catalog Prices for the New York Exchange and Bloomingdale's

	Range of Prices	
Item	New York Exchange	Bloomingdale's
cloaks	$9.00–18.00	$2.88–2.89
cambric shirts	1.75–3.50	0.65–1.18
boys shirts (linen, wool, and pique)	5.00–8.00	3.00–7.60
wrapper	3.00–5.00	1.29–2.75
flannel shirts	2.75	0.65–1.33
bibs	1.00	0.08–0.59
dresses (for ages 3–12)	3.00–12.00	2.53–5.15
sacques	2.00–6.00	0.50–1.25
slips	1.50	2.75

Sources: Bloomingdale Brothers, *Bloomingdale's Illustrated 1886 Catalog: Fashions, Dry Goods and Housewares* (1886, repr. New York: Dover Books, 1988), pp. 38, 42, 44, 103; New York Exchange for Woman's Work, *Catalogue and Price List,* 1900–1901, p. 33.

Table 6. Amounts (Commissions) Paid to Consignors in 1891 by Exchanges Reporting Payments

Exchange	Amount	Consignors
New York	$51,000	2,000
Boston, Mass.	34,510	525
Cincinnati, Ohio	26,992	315
San Francisco, Calif.	23,372	240
Wichita, Kans.	18,000	20 [a]
Baltimore, Md.	15,500	1,600
Philadelphia (Chestnut Street)	14,562	786
Columbus, Ohio	13,000	60
Pittsburgh, Pa.	12,549	n.a.
Topeka, Kans.	10,000	123
St. Paul, Minn.	9,054	118
Springfield, Ill.	9,000	85
Denver, Colo.	8,500	163
Philadelphia (Ladies' Depository)	8,094	300
New Orleans, La.	7,107	230
Stamford, Conn.	7,096	300
Utica, N.Y.	7,000	200
Los Angeles, Calif.	6,000	200
St. Joseph, Mo.	5,500	200
Louisville, Ky.	5,154	201
Lexington, Ky.	4,500	n.a.
Elizabeth, N.J.	4,216	155
Bridgeport, Conn.	4,017	400
Newport, R.I.	4,000	289
Englewood, N.J.	3,706	45
Little Rock, Ark.	3,688	20
Morristown, N.J.	3,500	190
Santa Barbara, Calif.	3,500	83
Charleston, S.C.	3,498	150

Exchange	Amount	Consignors
St. Louis, Mo.	3,475	942
Memphis, Tenn.	3,326	138
New York (Harlem)	3,145	110
Duluth, Minn.	3,000	70
Atchison, Kans.	2,957	30
Rochester, N.Y.	2,890	219
Albany, N.Y.	2,824	200
Hartford, Conn.	2,731	411
Decatur, Ill.	2,559	125
Newark, N.J.	2,251	319
New Bedford, Mass.	2,000	350
Norfolk, Va.	2,000	115
Augusta, Ga.	1,953	59
San Diego, Calif.	1,617	44
Bristol, R.I.	1,300	100
New Brunswick, N.J.	1,277	n.a.
Houston, Tex.	1,200	134
Northampton, Mass.	1,100	45
Charlottsville, Va.	1,000	119
Lancaster, Pa.	1,000	n.a.
Troy, N.Y.	500	152
	$370,720	

Sources: Frank Asa Lincoln, *The Directory of Exchanges for Woman's Work* (Springfield, Mass.: F. A. Lincoln, 1891); Lucy Salmon, "The Woman's Exchange: Charity or Business?" Forum 13 (March–Aug. 1892): 396.

Note: The Exchanges for which payments were not reported to the *Directory of Exchanges for Woman's Work* in 1891 include: Waterbury, Conn.; District of Columbia; Chicago and Jacksonville, Ill.; Amherst and Worcester, Mass.; Detroit; Plainfield, N.J.; Brooklyn, Buffalo, and Mt. Vernon, N.Y.; New York City (Madison Avenue); Cleveland; Providence; San Antonio; Lynchburg and Richmond, Va.; and Milwaukee and Oshkosh, Wis.

a. The Wichita Exchange indicated the amount paid to the twenty consignors was "about $75 monthly." Based on this figure, the annual amount paid to each consignor would have been $900.

Table 7. Amounts Paid to Consignors in 1891 by the Ten Largest Exchanges

New York Exchange for Woman's Work	$ 51,000
Boston Woman's Educational and Industrial Union	33,510
Cincinnati Woman's Exchange	26,992
San Francisco Woman's Exchange	23,372
Baltimore Woman's Industrial Exchange	15,500
Philadelphia Exchange for Woman's Work	14,562
Columbus Woman's Exchange	13,000
Minneapolis Woman's Exchange	12,791
Topeka Ladies' Exchange	10,000
Milwaukee Woman's Industrial Exchange	9,824
	$210,551

Source: Frank Asa Lincoln, *Directory of Exchanges for Woman's Work* (Springfield, Mass.: F. A. Lincoln, 1891).

Table 8. Member Exchanges in the Federation of Woman's Exchanges, 1997

Connecticut
    Fairfield Woman's Exchange
    Greenwich Exchange for Woman's Work
    Heritage Village Woman's Exchange
    The Woman's Exchange (West Hartford)
    The Woman's Exchange of Old Lyme
Florida
    The Woman's Exchange (St. Augustine)
Louisiana
    Christian Woman's Exchange (New Orleans)
Maryland
    The Woman's Industrial Exchange (Baltimore)
Massachusetts
    Dedham Women's Exchange
    The Hay Scales Exchange, Inc. (North Andover)
    Old Town Hall Exchange (Lincoln Center)
    Port O'Call Exchange (Gloucester)
    The Wayland Depot, Inc.
Missouri
    The Woman's Exchange of St. Louis
New Jersey
    The Depot (Midland Park)
    The Hunterdon Exchange (Flemington)
    Woman's Exchange of Monmouth County (Little Silver)
New York
    New York Exchange for Woman's Work (Manhattan)
    Scarsdale Woman's Exchange
    Brooklyn Woman's Exchange
North Carolina
    Sandhills Woman's Exchange
Ohio
    The Chagrin Valley Woman's Exchange, Inc. (The Sassy Cat)
Pennsylvania
    Chestnut Hill Woman's Exchange
    The Woman's Exchange of the Neighborhood League (Wayne)
    The Woman's Exchange of Reading
    The Woman's Exchange of West Chester
    The Woman's Exchange of Yardley
Tennessee
    The Woman's Exchange of Memphis, Inc.
Texas
    St. Michael's Woman's Exchange (Dallas)

Source: The Federation of Woman's Exchanges, *Directory,* 1997.

Appendix B:
The Woman's Exchange of Cincinnati

The formation of the Woman's Exchange of Cincinnati in 1883 exemplified how the decorative arts, the Woman's Christian Association, a ladies' depository, a formidable leader, and the new self-help–self-improvement philosophy combined to make a successful postbellum Exchange. The Cincinnati Exchange, composed of elements from the charitable and instructional programs of the Woman's Art Museum Association, the Women's Christian Association, and the Ladies' Depository, was successfully formed under the unswerving guidance of Annie Roelker, who remained at the helm for nearly six decades, until her death in 1938. It was a formula that laid the foundation for a business enterprise that would last for more than a century.

Although part of a continuum in the city's strong tradition of philanthropic activities, the Cincinnati Exchange, like the New York Exchange on which it was modeled, could identify the catalyst for its founding as the decorative arts movement spurred by the Philadelphia Centennial of 1876. Much as Candace Wheeler was inspired by the Royal School's exhibit to initiate the Society of Decorative Art and, a year later, the New York Exchange, so, too, were many of Cincinnati's wealthy women influenced by the idea of combining self-help and decorative arts standards in efforts to help working women. The Cincinnati Exchange intertwined benevolent women's artistic and charitable self-help activities and reflected the dual, and often overlapping, nature of many postbellum leisure-class women's interests.

Although they had been meeting for years in a "dusty, dirty attic above the Masonic Temple" to indulge their artistic impulses, Cincinnati's well-to-do women finally gave full vent to their creative flair after witnessing and participating in the arts and women's exhibits at the Centennial Exhibition.[1] Many former committee members continued their interest in furthering the arts movement by forming the Women's Art Museum Association in 1879.[2] Cincinnati women had already put the Queen City on the map as an important cultural center by establishing the Fine Arts Academy in 1854 to exhibit paintings and sculpture and encourage public interest in the fine arts. Fifteen years later, eager to show how art and industry were not mutually exclusive, they opened the School of Art and Design, whose students later displayed their art at the Cincinnati Room of the Women's Pavilion in 1876.

Eight of the eighteen founding Women's Art Museum Association (WAMA) members would become founders and charter members of the Cincinnati Exchange in 1883.[3] In its efforts to continue and promote the new decorative arts standard expressed at the Philadelphia Centennial, the WAMA rented classrooms and an exhibit hall in downtown Cincinnati to provide instruction in embroidery, china painting, and water color. The group invited artists to exhibit their work and presented a lecture on the South Kensington movement—"the ladies' favorite subject."[4] Sir Philip Cunliffe, director of the South Kensington Museum, which had sponsored the wildly popular exhibit at the Centennial, in 1883 paid a visit to the WAMA's exhibition hall, bringing with him Etruscan pottery and prized examples of the by-then famous South Kensington tapestries and embroideries.[5]

The Cincinnati chapter of the Woman's Christian Association also figured prominently in the formation of the Cincinnati Exchange. Minutes of the spring 1882 WCA meeting reveal that a member "first agitated" the idea to start an Exchange.[6] But it was several months later, at the regularly scheduled January 3, 1883, meeting that a member noted that she had seen an article in the *New York Evangelist* "giving an account of the workings of the Exchange in that city."[7] Several Cincinnati WCA members visited the New York Exchange, where they learned of the great success and profits to consignors. One New York consignor, they were told, in five years "had earned $7,000 baking angel food cake, and another a fabulous amount in pickles and preserves."[8] The Cincinnati women obtained a copy of the New York Exchange's bylaws, and by the January 30, 1883, WCA meeting the "committee on rules and regulations thought it advisable to adopt the rules used by the New York Exchange."[9] A "locality" committee of five members was appointed to find a store and agreed to locate in the Phoenix Building in the heart of the city's shopping area.

Several WCA members, representing the interest in the decorative arts, suggested exhibiting works of pottery made by WAMA members at the Exchange's opening. The idea was vetoed after others thought the exhibit might discourage less talented or less artistic women from becoming consignors.

To help another kind of impoverished women in their "continued struggle" in 1868, concurrent to the founding of the Women's Christian Association, another group of Cincinnati benevolent women formed the Ladies' Depository. Identical in mission and philosophy to the Philadelphia Ladies' Depository formed three decades earlier. The Cincinnati counterpart offered help to the "decayed gentlewoman" who had met with hard times and would offer assistance only to needy peers of the wealthy founders. Here, poverty-stricken gentlewomen, "persons in relieved circumstances," could conveniently and secretly sell their needlecraft through the consignment shop, "a medium between [its] patrons and depositors."[10] The Depository managers wrote of their hopes to provide a "means of support for that class of respectable women who are obliged to maintain themselves by sewing and whose duties to their families make it necessary that their work be done at home. Numberless instances might be given of women brought up in comfort and refinement, who are now dependent upon the scanty earnings of the needle for their own and their children's support."[11]

The establishment, and relatively quick demise, of the Cincinnati Ladies' Depository testified to the transformation in attitudes over the intervening decades concerning women's right to seek financial independence and who should benefit from leisure-class women's charitable efforts. Although the Depository recruited 450 members in its first two years, by its final year, 1872, membership had dropped to fewer than 150 subscribers. As in the dissolution of its counterpart in Pittsburgh, the Cincinnati Depository closed its doors after only five years because of lack of community interest and the narrow scope of its mission at a time when benevolent women nationwide increasingly sought to embrace a wider range of women through self-help. Despite its short life span, however, the Depository set the precedent for establishing a self-help consignment shop in Cincinnati. As with the WAMA and WCA, many directors and members would join forces a decade later after being inspired by the decorative arts movement at the Philadelphia Centennial to implement the Cincinnati Exchange.[12]

The Cincinnati Exchange was fortunate from its inception to have the guidance of an exceptionally strong leader. Annie Roelker, a physician's daughter from a well-connected local family, perhaps more than any other founding manager guided the Exchange through its formative period and helped it stay the course on its appointed mission to reach a range of women in need of earning income. Roelker was known to display the "keenest sympathy for those in need."[13] She served as treasurer for the Exchange's first seventeen years and became president in 1900. Her tenure proved among the most steadfast of her peers. She helped to conceive and implement the Exchange at the age of twenty-seven and remained active until her death at eighty-two. In her offices as treasurer and president she took a personal interest in the administration of all the committees, "having their interest greatly at heart. Her judgment in the running of the Exchange was said to be wise and always just."[14]

Although Roelker and the other managers publicly documented their vision and hopes for the Exchange each year in annual reports, her private sympathies for the plight of working women could also be found in her journals and scrapbooks. By the 1880s, as the suffrage movement gained increasing national visibility, Roelker apparently became intrigued by the clash between the "advanced women," women endorsing suffrage and woman's rights, and the "anti's," those opposed to getting the vote and liberalizing woman's rights. Of most concern was the perception that women of her own sheltered class could not sympathize with the harsh realities of life for the woman forced to earn income in the industrial workplace. In 1894 she made note of an article by a writer critical of well-to-do women's reticence to endorse suffrage and woman's rights: "What do these ladies know of the terrible realities of life which face the working woman? How can these ladies who have never felt the chilling cold of a winter's icy breath, save as they pass from furnace heated home to luxurious limousines, know ought of the relation of wages to the cost of living or the power of the vote to regulate such issues. The ladies of the anti-suffrage movement of Cincinnati cannot judge their working sisters or their needs."[15]

Through their efforts to create an alternative to work in the industrial and commercial mainstream, Roelker and her peers no doubt felt that they could identify with the "terrible realities of life which face the working woman." Like Exchange managers around the country, they were serious about their roles as social reformers in women's work issues and in their efforts to help women gain financial independence.

Notes

Introduction

1. Candace Wheeler, *Yesterdays in a Busy Life* (New York: Harper and Brothers, 1918), p. 422.

2. The Woman's Exchange of Cincinnati, *Twenty-fifth Anniversary Report,* 1908, p. 7, Cincinnati Historical Society Library, Cincinnati Museum Center.

3. "Commission" in this study refers both to the profits that consignors earned from the sale of their merchandise and the percentage of the sale that the Exchanges kept to cover overhead. In the antebellum years, managers charged 6 percent; in the postbellum Exchanges, the commission was 10 percent, with the balance earned by the consignor.

4. Lucy Salmon, "The Woman's Exchange: Charity or Business?" *Forum* 13 (March–Aug. 1892): 395.

5. The Philadelphia Ladies' Depository, *Eighth Annual Report,* 1840, p. 5, the Library Company of Philadelphia.

6. The Woman's Exchange of Cincinnati, *Annual Report,* 1889, p. 9, emphasis in the original, Cincinnati Historical Society Library, Cincinnati Museum Center.

7. F. A. Lincoln, *Directory of Exchanges for Woman's Work: With Methods for Dealing with Them: Giving Also Information as to the Object of These Organizations, Kinds of Goods Available, etc., to Which Are Added Other Practical Suggestions Pertinent Thereto: Designed for the Women of America* (Springfield, Mass.: F. A. Lincoln Publishers, 1891), p. 5. When it was first published, the *Directory* cost 5 cents a copy, "a price within the reach of all classes." "Tell your neighbors and friends about it," encouraged author and publisher Lincoln.

8. Ruth McEnery Stuart, "The Woman's Exchange of Simpkinsville," in *A Golden Wedding and Other Tales* (Freeport: Books for Library Press, 1893), p. 318.

9. *Life,* Aug. 31, 1899, pp. 170–71.

10. The Philadelphia Ladies' Depository, *Annual Report,* 1875, p. 1, the Library Company of Philadelphia.

11. Lincoln, *Directory,* p. 11.

Chapter 1: "To Win for Themselves That Blessed Independence"

1. The Philadelphia Ladies' Depository, *Annual Report,* 1834, p. 6, the Library Company of Philadelphia. Although the Depository was established in 1832, the managers did not publish their first annual report until 1834.

2. Lincoln, *Directory,* p. 12.

3. The Philadelphia Ladies' Depository, *Annual Report,* 1834, p. 3.

4. Cultural historians have long wrestled with the problems of defining class in the United States. The definitions that would best apply to this study are those that emphasize cultural, not exclusively economic, factors. Wealthy (in this study often called "well-to-do" or "elite") Americans of the nineteenth century took on dimensions beyond those of their income and assets and perceived themselves to be far removed from the vast "middling" or working classes because of unique experiences, life-styles, and identities.

5. The Philadelphia Ladies' Depository, *Annual Report,* 1834, p. 3.

6. The quotation is from the *New York Tribune,* Oct. 14, 1845.

7. George Ellington, *The Women of New York; or, the Under World of the Great City* (1869, repr. New York: Arno Press, 1972), p. 185.

8. Lincoln, *Directory,* p. 7. Anne Firor Scott, in *Natural Allies: Women's Associations in American History* (Urbana: University of Illinois Press, 1991), has found that all charities served the genteel poor when the need arose but none professed as their mission to serve this class exclusively, as did the founders of the first Exchanges: "Occasionally a 'dear sister of our society' was in need and was promptly helped" (p. 17).

9. The Philadelphia Ladies' Depository, *Annual Report,* 1849, p. 4, the Library Company of Philadelphia.

10. It is possible that an Exchange or Depository was established in Brooklyn in 1854. This Exchange in its early years might have been aligned with the Brooklyn Female Employment Society, a charity then popular in many cities of the Northeast that focused on helping destitute women and families. This organization was not like the Philadelphia Ladies' Depository or the New Brunswick Depository, both of which sought to help only formerly wealthy women. Lincoln, *Directory,* p. 12.

11. Lincoln, *Directory,* p. 11.

12. The Philadelphia Ladies' Depository, *Annual Report,* 1837, p. 4, the Library Company of Philadelphia.

13. Alice Hyneman Rhine, "Woman in Industry," in Annie Nathan Meyer, *Woman's Work in America* (New York: Henry Holt, 1891), p. 288.

14. James Gray, "Society for Industry," *American Monthly Critical Review,* Dec. 1830, p. 78.

15. Mathew Carey, *Essays on the Public Charities of Philadelphia* (Philadelphia: J. Clark, 1829), pp. 7, 10.

16. Carey, *Essays on the Public Charities of Philadelphia,* p. 6.

17. Lincoln, *Directory,* p. 12.

18. The Scottish influence on American women's philanthropy is undeniable. The first charity started by women in the United States, the Relief of Poor Widows and Small

Children, was founded in New York City in 1796 by a newly immigrated Scotswoman, Isabella M. Graham. At the time, there were no other charities that assisted women and children. See Merle Curti, "American Philanthropy and the American Character," *American Quarterly* 10 (1958): 425–32.

19. Quoted in "Many Women Benefit by Unique Charity," Philadelphia *Evening Bulletin*, Feb. 23, 1914, p. 17.

20. Lincoln, *Directory*, p. 12.

21. The six women were Sergeant, Markoe, Harlan, Chester, Hazlehurst, and Lippincott. Mrs. James Rush, one of Philadelphia's wealthiest women, who would become a member and not a manager of the Depository, also signed the petition. See Carey, *Essays on the Public Charities of Philadelphia*, p. 7.

22. Letter reprinted in Carey, *Essays on the Public Charities of Philadelphia*, p. 7.

23. Lincoln, *Directory*, p. 9.

24. Ibid., p. 13. Although stirred to create a "broad field of opportunity to help themselves" for their peers, founders of the first Exchange lived safely within the comfort of wealth and status in the upper brackets of Philadelphia's antebellum elite class. Stott's wealth was estimated between $100,000 and $250,000, among antebellum Philadelphia's largest fortunes. Census records reveal that she lived with a son or daughter and his or her spouse, each between the ages of thirty and forty, and three children (likely her grandchildren), one under the age of five and two between the ages of five and ten. See *United States Census, 1830* (Washington: Government Printing Office, 1830), 20:318.

During the 1830s and 1840s, assets of $150,000 were considered a fortune. Now, a similar fortune would require an amount twenty-five to forty times the antebellum figure. In *Riches, Class and Power before the Civil War* (Lexington: D. C. Heath, 1973), Edward Pessen finds that Philadelphia's top tier of wealth in 1846 included eight men and three family estates with wealth estimated more than $1 million. In the next tier, with estimated wealth between $250,000 and $1 million, were thirty-eight individuals and eleven family estates. In the third tier, with estimated wealth between $100,00 and $250,000, 241 individuals and 33 family estates were listed.

Many Exchange members and founders are represented in Pessen's categories. The other founders' wealth appears equal to or even greater than Stott's, well above the $100,000 to $250,000 range. Mrs. Joshua Lippincott (neé Sarah Wetherill), for example, came from a well-established New Jersey Quaker family of pre-Revolutionary land owners who also owned a great auction house in Philadelphia. The 1831 *Philadelphia City Directory* listed other founders as "gentlewomen," that is, widows of independent means or wives of merchants and daughters of wealthy families. See DeSilver's *Almanac and City Directory* (Philadelphia: DeSilver Publishing, 1831). Mrs. John Sergeant was the wife of a prominent Philadelphia attorney, scion of one of the most aristocratic and wealthiest families in the Northeast. Diarist Sidney George Fisher referred often to the opulent dinners and balls—"very handsome affair[s]"—held at the Sergeant mansion. See Nicholas Wainwright, ed., *A Philadelphia Perspective: The Diary of Sidney George Fisher Covering the Years 1834–1871* (Philadelphia: Historical Society of Pennsylvania, 1967), p. 17.

25. No comprehensive listing of charities in Philadelphia for 1832 can be located. Three years earlier, however, in 1829, Mathew Carey compiled a list of charities, complete with numbers of subscribers and total numbers of dollars contributed. In 1829, 3,561 people subscribed to charities in Philadelphia, with annual contributions of $6,933. See Carey, *Essays on the Public Charities of Philadelphia*, p. 22. Thirty-three philanthropies were located in Philadelphia in 1833. See Robert Bremner, *American Philanthropy* (Chicago: University of Chicago Press, 1988), p. 45.

26. Three charter members (subscribers) held assets listed at $250,000 to $1 million. One, Mrs. James Rush, was the daughter-in-law of one of Philadelphia's eight millionaires, Dr. Benjamin Rush, co-founder of the temperance and anticapital punishment movements and the most prominent American physician of his day. Mrs. Rush, who became a millionaire through inheritance, was by all accounts highly visible in Philadelphia society and unconfined by the conventions of the day. Sidney George Fisher in his diary noted that she was a "person of remarkable qualities, with virtues and defects strongly marked, much intellect, cultivated by books, society and traveling . . . excitable passions, and sentiments altogether elevated and free." See Wainwright, ed., *A Philadelphia Perspective*, p. 204. Fisher often found Rush's behavior extravagant and eccentric, however, for she had what he felt was the unpleasant trait of liking almost everyone she met: "She found agreeable people in every circle and therefore visited all and invited all to her house" (p. 204).

27. Frances Milton Trollope, *The Domestic Manners of the Americans* (1832, repr. New York: Alfred A. Knopf, 1949), pp. 280–81. The elite American women whom Trollope described did their best to imitate their counterparts in England. Her observations were occasionally harsh because she, once a member of England's wealthy class, had fallen into genteel poverty and was forced to earn a living.

28. The Philadelphia Ladies' Depository, *Annual Report*, 1840, p. 5.

29. The Philadelphia Ladies' Depository, *Annual Report*, 1834, p. 3.

30. Sarah Josepha Hale, "Family Lectures," *Ladies' Magazine* 5 (Feb. 1832): 87.

31. From Caroline Dall, *Woman's Right to Labor; or, Low Wages and Hard Work* (Boston: Lawrence, 1860), as quoted in *Women's America: Refocusing the Past,* ed. Linda Kerber and Jane Sherron DeHart (New York: Oxford University Press, 1991), p. 157.

32. The prolonged Panic of 1819, the first economic upheaval after the onset of industrialism, struck both rural and urban Americans with particular ferocity. Lasting more than three years, the depression lingered as banks and businesses failed, weakening the financial position of the new urban mercantile wealthy and western and southern farmers alike. The Panic of 1837, fueled by the specie crisis of the Bank of the United States and consequent failure of countless banks across the country, lasted well into 1843. It was followed by the Panic of 1857, which strengthened the southern economy through increased cotton sales but seriously weakened northern businesses. Suzanne Lebsock has noted the severity of the antebellum depressions and the inability of charities to keep up with helping the poor. "How people got by is a mystery," she concludes in *The Free Women of Petersburg: Status and Culture in a Southern Town, 1784–1860* (New York: W. W. Norton, 1984), p. 214.

33. The Philadelphia Ladies' Depository, *Annual Report*, 1840, p. 5.

34. Alexis de Tocqueville, *Democracy in America* (1835, repr. New York: Penguin Books, 1956), p. 213.

35. Wainwright, ed., *A Philadelphia Perspective*, p. 27.

36. Ibid., p. 128. George Templeton Strong, a wealthy New York attorney and diarist, concurred on the widespread effects of the antebellum depressions. During the Panic of 1837, he wrote that "all the best houses in New York are boarded up." Quoted in Page Smith, *A Nation Comes of Age: A People's History of the Antebellum Years* (New York: McGraw-Hill, 1981), p. 352.

37. Smith, *A Nation Comes of Age*, p. 187.

38. Quoted in Barbara Welter, "The Cult of True Womanhood, 1820–1860," *American Quarterly* 18 (1966): 165.

39. Sarah Josepha Hale, "Editor's Table," *Godey's Lady's Book* 34 (March 1852): 264.

40. See Fanny Fern, *Ruth Hall* (1854, repr. New York: W. W. Norton, 1971), p. xxi.

41. Quoted in Mathew Carey, *Female Wages and Female Oppression, 1835, Addressed to the Particular Attention of the Ladies of the United States* (Philadelphia: unknown publisher, 1835), pp. 6, 3.

42. Bremner, *American Philanthropy*, p. 45.

43. Quoted in Smith, *The Nation Comes of Age*, pp. 711–12.

44. Some expressed concern that even community charity work—"mingling with the great public movements of the day"—was too excessive an activity for women. In 1841 Mrs. A. J. Graves wrote *Woman in America: Being an Examination into the Moral and Intellectual Condition of American Female Society*, which outlined the expected boundaries for women in American society. Graves admonished women for venturing out of their "appropriate and proper sphere"—the home. "The home is her appropriate sphere of action; and that whenever she neglects these duties, or goes out of this sphere of action to mingle in any of the great public movements of the day, she is deserting the station which God and nature have assigned to her. She can operate far more efficiently in promoting the great interests of humanity by supervising her own household than in any other way." Reprinted in *Root of Bitterness: Documents of the Social History of American Women*, ed. Nancy Cott (New York: E. P. Dutton, 1972), p. 141.

45. Sermon of Jonathan F. Stearns, "Discourse on Female Influence," 1837, in *Up from the Pedestal: Selected Writings in the History of American Feminism*, ed. Aileen S. Kraditor (Chicago: University of Chicago Press, 1968), pp. 47–48. Frances Trollope added another interpretation for American women's keen interest in religious charity: "It is from the clergy only that women of America receive the sort of attention which is so dearly valued by every female heart throughout the world . . . [American women] seem to give their hearts and souls into their keeping. I never saw or read of any country where religion had so strong a hold upon the women or a slighter hold on the men." See *Domestic Manners of the Americans*, p. 75.

46. As quoted in Susan Porter Benson, "Business Heads and Sympathizing Hearts: The Women of the Providence Employment Society," *Journal of Social History* 12 (Winter 1978): 303.

47. Lucretia Mott to Anne Mott, Feb. 2, 1820, as quoted in Lori Ginzberg, *Women and the Work of Benevolence: Morality, Politics and Class in Nineteenth-Century America* (New Haven: Yale University Press, 1990), p. 39.

48. Lincoln, *Directory*, p. 13.

49. New Brunswick Depository, *Annual Report*, 1871, p. 4, Archives of the Mabel Smith Douglass Library of Rutgers, the State University of New Jersey.

50. Ralph Waldo Emerson, "Self-Reliance," 1841, as quoted in Bremner, *American Philanthropy*, p. 56.

51. Catharine Beecher, *Treatise on Domestic Economy for the Use of Young Ladies at Home and at School* (Boston: Marsh, Capen, Lyon, and Webb, 1841), p. 166.

52. Trollope, *Domestic Manners*, pp. 118–19. Trollope would have been interested in American philanthropy. She had undertaken her trip to America to recoup the family's misfortunes by establishing a bazaar in Cincinnati in 1830. The enterprise met with failure, but Trollope wrote and lectured of her travels and so was enabled to regain some of her lost fortunes. *The Domestic Manners of the Americans*, published on March 19, 1832, is an early example of travel books and social commentaries about the United States from an outsider's perspective.

53. The Philadelphia Ladies' Depository, *Annual Report*, 1840, p. 6.

54. The Philadelphia Ladies' Depository, *Annual Report*, 1849, p. 3.

55. The Philadelphia Ladies' Depository, *Annual Report*, 1834, p. 3.

56. There is evidence as early as the late eighteenth century that wealthy women and families formed cooperatives for their own benefit when financial reversal struck. In *Women in Industry: A Study of American Economic History* (New York: D. Appleton, 1910), Edith Abbott describes how daughters of formerly wealthy families in Boston formed a mutual aid society to provide employment in spinning and weaving: "The Boston factory was a large and unique establishment and it is not surprising that it attracted [George] Washington's attention. . . . There were four hundred people employed. . . . The spinners admit none into their company except by vote. President Washington at the time of his visit said of them: 'They are daughters of decayed families and are girls of character—none others are admitted'" (pp. 39–40).

57. Quoted in Christine Stansell, *City of Women: Sex and Class in New York, 1789–1860* (Urbana: University of Illinois Press, 1987), pp. 271–72.

58. "Many Women Benefit by Unique Charity," *Philadelphia Evening Bulletin*, Feb. 23, 1914, p. 17.

59. Lincoln, *Directory*, p. 12.

60. Ibid.; New Brunswick Woman's Depository, *Annual Report*, 1859, Archives of the Mabel Smith Douglass Library of Rutgers, the State University of New Jersey.

61. Quoted in Howard Zinn, *A People's History of the United States* (New York: HarperCollins, 1980), p. 216.

62. Trollope, *Domestic Manners*, p. 262. Trollope and Wright apparently were friends in England, and it is possible that Wright inspired Trollope to visit the United States. Wright visited Trollope's home in England shortly before Trollope embarked on her trip. Trollope was interested in the cooperative movement and sent her son to Robert

Owen's cooperative school in New Harmony, Indiana. See Introduction, Trollope *Domestic Manners*, pp. ii–xii, and p. 263.

63. The Philadelphia Ladies' Depository, *Annual Report*, 1859, p. 4. the Library Company of Philadelphia.

64. Lincoln, *Directory*, p. 14.

65. The Philadelphia Ladies' Depository, *Annual Report*, 1840, p. 5.

66. The Philadelphia Ladies' Depository, *Annual Report*, 1834, p. 3.

67. Ibid.

Chapter 2: "One of the Most Attractive Shops on the Street"

1. The Philadelphia Ladies' Depository, *Annual Report*, 1869, p. 5, the Library Company of Philadelphia.

2. The Philadelphia Ladies' Depository, *Annual Report*, 1840, p. 4.

3. Trollope, *Domestic Manners*, p. 260.

4. R. A. Smith, *Philadelphia as It Is in 1852: A Correct Guide* (Philadelphia: Linday and Blakiston, 1852), p. 15. Another antebellum commentator noted that "the houses were of the first class, well built and handsomely furnished in the interior, with broad open newel stairwells guarded by broad oaken handrails, leading to the upper apartments; the parlors, being in the second story, with an unrestricted view of the Delaware and its floating wealth. These parlors were handsomely furnished with carved mantels and some fancy work on the ceiling." See Abraham Ritter, *Philadelphia and Her Merchants: Portraits of Some of its Prominent Occupants* (Philadelphia: Abraham Ritter, 1860), p. 20.

5. Gary B. Nash and Roy Jeffrey, eds., *The American People: Creating a Nation and a Society*, 3d ed., vol. 1: *To 1877* (New York: HarperCollins, 1994), p. 337. In his diary, Sidney George Fisher often testified to the opulent and aristocratic ambiance of the wealthy residents of Girard Row. In 1839 he wrote of a party he had attended at the home of Mrs. George Cadwalader, a fellow charter member of the Philadelphia Ladies' Depository. He wrote on March 4 that he had gone to a "small but very recherché party at Mrs. Geo. Cadwalader's. . . . The rooms are very rich and splendid, & also in excellent taste, tho I think too costly for our style living and habits. Walls and ceilings painted in fresco by Monachesi, curtains, chairs, divans, ottomans of the richest white damask satin embroidered, vases, candelabra, enormous mirrors in great profusion . . . two large rooms . . . with about fifty well dressed and well bred men & women, sitting in quiet talk. . . . They have been accustomed to this thing all their lives, and do it with ease, propriety and grace." See Wainwright, ed., *A Philadelphia Perspective*, p. 76.

6. Using DeSilver's *Almanac and City Directory* for 1831, it appears that the founders of the Depository lived within a six- or seven-block radius of Girard Row. The listing includes the following addresses for the founders and their husbands (the occupations of the husbands appear in parentheses): Mrs. John Markoe, (gentleman), 293 Chestnut Street; Mrs. Elizabeth Stott, a gentlewoman, Twelfth and Arch; Mrs. Stephen Simmons, (lumber merchant), 198 Chestnut Street; Rebecca Chester, a gentlewoman, Sev-

enth Street; Mrs. Richard Alsop, (merchant), Fourth Street; Mrs. Richard Harlan, (physician), Ninth and George streets; Mrs. John Sergeant, (lawyer), Fourth Street; Mrs. Joshua Lippincott, (auctioneer), Clinton Square; Mrs. Lewis Clapier, (merchant), Walnut Street; Mrs. J. Colquhoun, a gentlewoman, Chestnut Street; and Mrs. James Coleman, (manufacturer), Mulberry Street. Two founders were not listed in the city directories: Adelaide Montmollin, a niece of Elizabeth Stott's, and Mary Hazlehurst, who was from the wealthy Hazlehurst family.

7. The Philadelphia Ladies' Depository, *Annual Report,* 1834, p. 4.

8. G. B. R. Cameron, *Chestnut Street, Philadelphia* (Philadelphia: Thronston Publishing, 1904), p. 9. The blocks surrounding Chestnut and Seventh boasted an illustrious and colorful chapter in Philadelphia's history. In 1793 the French "aeronaut" J. P. Blanchard made the first balloon ascension from the Walnut Street jailyard, where he later erected a grandiose rotunda to house the historic balloon. The imposing granite Masonic Temple dominated the area; it was converted to the Temple Theatre after a fire in 1855. Around the block, the Chestnut Street Theatre welcomed the greatest actors and performers of the early nineteenth century; it was here that "Hail Columbia" was first sung in 1798. In 1850 a little-known showman, P. T. Barnum, tested the public's affinity for the bizarre and grotesque in his first commercial venture, the Barnum Museum. Three weeks after the Philadelphia Ladies' Depository threw open its doors for business, Philadelphia celebrated the centennial of George Washington's birthday with the greatest parade the city had ever seen. Months later, a cholera epidemic swept through the city, killing hundreds within days. Federal Writers' Project, *Philadelphia: A Guide to the Nation's Birthplace* (Philadelphia: William Penn Association, 1937), p. 61.

9. Smith, *Philadelphia as It Is in 1852,* p. 91. New York, similarly, had a Merchants' Exchange, which was rebuilt in 1835 after fire destroyed the original. It was built on Wall Street as a testament to "the power and importance of businessmen; the land cost $750,000 and the building well over a million dollars." See Smith, *The Nation Comes of Age,* p. 756.

10. The Philadelphia Ladies' Depository, *Annual Report,* 1840, p. 3.

11. O'Brien's *Commercial Intelligencer: City and County Merchants,* Philadelphia, 1840, p. 51.

12. The Philadelphia Ladies' Depository, *Annual Report,* 1840, p. 3.

13. The Philadelphia Ladies' Depository, *Annual Report,* 1876, p. 4, the Library Company of Philadelphia.

14. The Philadelphia Ladies' Depository, *Annual Report,* 1864, p. 5, the Library Company of Philadelphia.

15. See, for example, the Philadelphia Ladies' Depository annual reports for 1834 and 1837.

16. The Philadelphia Ladies' Depository, *Annual Report,* 1869, p. 6.

17. The Philadelphia Ladies' Depository, *Annual Report,* 1837, p. 4.

18. The Philadelphia Ladies' Depository, *Annual Report,* 1869, p. 6. In the first year, managers received sixty-four cash contributions totaling $260.50. In-kind contribu-

tions of a piece of linen and two shawls and several books were contributed for sale in the shop. Over the years, income from fund-raising efforts fluctuated. By 1837 the managers received only $223 in contributions. Like the sales of the consigned and special-order goods, the income derived from fund-raising reflected the erratic economy. Unfortunately, then as now, charities most needed income when it was hardest to obtain.

19. Comparisons made between the Philadelphia Ladies' Depository, *Annual Report*, 1834, subscriber list and lists of members of Philadelphia social clubs quoted in Pessen. While the members of the Philadelphia Ladies' Depository were making history in women's voluntarism, members of the Philadelphia Club were setting records in their own right. Minutes of the Philadelphia Club indicate that members participated in heroic cultural efforts; one member "used to perform the uncommon feat of drinking a glass of madeira while standing on his head." Pessen, *Riches, Class and Power*, p. 223.

20. Male members of the Walking Club and the Philosophical Club who were husbands of Ladies' Depository members or who supported the Depository themselves included John Sargeant and Nicholas Biddle. Ibid., pp. 223–24.

21. The Philadelphia Ladies' Depository, *Annual Report*, 1837, p. 4.

22. The Philadelphia Ladies' Depository, *Annual Report*, 1869, p. 5.

23. The Philadelphia Ladies' Depository, *Annual Report*, 1837, p. 1.

24. The Philadelphia Ladies' Depository, *Annual Report*, 1834, p. 6.

25. The Philadelphia Ladies' Depository, *Annual Report*, 1864, pp. 1–2.

26. The Philadelphia Ladies' Depository, *Annual Report*, 1834, p. 5.

27. Ibid., pp. 4–5.

28. Ibid., p. 6.

29. The Philadelphia Ladies' Depository, *Annual Report*, 1840, pp. 4–5; the Philadelphia Ladies' Depository, *Annual Report*, 1837, p. 4.

30. The Philadelphia Ladies' Depository, *Annual Report*, 1840, p. 5.

31. The Philadelphia Ladies' Depository, *Annual Report*, 1837, p. 4.

32. See, for example, the Philadelphia Ladies' Depository annual reports for 1835 (p. 4) and 1843 (p. 4), the Library Company of Philadelphia.

33. The Philadelphia Ladies' Depository, *Annual Report*, 1843, p. 6.

34. The Philadelphia Ladies' Depository, *Annual Report*, 1834, p. 4; the Philadelphia Ladies' Depository, *Annual Report*, 1835, p. 4.

35. The Philadelphia Ladies' Depository, *Annual Report*, 1840, pp. 4–5.

36. Ibid.

37. One month before the Depository opened, *Godey's* pronounced the following to be the fashion look of the season for well-turned-out women: "The evening dress: Bird of Paradise coloured chaley with a deep fall of blond around the bosom; coronet, turban of crimson. Black canton crepe shawl embroidered with flowers. The walking dress: pelisse of royal purple merino trimmed with black velvet. Bows and strings of purple gauze and black gauze alternately." *Godey's Lady's Book* 4 (Jan. 1832): 1.

38. As quoted in Jack Larkin, *The Reshaping of Everyday Life, 1790–1840* (New York: Harper and Row, 1988), p. 190. Early feminist writers were not amused by women al-

lowing themselves to become frivolous "animals of dress." "How should we feel," asked Sarah Grimké in 1838, "if we saw ministers of the gospel rise to address an audience with earrings dangling from their ears, glittering rings on their fingers, and a wreath of artificial flowers on their brow, and the rest of their apparel in keeping?" From "The Dress of Woman," reprinted in *The Liberator*, Jan. 26, 1838, and quoted in *Up from the Pedestal: Selected Writings in the History of American Feminism*, ed. Alice S. Kraditor (Chicago: University of Chicago Press, 1968), p. 123.

39. The Philadelphia Ladies' Depository, *Annual Report*, 1849, p. 5.

40. Patsy Orlofsky and Myron Orlofsky, *Quilts in America* (New York: Abbeville Press, 1992), p. 42, note that "well-to-do young women attended private classes where they learned various forms of needlework—plain work, dresden, point work, tent stitch, cross stitch and how to make bone lace with pillows and bobbins."

41. The Philadelphia Ladies' Depository, *Annual Report*, 1834, p. 4.

42. The Philadelphia Ladies' Depository, *Annual Report*, 1835, p. 4.

43. The Philadelphia Ladies' Depository, *Annual Report*, 1840, p. 5.

44. Ibid., p. 7.

45. The first documented fixed prices occurred in 1827. See Robert Hendrickson, *The Grand Emporiums: An Illustrated Guide of America's Great Department Stores* (New York: Stein and Day, 1979), p. 28.

46. The Philadelphia Ladies' Depository, *Annual Report*, 1834, p. 5.

47. Ibid.

48. Lincoln, *Directory*, p. 12.

49. Trollope, *Domestic Manners*, p. 280.

50. The Philadelphia Ladies' Depository, *Annual Report*, 1834, p. 5.

Chapter 3: "The Time Was Ripe for a Change"

1. Quoted in Page Smith, *The Rise of Industrial America: A People's History of the Post Reconstruction Era* (New York: McGraw-Hill, 1984), p. 668.

2. Women's voluntarism "increased so rapidly that by 1900 no one had any idea how many different kinds of associations there were." Scott, *Natural Allies*, p. 81.

3. Rhine, "Women in Industry," p. 287.

4. Quoted in Bremner, *American Philanthropy*, p. 76. Kathleen McCarthy has found that the Sanitary Commission grew nationally from the grass-roots level as thousands of women organized soldiers' aid societies in every town and village in the North. Eventually, most of these local organizations were brought under the umbrella of the Sanitary Commission. Similarly, southern women responded to the cause, setting up large networks of associations to provide supplies to soldiers, to staff hospitals, and to set up wayside stations for wounded soldiers. See *Lady Bountiful Revisited: Women, Philanthropy and Power* (New Brunswick: Rutgers University Press, 1990), pp. 40–41.

5. Bremner, *American Philanthropy*, p. 85.

6. Quoted in Karen Blair, *The Torchbearers: Women and Their Amateur Arts Associations in America, 1890–1930* (Bloomington: Indiana University Press, 1994), p. 32.

7. In *Women's Culture: American Philanthropy and Art, 1830–1930* (Chicago: University of Chicago Press, 1991), Kathleen McCarthy notes of postbellum women's volunteerism that "nonprofit entrepreneurship (i.e., commercial ventures carried out by non-profit organizations that distribute the resulting revenues for charitable, cultural and educational purposes rather than to investors) was a crucial element of many female cultural ventures in the decades after the Civil War" (p. 61).

8. Ginzberg, in *Women and the Work of Benevolence,* p. 173, suggests that women masculinized their benevolence, disguising and tempering feminine rhetoric and applying more corporatelike structures and tactics to their voluntary organizations.

9. Rhine, "Women in Industry," p. 293.

10. *New York Evangelist,* Sept. 28, 1882, p. 1. The Woman's Exchange of Cincinnati was begun in 1883 after its founders read an article in the *New York Evangelist* about the success of the New York Exchange. Similarly, copies of the *New York Evangelist* are found among the records of the Richmond Exchange. It is probable that many late-century Exchange founders across the country would have had access to and been inspired by news of the New York Exchange in the *New York Evangelist* because it was the leading publication of a prominent national Protestant organization, the American Bible Tract Society.

11. Wheeler, *Yesterdays,* p. 222.

12. Cited in Doreen Bolger Burke et al., *In Pursuit of Beauty: Americans and the Aesthetic Movement* (New York: Metropolitan Museum of Art and Rizzoli Publishers, 1986), p. 32.

13. The Centennial Committees exemplified how nineteenth-century women's arts and charity associations were inextricably bound, with the Philadelphia Centennial Exhibition providing the linkage. Members of women's voluntary associations around the country formed Centennial Committees to represent their groups at the Centennial Exhibition. When they were dissolved after the Exhibition, the Centennial Committees often formed larger, longer-lasting women's organizations. In Cincinnati, for example, after the Centennial Committee disbanded in 1877, members laid the groundwork for what would within a year become the Cincinnati Women's Art Museum Association (WAMA). This, in turn, led to the establishment of the Cincinnati Art Museum. Of the eighteen founding members of WAMA, eight would become charter founders and members of the Cincinnati Exchange for Woman's Work in 1883. Taken from miscellaneous documents in the file of the Cincinnati Women's Art Museum Association, Cincinnati Historical Society Library, Cincinnati Museum Center. In Philadelphia a prestigious association for women, the New Century Club, evolved from that city's Centennial Committee. See Federal Writers Project, *Philadelphia: A Guide to the Nation's Birthplace* (Philadelphia: William Penn Association, 1937), p. 400.

14. Thomas J. Schlereth, *Victorian America: Transformations in Everyday Life, 1876–1915* (New York: HarperCollins, 1991), p. 4, notes that other exhibits in the Women's Pavilion "included a working steam engine run by Emma Allison. More than seventy-five women displayed their recently patented inventions. Implements in laundering, ironing, food preparation, and cooking represented the traditional sphere of home-

making. Others hinted at the fact that by 1876 women constituted close to 20 percent of the American labor force outside the home. Female workers ran the Pavilion's telegraph office, spooling machine, Jacquard loom, cylinder printing press, sewing and knitting machines."

15. "The Royal School of Art Needlework," *Art Amateur* 11 (Sept. 1884): 98.

16. Quoted in McCarthy, *Women's Culture*, pp. 41, 43.

17. Wheeler, *Yesterdays*, p. 210. After the Centennial Wheeler's "life changed abruptly." Burke et al., *In Pursuit of Beauty*, p. 481.

18. "The Society of Decorative Art," *Scribner's Monthly* 22 (Sept. 1881): 699.

19. "The Society of Decorative Art," pp. 699–700.

20. Ibid., p. 699. Wheeler notes in *Yesterdays*, p. 212, that the South Kensington stitch was not a new stitch—"centuries of needlework practice had exhausted every possibility in that line"—but one that had been recently revived and made more widely visible to a new audience.

21. Wheeler, *Yesterdays*, p. 211.

22. Ibid.

23. Ibid.

24. Candace Wheeler, *The Development of Embroidery in America* (New York: Harper and Brothers, 1921), p. 21.

25. Wheeler, *Yesterdays*, pp. 210–11.

26. Ibid., pp. 209–10.

27. Ibid., p. 211. It is not known if Wheeler was aware of the earlier Exchanges, although at the time of the opening of the New York Exchange in 1878 ladies' depositories operated in several cities.

28. Ibid., p. 222.

29. Ibid., p. 210.

30. Quoted in Burke et al., *In Pursuit of Beauty*, p. 28.

31. Wheeler, *Yesterdays*, pp. 212–13.

32. Ibid., p. 218.

33. Ibid., p. 224.

34. "The Society of Decorative Art," p. 701.

35. Wheeler, *Yesterdays*, p. 226.

36. "The Society of Decorative Art," p. 701.

37. McCarthy, *Women's Culture*, p. 49.

38. Wheeler, *Yesterdays*, p. 216.

39. Blair, in *The Torchbearers*, p. 84, pointed out that "American craft appealed to the clubwoman, whose object was to improve the American home. As soon as they became convinced that household decoration with well designed craft objects could achieve their ends, they championed lectures, exhibitions, and classes devoted to crafts."

40. Quoted in McCarthy, *Women's Culture*, p. 51.

41. Wheeler, *Yesterdays*, 220.

42. "The Society of Decorative Art," p. 706.

43. Wheeler, *Yesterdays*, pp. 226, 210.

44. Ibid., pp. 223, 224.

45. Quoted in McCarthy, *Women's Culture*, p. 56.

46. The reason for changing from the antebellum term *depository* to the postbellum term *exchange* is not made clear in the records. Merchants' exchanges, however, were a mainstay of men's commercial enterprises in many cities, and places where captains of industry traded goods and commodities. It is likely that postbellum managers wanted their own mercantile enterprises in the voluntary sector to carry the same prestige and status as did their male counterparts' ventures in the commercial sector. London, for example, had its Royal Exchange, where "cooperating merchants would operate various shops under one roof." See Hendrickson, *The Grand Emporiums*, pp. 77–79. Perhaps Exchange founders adopted this connotation for their retail shops. The word *exchange* also defines the goal of the enterprises: to exchange merchandise for monetary profit.

47. Wheeler, *Yesterdays*, p. 224.

48. In 1974 Rosemary Hall merged with the Choate School for Boys to become Choate Rosemary Hall.

49. Wheeler, *Yesterdays*, p. 224. Wheeler did not stay actively involved with the New York Exchange for too long after its implementation. She later founded L. C. Tiffany and Associated Artists, a for-profit decorating firm. "We are going after the money there is in art, but the art is there all the same," she said. See Isabelle Anscombe, *A Woman's Touch: Women in Design from 1860 to the Present Day* (New York: Viking Penguin, 1984), p. 37.

50. Wheeler, *Yesterdays*, p. 224. In *Women's Culture*, McCarthy notes that the Exchanges were "designed to broker the sale of 'any marketable object which a woman can make,' [and] drew their inspiration from the decorative arts movement, but relaxed the movement's artistic standards in a bow to their stated desire to help women in need" (p. 61).

51. Wheeler, *Yesterdays*, p. 227.

52. Ibid., p. 225.

53. Mary Choate, "For Many Women Who Must Earn Money at Home, the Exchange for Woman's Work Offers a Happy Solution of the Financial Problem," newspaper clipping from 1918 in the New York Exchange for Woman's Work Archives, New York City.

54. Wheeler, *Yesterdays*, p. 226.

55. The New York Exchange for Woman's Work, *Minutes*, March 6, 1878, New York Exchange for Woman's Work Archives, New York City. There were no minutes kept for the February 28 meeting, which is mentioned in the March 6 minutes.

56. Ibid.

57. Ibid.

58. Ibid.

59. The New York Exchange for Woman's Work, *Annual Report*, Nov. 1, 1879, p. 3, New York Exchange for Woman's Work Archives, New York City.

60. Choate, "For Many Women Who Must Earn Money," ca. 1918, clipping in the New York Exchange for Woman's Work Archives, New York City.

61. The minutes reveal that the gift was solicited by Mrs. Alex J. Stewart, a friend of one of the founding members. Like the members of the Philadelphia Ladies' Deposi-

tory, who were not shy about soliciting gifts from men, the New York managers' eagerness to raise money dispels earlier notions of women's hesitancy in directly asking men for money to support their causes.

62. Choate, "For Many Women Who Must Earn Money."

63. "An Exchange for Woman's Work," *New York Daily Tribune*, March 25, 1878, p. 5. The date of the organizing meeting of the Exchange differs between the minutes and the first annual report, which states that the "Society . . . organized in April, 1878." The minutes place the organizing meetings as February 28 and March 6.

64. Choate, "For Many Women Who Must Earn Money."

65. The New York Exchange for Woman's Work, *Minutes*, April 24, 1878, New York Exchange for Woman's Work Archives, New York City.

66. The New York Exchange for Woman's Work, *Annual Report*, Nov. 1, 1879, p. 1.

67. The speaker from the Society of Decorative Art, whether Candace Wheeler or someone else, is not identified in the minutes.

68. The New York Exchange for Woman's Work, *Minutes*, April 24, 1878. Actually, the Exchanges focused on education as well, considering a part of their mission to provide vocational training.

69. "An Exchange for Woman's Work," p. 5.

70. Lincoln, *Directory*, p. 23.

71. "The Society of Decorative Art," p. 698.

72. Salmon, "The Woman's Exchange," p. 404.

73. The New York Exchange for Woman's Work, *Annual Report*, Nov. 1, 1879, p. 1.

74. Choate, "For Many Women Who Must Earn Money."

75. Lincoln, *Directory*, p. 27.

76. The New York Exchange for Woman's Work, *Catalogue and Price List*, 1900–1901, New York Exchange for Woman's Work Archives, New York City.

77. Lincoln, *Directory*, pp. 27–28. It is possible that smaller Exchanges did not offer such a range of merchandise. The Richmond Exchange, for example, remained small in comparison to those in New York or Cincinnati. In 1890 Richmond paid consignors $490, whereas consignors received $51,000 in New York and $27,000 in Cincinnati. The Richmond Exchange listed items similar to those found in the reports of the Philadelphia Ladies' Depository: aprons, handkerchiefs, embroidered towels and nightshirts, needle cases, doll clothes, and toy animals, among others. Richmond Exchange for Woman's Work, *Annual Report*, 1899, p. 9, Valentine Museum, Richmond, Va.

78. The New York Exchange for Woman's Work, *Annual Report*, Nov. 1, 1879, p. 2.

79. Lincoln, *Directory*, p. 17.

80. Choate, "For Many Women Who Must Earn Money."

Chapter 4: A "Prosperous Existence in Every Town"

1. Lincoln, *Directory*, p. 17.

2. Ibid.

3. Salmon, "The Woman's Exchange," p. 396.

4. Wheeler, *Yesterdays*, p. 228.

5. Rhine, "Women in Industry," p. 296.

6. Individual Exchange records examined for this study reveal almost identical organizational structures for each Exchange: boards of managers, committees, bylaws, rules for consignors, and financial records are all similar.

7. Martha Louise Rayne, *What Can a Woman Do? or, Her Position in the Business and Literary World* (1893, repr. New York: Arno Press, 1974), p. 149.

8. Lincoln provides a complete listing of all Exchanges in operation in 1891 (*Directory*, pp. 43–87).

9. After the Centennial in 1876 critics occasionally noted that "art education had not reached the working class, whom educators claimed they wish to serve," stating that the decorative arts and art schools were "run for the accommodation of ladies, mostly the wives and daughters of our wealthy citizens." See Burke et al., *In Pursuit of Beauty*, p. 36. As Exchanges spread throughout the country they helped in this effort by bringing art education to working-class women through vocational training.

10. Quoted in Scott, *Natural Allies*, p. 104.

11. Ibid.

12. Ibid., pp. 104–5.

13. Joanne Meyerowitz, *Women Adrift: Independent Wage Earners in Chicago, 1880–1930* (Chicago: University of Chicago Press, 1988), p. 46.

14. Josephine Shaw Lowell, a writer and a feminist, noted in 1891 that WCA chapters were run by "women who have leisure and education [and] who devote both to efforts to help and succor women who have neither," adding that "the Woman's Christian Association, of which there are more than fifty in the country, open rooms for evening entertainment and study, give instruction in intellectual and manual branches, find situations for those who need them, help working girls in every way." See Josephine Shaw Lowell, "Charity," in Annie Nathan Meyer, *Woman's Work in America* (New York: Henry Holt, 1891), p. 337.

15. By 1883 Exchanges operated in Philadelphia, New Brunswick, New York (Manhattan and Brooklyn), Baltimore, Boston, Rochester, New Orleans, New Bedford, Newark, Albany, Providence, St. Paul, and Milwaukee.

16. The Richmond Exchange for Woman's Work, *Annual Report*, 1884, p. 11, Valentine Museum, Richmond, Va.

17. Ibid. Mrs. C. R. Agnew, a founder of the New York Exchange for Woman's Work, was serving as recording secretary at the time she wrote the letter to the organizers of the Richmond Exchange.

18. The Richmond Exchange for Woman's Work, *Annual Report*, 1887, p. 11, Valentine Museum, Richmond, Va.

19. It is not known how many other Exchanges were started as joint-stock ventures. It is possible that most Exchanges were started more informally, by raising donations and in-kind contributions rather through the sale of shares of stock.

20. Lincoln, *Directory*, p. 16.

21. Charles L. Dufour, *Women Who Cared: The One Hundred Years of the Christian Woman's Exchange* (New Orleans: Upton Printing, 1980), p. 7.

22. Lincoln, *Directory*, p. 16.

23. Dufour, *Women Who Cared*, p. 12.

24. Lincoln, *Directory*, p. 16.

25. Dufour, *Women Who Cared*, p. 11. Dufour adds, "Can there be any doubt that 'a Church Member' was a member of the Christian Woman's Exchange? Is it a wild surmise that may have raised this subject at the April 5 meeting and had been rebuked by the ruling from the chair?"

26. The New Orleans founders established an ambitious platform for their organization: "The object of the Christian Woman's Exchange can be indicated by the words 'encouragement, improvement, and reclamation,' and are illuminated as follows: (1) To provide ways and means for the encouragement and relief of our impoverished women, who cannot be crushed into beggary and sin, but who earnestly seek to help themselves; (2) to provide some means of improvement in the education of our young women in which they can become artistic workers in all the great and grand affairs of human life, both practical and ornamental; and (3) we mean an honest effort to reclaim the Lord's own from the pernicious amusements and allurements of the world and to cultivate in our hearts the high Christian grace of compassion, as shown by our Lord's example when he said to that guilty woman: 'Go and sin no more.'" Ibid., p. 7.

27. Dufour, *Women Who Cared*, pp. 11, 12.

28. Ibid. The Countess met with an unfortunate end, but not before leading an adventurous life as a novelist and reformer. Like many young, wealthy American women of the late nineteenth century, she married a titled European, an Italian nobleman, and was known to have written novels and crusaded for progressive causes. In 1895 she became enmeshed in the sensational murder trial of Maria Barbella, the first American woman to be sentenced to die in the electric chair. Ten years later the Countess went suddenly insane while trying on a dress and spent the next thirty-eight years in a mental hospital. Her great-granddaughter, Idanna Pucci, wrote of the Countess's tumultuous life and the Barbella trial in *The Trials of Maria Barbella: The True Story of a Nineteenth-Century Crime of Passion* (New York: Four Walls Eight Windows, 1996).

29. Lincoln, *Directory*, p. 61.

30. Ibid., p. 47.

31. Ibid., p. 45.

32. Rhine, "Women in Industry," pp. 400–401.

33. Ibid., p. 292.

34. See Louisa May Alcott, *Work: A Story of Experience* (1873, repr. New York: Schocken Books, 1977). By age thirteen, Alcott already was contributing to the family income after her father's Transcendentalist experiment at farming met with failure. Alcott turned to fashioning doll dresses for the neighbors' children. *Work: A Story of Experience* tells of a middle-class woman's efforts to find acceptable employment. Like Alcott, the heroine, Christie, is "one of that large class of women, who moderately endowed with talents, earnest and true-hearted, are driven by necessity, temperament, or principle out into the

world to find support, happiness and homes for themselves" (p. 11). Although it was published in 1873, Alcott had begun the book twelve years earlier.

35. Lowell, "Charity," p. 337.

36. Rhine, "Women in Industry," p. 292.

37. Margaret F. Buck, *One Hundred Years of the Woman's Exchange* (West Hartford: Woman's Exchange, 1988), p. 8.

38. Ibid. Such activities apparently kept the "older" girls occupied, but the Hartford managers fretted about others, noting that "what to do with the younger girls has been a problem and a variety of schemes have been devised for their amusement. The young-sters are only desirous of being entertained" (*Annual Report,* 1889, Archives of the Fed-eration of Woman's Exchanges, Scarsdale, N.Y.). The managers found that reading Shakespeare and organizing choral groups solved the problem.

39. Mrs. Arthur Fisher. *The History of the St. Augustine Woman's Exchange,* p. 1. The King's Daughters Society eventually became a national federation of community chap-ters dedicated to women's issues; many King's Daughters chapters became affiliated with hospital auxiliaries.

40. Ibid. Minutes of the St. Augustine Exchange, as cited in Fisher, *History of the St. Augustine Woman's Exchange,* indicate that consigned work was accepted only from needy women. The minutes also reveal that "in 1916 a woman opened a shop on St. George Street and called it 'The New Woman's Exchange,' and the Board of Managers called upon her to persuade her to discontinue the use of the name and she complied. Through the years, in other parts of the country, others have attempted to use the name 'Woman's Exchange,' and this was the reason the Federation [of Woman's Exchanges] was formed in 1934."

41. Ibid.

42. Ibid.

43. Dufour, *Women Who Cared,* p. 13.

44. Ibid., pp. 14–15. The extent to which nineteenth-century women made large cash contributions to philanthropies is only now being examined. McCarthy, in *Lady Boun-tiful Revisited,* pp. 17–19, cites several examples of women's largess. In Chicago, for example, women donors collectively gave more than $700,000 in gifts of $5,000 or more. Other examples include a $625,000 bequest from Clarissa Peck to the Home for the Incurables and Mary Elizabeth Garrett's $307,000 gift to the Johns Hopkins Uni-versity, with the caveat that women be admitted to the School of Medicine.

45. Ibid., p. 15.

46. "We're Very Old-Fashioned," *Baltimore Sun,* Sept. 15, 1971, p. B1. Others who helped to establish the Baltimore Industrial Exchange include Mary N. Perry, Isabelle Tyson, Anne D. Kirk, Jane E. White, Mary Leyser Thomas, Anne S. Thompkins, Mary Stow, Helen Coale, Sophia G. Orem, Elizabeth R. Hopkins, and Leorice Josephine Stew-art. See "Sympathy and Practical Aid," *Baltimore Sun,* June 27, 1954, n.p.

47. "Sympathy and Practical Aid."

48. Nellie Fisher, *Baltimore American,* 1896, quoted in "We're Very Old-Fashioned."

49. Elizabeth Kolmer, "Ariadne Lawnin and the Woman's Exchange: 'To Help Women

Help Themselves,'" paper presented to the St. Louis Historical Society, April 10, 1988, p. 3.

50. It appears that depositories, based on the template of the Philadelphia Ladies' Depository to assist the genteel poor, were started in several cities—Pittsburgh, Chicago, and St. Louis, among others—right after the Civil War. These organizations laid the groundwork for the newer Woman's Exchanges that opened in the last two decades of the century. (See Table 2, Appendix A for listing of depositories.)

51. This is a favorite anecdote often told by Lawnin's granddaughter, Julia Lawnin Gordon. Quoted in the "Woman's Exchange: A Century Old," *St. Louis Globe Democrat,* May 23, 1984, p. 3D.

52. Memorial booklet for Richmond founder, Mrs. S. H. Hawes, the Richmond Exchange for Woman's Work Archives, Valentine Museum, Richmond, Va.

53. Pittsburgh Ladies' Depository, *Minutes,* March 6, 1873, Library and Archives Division, Historical Society of Western Pennsylvania, Pittsburgh.

54. Pittsburgh Ladies' Depository, *Minutes,* March 13, 1879, Library and Archives Division, Historical Society of Western Pennsylvania, Pittsburgh.

55. Pittsburgh Ladies' Depository, *Minutes,* May 15, 1873, Library and Archives Division, Historical Society of Western Pennsylvania, Pittsburgh.

56. Pittsburgh Ladies' Depository, *Minutes,* Aug. 7, 1873, Library and Archives Division, Historical Society of Western Pennsylvania, Pittsburgh.

57. Lincoln, *Directory,* p. 79.

58. Ibid., p. 17.

59. The Depository and Philadelphia Exchange for Woman's Work, *Catalogue,* 1904, p. 4, the Pennsylvania Historical Society, Philadelphia. By the year of the merger, 1894, the Philadelphia Ladies' Depository was losing business. Between 1869 and 1876, for example, commissions paid to consignors dropped 18 percent (Table 1, Appendix A).

60. Ibid.

61. Ibid., pp. 5, 4.

62. Salmon, "The Woman's Exchange," p. 395.

63. Lincoln, *Directory,* p. 8.

64. Ibid.

65. Buck, *One Hundred Years of the Woman's Exchange,* p. 9.

66. Dufour, *Women Who Cared,* p. 7.

67. Lincoln, *Directory,* p. 86

68. The Milwaukee Woman's Exchange, *Annual Report,* 1888, p. 8, Milwaukee County Historical Society.

69. The Richmond Exchange for Woman's Work, *Annual Report,* 1888, p. 10, Valentine Museum, Richmond, Va.

70. Kolmer, "Ariadne Lawnin," p. 5.

71. *The Woman's Exchange Mirror,* Dec. 1886, as quoted in Kolmer, "Ariadne Lawnin," p. 5.

72. "Where Gentility Is a Bulwark against Change," *Washington Post,* May 25, 1989.

73. Dufour, *Women Who Cared,* p. 17.

74. Lincoln, *Directory,* p. 54.

75. The New York Exchange for Woman's Work, *Annual Report,* Nov. 1, 1879, p. 2. The New York Exchange was not able to purchase its own building until 1911 because of the city's exceptionally high real estate prices. In that year, the managers paid $150,000 for the building they had been renting for many years.

76. The New York Exchange for Woman's Work, *Annual Report,* Nov. 1, 1879, p. 1.

77. The New York Exchange for Woman's Work, *Minutes,* April 16, 1892, New York Exchange for Woman's Work Archives, New York City.

78. Lincoln, *Directory,* p. 18.

79. Ibid.

80. Ibid., p. 42.

81. Smith, *The Rise of Industrial America,* p. 675.

82. Charlotte Perkins Gilman, *The Home: Its Work and Influence* (1903, repr. Urbana: University of Illinois Press, 1972), p. 203.

83. Quoted in Mary Richmond, *Friendly Visiting among the Poor: A Handbook for Charity Workers* (Montclair: Patterson-Smith, 1899), p. 73.

84. William Leach maintains that "women sought to organize women's working experiences, both within and without marriage, according to cooperative principles. In place of individual competition, they increasingly sought cooperative industry, cooperative sharing and national organizations." *True Love and Perfect Union: The Feminist Reform of Sex and Society* (New York: Basic Books, 1980), p. 191. "The idea of cooperation took an even stronger hold on the feminine mind; articles appeared on cooperative industries, cooperative buses for girls, and cooperative associations" (p. 190).

85. From papers read at the Third Women's Congress of the Association for the Advancement of Women, Syracuse, New York, quoted in Cott, ed., *Root of Bitterness,* p. 355.

86. The Woman's Exchange of Cincinnati, *Annual Report,* 1885, p. 11, Cincinnati Historical Society Library, Cincinnati Museum Center.

87. Annie Roelker and Roelker family journals and scrapbooks, Cincinnati Historical Society Library, Cincinnati Museum Center.

88. The Woman's Exchange of Cincinnati, *Annual Report,* 1894, p. 19, Cincinnati Historical Society Library, Cincinnati Museum Center.

89. Lincoln, *Directory,* pp. 12, 5.

Chapter 5: "We Sell Everything Good, from a Pickle to a Portiere"

1. Salmon, "The Woman's Exchange," pp. 394, 386.

2. Dufour, *Women Who Cared,* p. 7.

3. Lincoln, *Directory,* pp. 13–14.

4. The Richmond Exchange for Woman's Work, *Twenty-fifth Anniversary Report,* 1908, Valentine Museum, Richmond, Va.

5. The Richmond Exchange for Woman's Work, *Annual Report,* 1889, p. 19, emphasis in original, Valentine Museum, Richmond, Va.

6. Lincoln, *Directory*, p. 37.

7. Salmon, "The Woman's Exchange," p. 397.

8. The New York Exchange for Woman's Work, *Minutes*, Sept. 2, 1892, New York Exchange for Woman's Work Archives, New York City.

9. The Woman's Exchange of Cincinnati, *Annual Report*, 1899, p. 17, Cincinnati Historical Society Library, Cincinnati Museum Center.

10. The Woman's Exchange of Cincinnati, *Minutes*, Dec. 4, 1892, Cincinnati Historical Society Library, Cincinnati Museum Center.

11. Hendrickson, *The Grand Emporiums*, p. 44.

12. Ibid., p. 78.

13. Ibid.

14. Quoted in Susan Porter Benson, *Counter Cultures: Saleswomen, Managers, and Customers in American Department Stores, 1890–1940* (Urbana: University of Illinois Press, 1986), p. 79.

15. Quoted in Benson, *Counter Cultures*, p. 17.

16. Quoted in Elaine S. Abelson, *When Ladies Go a-Thieving: Middle Class Shoplifters in the Victorian Department Store* (New York: Oxford University Press, 1989), p. 29.

17. Quoted in David Cohen, "Grand Emporiums Peddle Their Wares in a New Market," *Smithsonian* 23 (March 1993): 130.

18. The New York Exchange for Woman's Work, *Annual Report*, Nov. 1, 1879, p. 1; Hendrickson, *The Grand Emporiums*, p. 65.

19. Rhine, "Women in Industry," p. 296.

20. The Woman's Exchange of Cincinnati, *Annual Report*, 1896, p. 15, Cincinnati Historical Society Library, Cincinnati Museum Center.

21. The Woman's Exchange of Cincinnati, *Annual Report*, 1884, p. 7, Cincinnati Historical Society Library, Cincinnati Museum Center.

22. Wendy Gamber, "A Precarious Independence: Milliners and Dressmakers in Boston, 1860–1890," *Journal of Women's History* 4 (Spring 1992): 67. Gamber has found that women shopkeepers of the nineteenth century "hailed from middling or working class backgrounds," daughters of laborers and artisans. Although there was a "sprinkling of distressed gentlewomen," only a "few could claim upper-class pedigrees." Lucy Eldersveld Murphy, "Business Ladies: Midwestern Women and Enterprise, 1850–1880," *Journal of Women's History* 3 (Spring 1991): 75, finds the same of midwestern women shopkeepers: 71 percent were of the middle class and the rest fell below that level.

23. The Richmond Exchange for Woman's Work, *Annual Report*, 1885, p. 6, Valentine Museum, Richmond, Va.

24. The Richmond Exchange for Woman's Work, *Annual Report*, 1889, p. 16.

25. "The unique character of the exchanges has helped build a following whose demographics any retailer would envy. . . . Why such loyalty? 'Because the exchanges offer things you can't find anywhere else,'" observed a contemporary patron of the Wayne, Pennsylvania, Exchange. See Jack Smith, "Women's Exchanges: The Nicest Shops," *Town & Country* 145 (May 1991): 82.

26. The New York Exchange for Woman's Work, miscellaneous document, p. 3, New York Exchange for Woman's Work Archives, New York City.

27. The Milwaukee Woman's Exchange, *Annual Report,* 1888, p. 9.

28. Lincoln, *Directory,* p. 31.

29. Rhine, "Women in Industry," p. 295.

30. Ibid., pp. 295–96.

31. The Richmond Exchange for Woman's Work, *Annual Report,* 1890, p. 6, Valentine Museum, Richmond, Va.

32. Lincoln, *Directory,* p. 7.

33. Rayne, *What Can a Woman Do?* p. 149.

34. Rhine, "Women in Industry," p. 297.

35. Lincoln, *Directory,* p. 37.

36. Ibid.

37. Ibid., pp. 38–39.

38. The Woman's Exchange of Cincinnati, *Minutes,* Jan. 2, 1884, Cincinnati Historical Society Library, Cincinnati Museum Center.

39. The St. Louis Exchange's unrelenting quest for the most desirable location revealed "a history of the city's most fashionable shopping areas." The managers "faced the difficulty of finding a low rent building in a fashionable district. By 1884, the women purchased a building for $15,000 at 617 Locust Street, the money raised by donations and benefits. They moved the Exchange again in 1898 to Tenth and Olive, the building on Locust now becoming the source of revenue from its rental. In 1899 they moved to the fashionable North Grand area, near Vandeventer Place . . . to remain near to their market." Kolmer, "Ariadne Lawnin," p. 4.

40. The Woman's Exchange of Cincinnati, *Annual Report,* 1894, p. 16. Benson, in *Counter Cultures,* p. 128, notes that by the 1890s display windows had become one of the most important aspects of retailing.

41. The New York Exchange for Woman's Work, *Minutes,* April 24, 1878.

42. The New York Exchange for Woman's Work, *Minutes,* Sept. 6, 1892, New York Exchange for Woman's Work Archives, New York City. It is not known if the managers' expected goal of $1,500 ever materialized; the records and treasurer's reports do not show this kind of income.

43. The New York Exchange for Woman's Work, *Annual Report,* Nov. 1, 1879, p. 1.

44. The Philadelphia Exchange for Women's Work, *Catalogue,* 1904, p. 5, the Pennsylvania Historical Society, Philadelphia.

45. The New York Exchange for Woman's Work, *Annual Report,* Nov. 1, 1879, p. 5.

46. The Richmond Exchange for Woman's Work, *Annual Report,* 1889, p. 12.

47. The Milwaukee Woman's Exchange, *Annual Report,* 1888, p. 6.

48. Lincoln, *Directory,* p. 18.

49. Ibid.

50. Salmon, "The Woman's Exchange," p. 395.

51. The New York Exchange for Woman's Work, *Annual Report,* Nov. 1, 1879, p. 1, emphasis in the original.

52. The New York Exchange for Woman's Work, *Minutes,* Nov. 14, 1880, New York Exchange for Women's Work Archives, New York City.

53. Lincoln, *Directory,* p. 11.

54. Salmon, "The Woman's Exchange," p. 400.

55. The Richmond Exchange for Woman's Work, *Annual Report,* 1888, p. 16.

56. Rayne, *What Can a Woman Do?* p. 150.

57. Lincoln, *Directory,* p. 8.

58. Salmon, "The Woman's Exchange," pp. 402, 404–5. Susan Burrows Swan, in *Plain and Fancy: American Women and Their Needlework, 1700–1850* (New York: Holt, Rinehart and Winston, 1977), has observed that "needlework was the most expressive contribution women made to the decorative arts" (p. 12).

59. The Woman's Exchange of Cincinnati, *Annual Report,* 1888, p. 11, Cincinnati Historical Society Library, Cincinnati Museum Center.

60. Rayne, *What Can a Woman Do?* p. 150.

61. The New York Exchange for Woman's Work, *Annual Report,* Nov. 1, 1879, p. 2.

62. The New York Exchange for Woman's Work, *Catalogue and Price List,* 1900–1901, p. 31. The Exchanges sold such items under the same conditions as consigned needlework and baked goods, keeping a 10 percent commission.

63. Lincoln, *Directory,* p. 69.

64. "Sympathy and Practical Aid," p. 18.

65. The Richmond Exchange for Woman's Work, *Catalogue of Goods,* 1899, Valentine Museum, Richmond, Va.

66. Lincoln, *Directory,* p. 26.

67. The Woman's Exchange of Cincinnati, *Annual Report,* 1891, pp. 10–11, Cincinnati Historical Society Library, Cincinnati Museum Center.

68. Lincoln, *Directory,* p. 26.

69. The Woman's Exchange of Cincinnati, *Annual Report,* 1893, p. 17, Cincinnati Historical Society Library, Cincinnati Museum Center. According to the New York Exchange for Woman's Work, *Minutes,* Sept. 2, 1892, the managers discussed holding an exhibit of consignors' goods at Madison Square Garden on November 15 and 16 of that year. The board also discussed joining forces with other New York State Exchanges—there were nine others in the state at that time—to stage an exhibit during the upcoming Columbian Exhibition at the World's Fair in Chicago. The records do not indicate if either effort materialized.

70. Salmon, "The Woman's Exchange," p. 395.

71. Lincoln, *Directory,* p. 29.

72. The New York Exchange for Woman's Work, fund-raising letter, 1880, emphasis in the original, New York Exchange for Woman's Work Archives, New York City.

73. The Woman's Exchange of Cincinnati, *Annual Report,* 1894, p. 16.

74. Hendrickson, *The Grand Emporiums,* p. 46.

75. Lincoln, *Directory,* p. 23.

76. "Sympathy and Practical Aid."

77. For decades, the Down Under Club was a popular and convenient lunch spot for

businessmen. It closed at some point in the 1940s or 1950s, and men were invited to eat upstairs. They quickly lost interest after their inclusion in the tearoom, however.

78. The Woman's Exchange of Cincinnati, *Annual Report*, 1885, p. 8.

79. The Woman's Exchange of Cincinnati, *Twenty-fifth Anniversary Report*, 1908, p. 2.

80. The Woman's Exchange of Cincinnati, *Annual Report*, 1885, p. 8.

81. The Woman's Exchange of Cincinnati, *Annual Report*, 1887, p. 7, Cincinnati Historical Society, *Annual Report*, 1891, p. 11.

82. The Woman's Exchange of Cincinnati, *Annual Report*, 1894, p. 17.

83. The Woman's Exchange of Cincinnati, *Annual Report*, 1896, p. 14. The Baltimore Exchange had a similar experience. After a great fire ravaged most of downtown Baltimore in 1904, businesses began to spring up in the blocks surrounding the Baltimore Exchange's building on North Charles Street at Pleasant Street, and the Exchange's lunchroom was unable to keep up with the increasing number of customers that resulted. Dozens of small lunch counters, perhaps inspired by the success of the nearby Baltimore Exchange, opened to accommodate the crowds: "The Woman's Industrial Exchange has been unable to keep up with all the hungry people. Realizing the possibilities of the lunchroom trade, several prominent women have rented quarters in the section of the city where corporations and commercial ventures have transferred their forces." From an unidentified newspaper clipping, 1904, Archives, Baltimore Industrial Exchange.

84. The Richmond Exchange for Woman's Work, *Annual Report*, 1890, p. 10; the Milwaukee Woman's Exchange, *Annual Report*, 1884, p. 7, Milwaukee County Historical Society.

85. Lincoln, *Directory*, pp. 23–26.

86. The Milwaukee Woman's Exchange, *Annual Report*, 1894, p. 8, Milwaukee County Historical Society.

87. Rayne, *What Can a Woman Do?* p. 151.

88. The Milwaukee Woman's Exchange, *Annual Report*, 1897, p. 6, Milwaukee County Historical Society.

89. The New York Exchange for Woman's Work, *Annual Report*, Nov. 1, 1879, p. 2.

90. The Milwaukee Woman's Exchange, *Annual Report*, 1894, p. 10.

91. The Richmond Exchange for Woman's Work, *Annual Report*, 1889, p. 12.

92. Lincoln, *Directory*, p. 16.

93. Quoted in Abelson, *When Ladies Go a-Thieving*, p. 111.

94. The Woman's Exchange of Cincinnati, *Annual Report*, 1897, pp. 18–19, Cincinnati Historical Society Library, Cincinnati Museum Center.

95. Salmon, "The Woman's Exchange," p. 400.

96. The Milwaukee Woman's Exchange, *Annual Report*, 1894, p. 10, Milwaukee County Historical Society.

97. Ibid.

98. The Milwaukee Woman's Exchange, *Annual Report*, 1884, p. 3.

99. Stuart, "The Woman's Exchange of Simpkinsville." There is no evidence that Exchange managers used their affiliation with Exchanges for personal financial gain.

100. Ibid., pp. 314, 336.

101. Lincoln, *Directory*, p. 11.

102. The Woman's Exchange of Cincinnati, *Annual Report*, 1887, p. 10, Cincinnati Historical Society Library, Cincinnati Museum Center.

103. *Cincinnati Commercial Tribune*, Feb. 25, 1900, p. 32.

104. The Richmond Exchange for Woman's Work, *Annual Report*, 1888, p. 12. This amount cannot be substantiated in any documents. Three years later, in 1891, Lincoln, in the *Directory*, reported that $1.1 million in commissions had been paid to consignors between 1878 and 1891 (see Table 3, Appendix A).

105. The Woman's Exchange of Cincinnati, *Annual Report*, 1888, p. 5.

Chapter 6: "An Excellent Way to Earn an Income"

1. Lincoln, *Directory*, p. 8.

2. Rhine, "Women in Industry," p. 297.

3. Lincoln, *Directory*, p. 21.

4. Ibid., p. 14.

5. Wheeler, *Yesterdays*, p. 222, emphasis in the original.

6. Salmon, "The Woman's Exchange," p. 402.

7. Rhine, "Women in Industry," pp. 285–86.

8. Muriel Dobbin, "Charles Street Landmark," *Baltimore Sun*, Nov. 29, 1959, p. C1.

9. Salmon, "The Woman's Exchange," p. 402.

10. Lincoln, *Directory*, p. 14.

11. Salmon, "The Woman's Exchange," p. 403.

12. Lincoln, *Directory*, pp. 17, 9.

13. Wheeler, *Yesterdays*, p. 212.

14. Salmon, "The Woman's Exchange," p. 403.

15. Lincoln, *Directory*, p. 9.

16. The Milwaukee Woman's Exchange, *Annual Report*, 1897, p. 5.

17. The Milwaukee Woman's Exchange, *Annual Report*, 1894, p. 11; the Richmond Exchange for Woman's Work, *Annual Report*, 1889, p. 9.

18. Lincoln, *Directory*, p. 9.

19. Ida Van Etten, "The Sweating System, Charity, and Organization," in Nancy F. Cott, ed., *Root of Bitterness: Documents of the Social History of American Women* (New York: E. P. Dutton, 1972), p. 331.

20. Ibid.

21. Josephine S. Lowell, in *Charities Review* 5 (1896): 390.

22. Salmon, "The Woman's Exchange," p. 399.

23. Ibid., p. 406.

24. Lincoln, *Directory*, pp. 33–37, 12.

25. The Richmond Exchange for Woman's Work, *Annual Report*, 1888, pp. 13–14.

26. Lincoln, *Directory*, pp. 62, 52.

27. The New York Exchange for Woman's Work, *Annual Report*, Nov. 1, 1879, p. 2.

28. Salmon, "The Woman's Exchange," p. 403.

29. Lincoln, *Directory*, p. 29.

30. Salmon, "The Woman's Exchange," p. 403.

31. Rhine, "Women in Industry," p. 297; Salmon, "The Woman's Exchange," p. 400.

32. Rhine, "Women in Industry," pp. 297–98.

33. Lincoln, *Directory*, p. 31.

34. The Richmond Woman's Exchange, *Annual Report*, 1888, p. 12, emphasis in the original.

35. Rhine, "Women in Industry," p. 296.

36. The New York Exchange for Woman's Work, *Annual Report*, 1892, New York Exchange for Woman's Work Archives, New York City.

37. The Woman's Exchange of Cincinnati, *Annual Report*, 1885, p. 8.

38. Rhine, "Women in Industry," p. 298.

39. Ibid., p. 295.

40. Lincoln, *Directory*, p. 21, emphasis in the original.

41. The Milwaukee Woman's Exchange, *Annual Report*, 1884, p. 3.

42. The Milwaukee Woman's Exchange, *Annual Report*, 1888, p. 10. The Richmond Exchange suffered a major setback when a fire destroyed its salesroom in February 1886. Although the Exchange's bylaws stated that the managers were not responsible for replacing or compensating consignors for their loss, they nonetheless felt morally bound to do so. They voted that "those persons whose handiwork had been injured or destroyed by the fire should in time be fully remunerated" and noted that "liberal and philanthropic friends in New York, Philadelphia, and Newark donated $425.83" to the cause. More than likely, the contributions were from Exchanges located in those cities. See the Richmond Woman's Exchange, *Annual Report*, 1888, p. 6.

43. Lincoln, *Directory*, p. 31.

44. The Richmond Woman's Exchange, *Annual Report*, 1887, p. 10.

45. Salmon, "The Woman's Exchange," p. 401.

46. The Milwaukee Woman's Exchange, *Annual Report*, 1894, p. 11.

47. Alcott, *Work: A Story of Experience*, p. 442; the Woman's Exchange of Cincinnati, *Annual Report*, 1884, p. 9.

48. The Milwaukee Woman's Exchange, *Annual Report*, 1894, p. 12.

49. Rayne, *What Can a Woman Do?* p. 16.

50. Rhine, "Women in Industry," pp. 288–89.

51. Lincoln, *Directory*, p. 75.

52. Ibid., p. 68.

53. "What to Make for Women's Exchanges," *The Modern Priscilla* (Oct. 1890): 34–40.

54. Rhine, "Women in Industry," p. 288.

55. Ibid.

56. Ibid., p. 289.

57. Rayne, *What Can a Woman Do?* pp. 16, 150–51.

58. Lincoln, *Directory*, p. 31.

59. The Milwaukee Woman's Exchange, *Annual Report*, 1894, p. 7.

60. The Richmond Exchange for Woman's Work, *Annual Report*, 1887, p. 4.

61. Lincoln, *Directory*, p. 15.

62. The Richmond Exchange for Woman's Work, *Annual Report*, 1890, p. 9.

63. Lincoln, *Directory*, pp. 17–18.

64. Helen Stuart Campbell, *Women Wage Earners* (1893, repr. New York: Arno Press, 1972), p. 252.

65. The Richmond managers made note of this meeting in their 1888 *Annual Report*, p. 11.

66. Ibid., p. 10.

67. Lincoln, *Directory*, p. 14.

68. The Woman's Exchange of Cincinnati, *Annual Report*, 1887, p. 7.

Epilogue

1. The six Exchanges represented at the 1934 meeting included those in Greenwich, Connecticut; Cedarhurst, New York; Philadelphia (Old York Road) and Wayne, Pennsylvania; New York (Manhattan); and Morristown, New Jersey.

2. It is difficult to know, without examining the individual records, what happened to most of the Exchanges after the turn of the twentieth century. Between Lincoln's publication of the *Directory* in 1891 and the inception of the Federation of Woman's Exchanges in 1934, no comprehensive listing is known to exist. In 1934 at least eighteen Exchanges are known to have been in operation, with six represented at the meeting to form the Federation. Some may have carried over to the twentieth century, changing addresses or closing and starting up again, breaking the continuity.

3. New York Exchange, promotional brochure, 1990. The New York Exchange still uses the crinoline-clad lady for its logo.

4. After experiencing a decline in business for several consecutive years, in the summer of 1997 the Baltimore Exchange closed for a month to reorganize its board and plan a strategy for the future. The managers appealed to the public: "Damsel in Distress!" read a banner across the front of the Exchange. On Monday, August 4, the Exchange once again opened for business and was greeted by a block-long line of loyal patrons eager to support their beloved Exchange. A reporter for the *Baltimore Sun*, Jacques Kelly, a native Baltimorean who has spent decades observing—and enjoying—the Exchange, noted: "In a city that has seen its great department stores close . . . [the] Exchange has exhibited a fragile antique strength, a staying power that has eluded larger restaurants and national retail chains." "Soup's on at Industrial Exchange," *Baltimore Sun*, Aug. 4, 1997, p. 1B.

5. The Boston Women's Educational and Industrial Union is not listed as a member of the Federation of Woman's Exchanges in 1997.

6. Buck, *One Hundred Years of the Woman's Exchange*, p. 31.

7. *Cincinnati Enquirer*, March 16, 1958, p. C1.

8. *Baltimore Sun*, Sept. 12, 1992, p. 3B.

Appendix B

1. Charles F. Gross, *Cincinnati: The Queen City* (Cincinnati: S. J. Clarke, 1912), 1:370.

2. The Women's Art Museum Association could claim much of the credit for the establishment of the Cincinnati Art Museum. Members helped raise more than $162,000, which was matched by an equal contribution from Cincinnati philanthropist Charles W. West, and in May 1886 the museum opened to the public. WAMA members contributed all of the painting, pottery, and carvings that they had been inspired to create following the Philadelphia Centennial a decade before. In turn, the women's arts movement in Cincinnati gave rise to the national interest in art pottery. Two Cincinnati women artists, who would also become founding members of the Cincinnati Exchange, in 1880 formed Rookwood Pottery, which through the remaining decades of the nineteenth century and well into the twentieth manufactured the renowned handcrafted pottery. One of the founders, Maria Nichols, was encouraged by her father in the enterprise "to give employment to the idle rich." See Cincinnati Art Museum, *The Ladies, God Bless 'em* (Cincinnati: The Museum, 1976), p. 12. The *New York Evangelist* reported on January 12, 1892, that "two prominent Cincinnati women, Mrs. George W. Nichols and Miss McLaughlin, have built a pottery in Cincinnati, where an elegant quality of ceramic ware is made, decorated with their own designs" (p. 2).

3. WAMA members who later founded the Woman's Exchange included Mrs. A. F. Perry, Mrs. John Shillito, Mrs. O. J. Wilson, Mrs. A. D. Dodd, Mrs. John Gano, Caroline Hulbert, Mary Huntington, and Ellen Starwood. The WAMA laid the organizational groundwork for the art museum. In 1883, as plans were being finalized to build the museum, a new association, the Cincinnati Museum Association, composed of prominent men, took over the management of the new museum. Many WAMA members, possibly feeling snubbed at the exclusion, channeled their creative energies into forming the Woman's Exchange of Cincinnati.

4. Cincinnati Art Museum, *The Ladies, God Bless 'em*, p. 11.

5. Following the Philadelphia Centennial Exhibition, Cincinnati women became smitten with the work and mission of the Royal School. Correspondence in the files of the Cincinnati Women's Art Museum Association shows a letter dated January 28, 1878, from Charles Taft, a prominent Cincinnati attorney, to Mrs. A. F. Perry, the WAMA's president, in which he agrees to "deliver the third lecture on the South Kensington Museum on any evening during the last week of March."

6. The Woman's Exchange of Cincinnati, *Minutes*, Jan. 3, 1883, p. 1, Cincinnati Historical Society Library, Cincinnati Museum Center.

7. Ibid.

8. The Woman's Exchange of Cincinnati, *Minutes*, Sept. 12, 1883, Cincinnati Historical Society Library, Cincinnati Museum Center. The New York consignor of "pickles and preserves" cited likely worked under far more favorable conditions than her counterparts in industry. The canning industry was a particularly brutal one, with workers often putting in a fifteen-hour day, sorting, pickling, labeling, and bottling during the

peak canning season. In a business where quickness and dexterity mattered, women workers could earn up to $1.50 an hour. Generally, most canning workers earned about the same as women wage-earners in the needle trades. See Elizabeth Beardsley Butler, *Women and the Trades: Pittsburgh, 1907–1908* (1909, repr. Pittsburgh: University of Pittsburgh Press, 1984), pp. 38–39.

9. The Woman's Exchange of Cincinnati, *Minutes,* Jan. 30, 1883, Cincinnati Historical Society Library, Cincinnati Museum Center.

10. The Cincinnati Ladies' Depository, *Annual Report,* 1867, p. 5, Cincinnati Historical Society Library, Cincinnati Museum Center.

11. The Cincinnati Ladies' Depository, *Annual Report,* 1871, pp. 5–6, Cincinnati Historical Society Library, Cincinnati Museum Center.

12. Of the twenty-four founders of the Ladies' Depository in 1868, eight would help to establish the Woman's Exchange in 1883: Mrs. William Procter, Mrs. William Resnor, Mrs. William McAlpin, Mrs. W. P. Hurlburt, Mrs. Alice Neave, Mrs. Murray Shipley, Mrs. J. P. Harrison, and Miss Fanny Carlisle.

13. From the eulogy read by Mrs. Howard Van Buren at Annie Roelker's funeral in 1938, and from the records of the Woman's Exchange of Cincinnati, miscellaneous documents. Cincinnati Historical Society, Cincinnati Museum Center.

14. Ibid.

15. *Cincinnati Enquirer,* Feb. 8, 1894, p. 21.

Index

Addams, Jane, 80
Aesthetic movement, 45, 61
"Age of the Benevolent Empire," 19. *See also* Women's voluntarism
Alcott, Louisa May, 66, 110. *See also* Women's Educational and Industrial Union
Anonymity. *See* Consignors
Anthony, Susan B., 45
Arch Street Theatre (Philadelphia), 24
Art Amateur, 45
Art Exchange of Harrisburg, Pa., 61
Astor, Mrs. John Jacob, 53

Baltimore American, 68, 93
Baltimore Exchange. *See* Woman's Industrial Exchange of Baltimore
Bartlett, Mrs. H. W., 63, 76. *See also* Christian Woman's Exchange
Beecher, Catharine, 21, 74
Bellamy, Edward, 75
Bellows, Rev. Henry W., 41. *See also* United States Sanitary Commission
Blackwell, Antoinette, 75
Bloomingdale Brothers (Bloomingdale's), 90, 91, 116
Boardinghouses (rooms), 71–72; Christian Woman's Exchange, 72; Exchange for Woman's Work of Richmond, 72; New York Exchange for Woman's' Work, 72; Woman's Industrial Exchange of Baltimore, 72
Board of advisors: New York Exchange for Woman's Work, 55, 94; Woman's Exchange of Cincinnati, 88

Boston Exchange. *See* Women's Educational and Industrial Union
Brown, Mrs. G. Harmon, 68, 76. *See also* Woman's Industrial Exchange of Baltimore
Buckingham, James Silk, 20

Campbell, Helen, 113
Canada (Exchanges in), 60
Carey, Mathew, 13–14, 23, 75
Centennial committees, 44, 141n
Charities (antebellum), 12, 135n; criticism of postbellum charities, 104–5; houses of industry, 22; in Philadelphia, 16, 134n
Cheney, Edith Dow Littlehale, 42
Choate, Mary Atwater, 2, 68, 76, 80, 87, 98, 116; founding of New York Exchange for Woman's Work, 53–59. *See also* Wheeler, Candace Thurber
Choate, William G. (Choate School for Boys), 53. *See also* Choate, Mary Atwater
Christian Woman's Exchange: as boardinghouse, 72; consignors, 71, 79; criticism of, 64; founding of, 63–64, 67; in twentieth century, 117; mission, 146n; services to women workers, 73; solvency, 97–98
Cincinnati: Cincinnati Room (at Centennial), 44; Ladies' Depository, 127; School of Art and Design, 128; suffrage, 130; Woman's Art Museum Association, 127–28, 129, 157n; Women's Centennial Executive Committee, 44, 141n. *See also* Roelker, Annie; Woman's Exchange of Cincinnati
Cincinnati Enquirer, 117–18

Cincinnati Exchange. *See* Woman's Exchange of Cincinnati
Cincinnati Times Star, 117
City Infant School (Philadelphia), 16
Civil War, 1, 41, 46, 52, 68, 91, 102, 110
Clisby, Harriet, M.D., 66. *See also* Women's Educational and Industrial Union
Commissions, 131n. *See also* Consignors (antebellum); Consignors (postbellum); individual listings of Exchanges
Consignors (antebellum), 7; anonymity, 6, 31, 35; as producers, 24, 33–35; commissions earned (income), 24, 35; descriptions in annual reports, 29, 31–32; entrepreneurship of, 2, 35; identities, 1, 12–13; numbers of, 32; permits, 24, 31, 35; self-employment, 35; skills required, 33–34
Consignors (postbellum), 7; anonymity, 107, 109, 116; commissions earned (income), 86, 100, 101, 105–6, 107–9, 117, 144n; entrepreneurship, 2, 85; from abroad, 106; identities, 2, 70, 102, 107–9; national network, 105–7; self-sufficiency, 103, 112–13; work opportunities at Exchanges, 93–94; 101–14
Conspicuous consumption, 47
Consumerism: antebellum, 28; postbellum, 2, 82–83
Cooper, Peter (Cooper Institute), 111
Cooperation: as a work alternative, 23–24, 49–50, 75–76, 136n; influence on Exchange movement, 22–25, 26, 36, 42, 49, 85–87, 149n
Cooperative retail stores, 23, 86
Countess di Brazza (Cora Slocum), 64, 146n. *See also* Christian Woman's Exchange
Craftsmanship, 45, 48, 89
Crinoline Bar, 115. *See also* New York Exchange for Woman's Work
Cross-class efforts (postbellum), 36, 69–73, 101, 102, 114. *See also* Woman's Exchange movement
Custer, Elizabeth (Libbie), 1, 7, 50, 76

Daily Chronicle (Philadelphia), 19
Dall, Caroline, 17
Day care ("creche"), 73. *See also* Christian Woman's Exchange

"Decayed gentlewomen," 2, 7, 11, 22, 24, 29, 48, 129
Decorative arts, 43, 46–47, 102
Department stores: influence on postbellum Exchanges, 81–84, 90, 98, 107, 115, 116
Diaz, Abby Morton, 66. *See also* Women's Educational and Industrial Union
Directory of Exchanges for Woman's Work: With Methods of Dealing with Them, 6, 106, 116, 131n. *See also* Lincoln, Frank Asa
Display windows, 28, 88
Domesticity, 23, 65
Dorcas Society (Philadelphia), 16

Economy (antebellum): instability, 17–18, 134n; postbellum, 97
Edible departments, 93, 96–97
Edinburgh Depository, 14–15, 45
Edwards House (New Orleans), 67
Elliot, Charles, 74. *See also* New York Evangelist
Emerson, Ralph Waldo ("Self-Reliance"), 21
Entrepreneurial philanthropy, 3, 25, 36
Entrepreneurship, 2, 36, 42, 43, 45, 46, 48, 53, 79, 84, 112, 114, 115, 119, 141n
Ephon, Nora, 119. *See also* Woman's Industrial Exchange of Baltimore
Exchange for Woman's Work of Bridgeport (Conn.), 106
Exchange for Woman's Work of Richmond (Va.), 6, 96, 100, 113; boardinghouse, 72; consignors, 71, 80, 97, 104, 106, 109; founding of, 62–63, 68; in twentieth century, 118; merchandise, 89, 91, 155n; merchandise catalog, 90; status in community, 84–85; vocational training, 112. *See also* Hawes, Mrs. S. H.
Exchange tearooms. *See* Tearooms (restaurants)

"Fancy fairs," 14
Fashion (women's), 33, 84, 139–40n
Federation of Woman's Exchanges, 115, 156n. *See also* Woman's Exchanges: contemporary
Female Improvement Society, 23
Female Moral Reform Society, 20

Female-run shops: influence on antebellum Exchanges, 28; influence on postbellum Exchanges, 84–85, 115, 150n

Financial independence (for women), 2, 7, 13, 19, 35, 49, 130; arguments for and against, 73–76

Financial instability (for wealthy women), 17–18

Financial reversal (women), 4, 11, 12, 15 17, 18, 52; "instant aid" to poverty-stricken consignors, 32. See also Poverty

Fisher, Nellie, 68. See also Woman's Industrial Exchange of Baltimore

Fisher, Sidney George, 18, 133n, 134n. See also Philadelphia Ladies' Depository

Fourier, Charles, 22

Fund-raising (by Exchange managers), 29–31, 63, 67, 86, 94, 143–44n, 145n, 147n

Genteel poor (women), 1, 13, 14, 15, 17, 19, 21, 22, 26

Gilman, Charlotte Perkins, 41, 74

Gimbel's, 81

Girard Row (Philadelphia), 11, 16, 23, 27, 28, 31, 35, 137n, 138n. See also Philadelphia Ladies' Depository

Godey's Lady's Book, 17, 33, 34, 139n. See also Hale, Sarah Josepha

Gordon, Julia Lawnin, 116. See also Woman's Exchange of St. Louis

Goshorn, Alfred T., 44

Gray, Letitia, 98, 112. See also Milwaukee Woman's Industrial Exchange

Gray, Rev. James, 13–14

Great Depression, 117

Greeley, Horace, 12

Hale, Rev. Edward Everett, 113, 115

Hale, Sarah Josepha, 17, 18, 23. See also Godey's Lady's Book

Hartford Exchange. See Woman's Exchange of Hartford (Conn.)

Hawes, Mrs. S. H., 68, 76. See also Exchange for Woman's Work of Richmond

Hermann-Grima House (New Orleans), 117. See also Christian Woman's Exchange

Homework (home production), 1, 4, 7, 43, 46, 48–49, 51, 80, 102–4, 114, 119; criticism of, 104; history of, 103

Horne, Mrs. Joseph, 89. See also Pittsburgh Woman's Industrial Exchange

"Household Exchange," 105

Houses of industry (fragment societies, employment societies), 22. See also Charities (antebellum)

Howard, Mrs. Charles T., 67. See also Christian Woman's Exchange

Howe, Julia Ward, 66. See also Women's Educational and Industrial Union

Industrial and Charitable Union of Decatur (Ill.), 72

Industrialism, 13; cooperation as a countermovement to, 22–25; labor turmoil, 23

Industrial schools, 108, 110–11. See also Vocational training

Jackson, Mrs. Thomas "Stonewall", 64. See also Christian Woman's Exchange

Jewett, Sarah Orne ("The Flight of Betsey Lane"), 44. See also Philadelphia Centennial Exhibition

King's Daughters, 66–67, 147n. See also Woman's Exchange of St. Augustine

"Labor directory," 72

Ladies' Christian Association, 63. See also Woman's Christian Association

Ladies' Depositories, 143n, 148n; Cincinnati Ladies' Depository, 128–29; Pittsburgh Ladies' Depository and Employment Office, 68–69. See also Philadelphia Ladies' Depository

Ladies' Garland, 34

Ladies' Repository, 34

LaFarge, John, 50

Lawnin, Ariadne, 68, 76, 116

Letters to Young Ladies, 18

Life magazine, 6

Lincoln, Frank Asa, 6, 14, 15, 23, 58, 60, 70, 73, 76, 80, 86, 87, 90, 94, 97–98, 101, 103, 107, 108, 109, 111–12, 131n. See also Directory of Exchanges for Woman's Work

Looking Backward, 75
Lowell, Josephine Shaw, 66, 74, 105, 145n

Macy's, 81, 83
Managers (antebellum) 14–16. *See also* Philadelphia Ladies' Depository
Managers (postbellum): as entrepreneurs, 28, 29, 79–100, 114; as social and economic reformers, 73–76, 80, 99, 100, 114, 130; benefits accrued from affiliation with Exchanges, 2–3, 7, 29, 31, 73–76, 79–100; status in community, 84, 141n. *See also* listings of individual Exchanges
Marshall Field, 81
McAlpin, Mrs. George, 89. *See also* Woman's Exchange of Cincinnati
McAlpin's, 84
Merchandise (offered at Exchanges): at New York Exchange for Woman's Work, 55–58, 83; at Woman's Exchange of Cincinnati, 84; mass-produced versus handmade, 33, 90–92; national distribution network, 106–7; prices at Philadelphia Ladies' Depository, 34–35; produced at Philadelphia Ladies' Depository, 34; types of, 89–92, 106, 144n. *See also* listings for individual Exchanges
Merchandise catalog, 90
Middle class, 47, 132n; as consignors, 108
Milwaukee Woman's Industrial Exchange, 85, 97; consignors, 71, 103–4, 108–9; lunchroom, 96, 97; twentieth century, 118; visiting committee, 97; vocational training, 110, 112. *See also* Gray, Letitia
The Modern Priscilla, 110–11
Montmollin, Adelaide, 15, 138n. *See also* Philadelphia Ladies' Depository
Mott, Lucretia, 20

Needlework: for wages, 1, 12, 49, 51, 103, 129; regaining lost status, 26, 46, 47–48, 51, 52; skills needed by consignors, 33–35. *See also* Royal School of Art Needlework; Wheeler, Candace Thurber
Neurasthenia, 82; "feeble and delicate" women, 74. *See also* Beecher, Catharine
New Brunswick Depository. *See* Woman's

Depository and Exchange of New Brunswick
New Orleans Exchange. *See* Christian Woman's Exchange
New Orleans Picayune, 63, 64
New York American, 116
New York Daily Tribune, 55, 56–57
New York Evangelist, 7, 43, 62, 71, 74, 75, 141n
New York Exchange for Woman's Work, 1, 2, 43, 87, 113; amounts earned by consignors, 83, 107–8; as a brokerage service, 92–93; boarding rooms, 72; consignors, 56, 57–58; description of, 83; distinction from Society of Decorative Art, 53–57; edible department, 97; founders, 54–55; founding of, 53–58, 144n; fund-raising, 94; incorporation, 56; influence on other Exchanges, 58, 61–64, 127–28; merchandise, 57, 90–91; merchandising techniques, 88, 90; services offered to women workers, 72; solvency, 98; success of, 58, 60, 128; twentieth century, 115–16; vocational training, 112. *See also* Choate, Mary Atwater; Society of Decorative Art; Wheeler, Candace Thurber
Noblesse oblige, 12
Northern Liberties Society, 16

Owen, Robert, 22

Paid work (for women): cultural restrictions against, 12; heightened status, 75, 76, 102–3, 113–14; perils of workplace, 12, 25; remuneration, 46, 47, 75, 114; stigma of, 1, 11, 45, 68, 69–70, 80, 114, 116, 117; working conditions, 12, 13, 15, 19, 20, 22, 31, 103, 104–5, 114, 130, 157–58n
Panic of 1873, 52, 102
Panic of 1893, 97
Philadelphia, 13, 14, 16, 17, 27; Merchants' Exchange, 27, 138n; retailers, 28, 81–82; wealthy classes, 26–27. *See also* Girard Row; Philadelphia Ladies' Depository
Philadelphia Centennial Exhibition, 2, 43–49, 50, 61, 128
Philadelphia Club, 30
Philadelphia Exchange for Woman's Work, 69–70, 89, 117

Philadelphia Female Academy, 13

Philadelphia Ladies' Depository, 4, 36, 45, 128–29; as a business, 11, 29; as a charity, 29; founders 15, 133n, 137–38n; founders' goals, 1, 24–25, 36, 37, 49; founding of, 1, 11–25, 26–29; influence of cooperation, 22–25; influence of self-help, 21–22; influence on postbellum Exchange movement, 51; membership, 16, 30, 133n, 134n, 137n; merchandise, 26, 33–35; merchandise prices, 24; merchandising techniques, 26, 28; merger with Philadelphia Exchange for Woman's Work, 69–70, 117, 148n; patrons, 26; sources of income, 29–30

Philosophical Society, 30

Pittsburgh Woman's Industrial Exchange, 69

A Plea for the Poor, 23. *See also* Carey, Mathew

Pogue's, 84. *See* Woman's Exchange of Cincinnati

Portland, Me.: women's voluntary associations in, 41

Poverty: changing ideas about, 42. *See also* Financial reversal (women)

Princess Beatrice, 113. *See also* Working Woman's Guild

Prohibition (Twenty-first Amendment), 115. *See also* New York Exchange for Woman's Work

Prostitution, 19

Proudfit, Mrs. Alexander, 21; *See also* Woman's Depository and Exchange of New Brunswick

Providence Employment Society, 20

Public sphere, 18. *See also* Paid work (for women)

"Putting out" (piecework) system, 22

Queen Olga of Greece, 64

Queen Victoria, 45, 113, 118. *See also* Philadelphia Centennial Exhibition; Working Woman's Guild

Rayne, Martha Louise, 61, 86, 91, 92, 97, 110, 111

Remarriage, 19

Rev. Proudfit of Philadelphia, 21

Rhine, Alice Hyneman, 13, 41, 42, 60–61, 66, 85–86, 101, 102, 105, 107, 108, 110

Richmond Exchange. *See* Exchange for Woman's Work of Richmond

Roelker, Annie, 76, 129–30. *See also* Cincinnati; Woman's Exchange of Cincinnati

Rosemary Hall. *See also* Choate, Mary Atwater

Royal School of Art Needlework, 45–53, 113; influence on Society of Decorative Art, 50–51; influence on Woman's Exchanges, 65–66, 116, 128, 157n. *See also* Wheeler, Candace Thurber

Rutgers College, 21. *See also* Woman's Depository and Exchange of New Brunswick

Ruth Hall, 19

Ruutz-Rees, Caroline, 53. *See also* Choate, Mary Atwater

Saleswomen (at Exchanges) 35, 56

Salmon, Lucy, 2, 4, 57, 70, 79, 80–81, 91, 98, 102, 103, 105, 106–7, 109

Scottish philanthropy: influence on first Exchanges, 14, 132–33n

Scribner's, 46, 47, 50, 5, 57

Self-help: application of, 2, 7, 21–22, 26, 32, 36, 42, 43, 45, 46, 48, 114; Candace Wheeler on, 52; change of meaning over nineteenth century, 43, 46, 48–49, 53, 59, 79, 127; European influence on Exchange movement, 1, 21–22, 45, 59

Self-improvement (self-development for women), 43, 48, 61, 66, 127

Shillito, Mrs. John, 89. *See* Woman's Exchange of Cincinnati

Shillito's, 84

Shipley, Mrs. Murray, 89. *See* Woman's Exchange of Cincinnati

"Shopping as a Fine Art," 82

Sleepless in Seattle, 119. *See also* Woman's Industrial Exchange of Baltimore

Smith, Walter, 50

Society of Decorative Art (New York): beneficiaries, 51; founding of, 49–53; influence on Woman's Exchange movement, 53–59; 102, 111; membership, 51; spread of idea, 51–52; vocational training, 52. *See also*

Royal School of Art Needlework; Wheeler, Candace Thurber
Southern Art Union (New Orleans), 64
South Kensignton School. *See* Royal School of Art Needlework
Stansbury, Mrs. S. C., 67. *See* Woman's Exchange of St. Augustine
Stanton, Elizabeth Cady, 45, 82–83
St. Augustine Exchange. *See* Woman's Exchange of St. Augustine
Stearns, Rev. Jonathon ("Discourse on Female Influence"), 20
St. Louis Exchange. *See* Woman's Exchange of St. Louis
Stocks: investment in, 29. *See also* Philadelphia Ladies' Depository
A Story of Experience, 66, 146–47n. *See also* Alcott, Louisa May
Stott, Elizabeth, 1, 14–15, 17, 21, 23, 26, 46, 54, 85. *See also* Edinburgh Depository; Philadelphia Ladies' Depository
Stuart, Ruth McEnery ("The Woman's Exchange of Simpkinsville"), 6, 99
Sweden (Exchanges in), 60

Tearooms (restaurants), 83, 94–96
Tiffany, Louis Comfort, 50, 143n
Tocqueville, Alexis de, 17–18
Trollope, Frances, 16, 21, 24, 36, 41, 136n, 136–37n
Tulane, Paul, 63. *See also* Christian Woman's Exchange

United States Sanitary Commission, 41, 140n

Van Etten, Ida M., 104–5
Vocational skills: importance of for women, 2, 36
Vocational training, 48, 79, 109, 110–13, 145n; schools, 108. *See also* Industrial schools
Voluntary sector: and employment opportunities for women, 2, 7, 36, 42, 43, 49, 50–51, 59, 101–14, 119; as economic alternative, 7, 50, 73; lines blurred with commercial sector, 3, 100, 119; nonmonetary careers for Exchange managers, 79–100; remunerative opportunities for consignors, 101–14

"Wages of charity," 22
Walking Club (Philadelphia), 30
Walmsley, Caroline Gratia Williams, 67. *See also* Christian Woman's Exchange
Wanamaker's, 81, 94; Grand Depot, 82; restaurant, 94. *See also* Tearooms (restaurants)
Wheeler, Candace Thurber, 1, 2, 43, 51, 60, 87, 101–2, 103, 116, 143n; founding of New York Exchange for Woman's Work, 53–59; founding of Society of Decorative Art, 46–51. *See also* Choate, Mary Atwater; New York Exchange for Woman's Work; Society of Decorative Art
Whitney, Mrs. M. L., 67. *See also* Christian Woman's Exchange
Willard, Frances, 65. *See also* Woman's Christian Temperance Union
Willis, Sara ("Fanny Fern"), 19. *See also* Hall, Ruth
Woman's Christian Association, 58, 61, 62–65, 101, 102, 145n; Cincinnati chapter, 127–28; New York chapter, 62; St. Louis chapter, 68
Woman's Christian Temperance Union, 58, 61, 65, 80, 101, 102
Woman's City Club (Philadelphia), 115. *See also* Federation of Woman's Exchanges
Woman's culture, 42
Woman's Declaration of Independence, 45
Woman's Depository and Exchange of New Brunswick (N.J.), 12, 36; founding of, 21; influence of cooperation, 22–25
Woman's Exchange movement: change of mission over nineteenth and twentieth centuries, 6–7, 36, 53–54, 57–58, 69–73, 76, 99, 102, 129, 143n; founding of, 4; in twentieth century, 115–19; legacy of, 113–14; spread of, 2, 3, 7, 53, 58–59, 60–76
Woman's Exchange of Cincinnati, 76; as a brokerage service, 93; case study, 127–30; commissions earned by consignors, 60, 117; committees, 83–84; edible department, 96–97; founding of, 62–63, 157–58n; influence of department stores, 84; in twentieth century, 117–18; managers, 2, 81, 88, 92, 93, 100, 114; merchandise, 98; merchandise

catalog, 90; sources of income for Exchange, 93–94; success of, 84; tearoom 94, 95–96. See also Cincinnati; Ladies' Depositories; Roelker, Annie

Woman's Exchange of Hartford, 66, 71; West Hartford, 116

Woman's Exchange of St. Augustine, 66–67, 116, 147n

Woman's Exchange of St. Joseph (Mo.), 106

Woman's Exchange of St. Louis: consignors, 71; founding of, 62, 68; location, 88, 151n; services to women workers, 73. See also Gordon, Julia Lawnin; Lawnin, Ariadne

Woman's Exchange of Troy (N.Y.), 64

Woman's Exchange of Worcester (Mass.), 65

Woman's Exchanges (antebellum), 2, 7, 11–25. See also Philadelphia Ladies' Depository; Woman's Depository and Exchange of New Brunswick

Woman's Exchanges: as businesses, 5, 7, 79–100; as charities, 7, 79; as documentation of women's lives, 5; economic benefits for women, 3–4, 36; historical records of, 5, 7; similarities, 5; used for economic opportunities for women, 5, 53

Woman's Exchanges: consignors. See Consignors

Woman's Exchanges: contemporary, 3, 115–19, 150n. See also Federation of Woman's Exchanges

Woman's Exchanges: managers. See Managers

Woman's Exchanges (postbellum), 7; as brokerage services, 92–93; as work alternatives, 75–76, 79–80, 101, 104, 105, 107–9, 112–13, 113–14; benefits to consignors, 86; criteria for founding 87; criticism of, 99, 104–5, 109; location of shops, 87; merchandise, 90–92; merchandise standards, 89, 97, 98; merchandising techniques, 88, 89–90; patrons, 85, 90; restaurants (tearooms), 94–96; services offered to women workers, 72–73; sources of income for consignors, 92–94; work opportunities, 108–9. See also listing of individual Exchanges

Woman's Industrial Exchange of Baltimore: as brokerage service, 93; boardinghouse, 72; consignors, 102; founding of, 68, 147n; in twentieth century, 116, 119, 156n; lunchroom, 95, 152–53n, 153n; Nellie Fisher (historian), 68. See also Brown, Mrs. G. Harmon

Woman's sphere, 7, 20, 23, 44, 53, 73–76, 135n

Woman's Work and Art Exchange of Morristown, N.J., 61

Woman's Work Exchange and Decorative Art Society of Brooklyn, 61, 132n

Women: and responsibility toward the poor, 1, 13, 59, 75–76, 145n; arguments about domestic responsibility vs. financial security, 23, 73–76; as consumers, 82–83; employment options, 18, 73–74, 101, 102; gifts to charities, 67; of wealth, 132n; working-class, 71, 111, 108, 130

Women's Educational and Industrial Union, 58, 61, 80, 102; of Boston, 65–66, 116

Women's Pavilion (Philadelphia Centennial Exhibition), 44–45, 128, 141–42n

Women's voluntarism (voluntary associations): antebellum, 19–20, 28; as careers, 29, 80; history of, 3, 4; masculinization of, 4, 42; national network, 52, 58–59, 61, 80; postbellum spread of, 37, 41–42; separatism, 65. See also Woman's Exchange movement

Working Woman's Guild (London), 113, 118. See also Princess Beatrice; Queen Victoria

Wright, Frances, 23–24, 136–37n

Kathleen Waters Sander has worked in higher education development and communications since the late 1970s, most recently as
director of development for the Department of Medicine at the
Johns Hopkins University. She also teaches history at the University of Maryland University College. She holds a Ph.D. from the
University of Maryland, College Park.

Women in American History

Women Doctors in Gilded-Age Washington: Race, Gender, and
Professionalization *Gloria Moldow*

Friends and Sisters: Letters between Lucy Stone and Antoinette Brown Blackwell,
1846–93 *Edited by Carol Lasser and Marlene Deahl Merrill*

Reform, Labor, and Feminism: Margaret Dreier Robins and the Women's Trade Union
League *Elizabeth Anne Payne*

Private Matters: American Attitudes toward Childbearing and Infant Nurture in the
Urban North, 1800–1860 *Sylvia D. Hoffert*

Civil Wars: Women and the Crisis of Southern Nationalism *George C. Rable*

I Came a Stranger: The Story of a Hull-House Girl *Hilda Satt Polacheck; edited by
Dena J. Polacheck Epstein*

Labor's Flaming Youth: Telephone Operators and Worker Militancy, 1878–1923
Stephen H. Norwood

Winter Friends: Women Growing Old in the New Republic, 1785–1835 *Terri L. Premo*

Better Than Second Best: Love and Work in the Life of Helen Magill
Glenn C. Altschuler

Dishing It Out: Waitresses and Their Unions in the Twentieth Century
Dorothy Sue Cobble

Natural Allies: Women's Associations in American History *Anne Firor Scott*

Beyond the Typewriter: Gender, Class, and the Origins of Modern American
Office Work, 1900–1930 *Sharon Hartman Strom*

The Challenge of Feminist Biography: Writing the Lives of Modern American
Women *Edited by Sara Alpern, Joyce Antler, Elisabeth Israels Perry, and
Ingrid Winther Scobie*

Working Women of Collar City: Gender, Class, and Community in Troy,
New York, 1864–86 *Carole Turbin*

Radicals of the Worst Sort: Laboring Women in Lawrence, Massachusetts, 1860–1912
Ardis Cameron

Visible Women: New Essays on American Activism *Edited by Nancy A. Hewitt and
Suzanne Lebsock*

Mother-Work: Women, Child Welfare, and the State, 1890–1930 *Molly Ladd-Taylor*

Babe: The Life and Legend of Babe Didrikson Zaharias *Susan E. Cayleff*

Writing Out My Heart: Selections from the Journal of Frances E. Willard, 1855–96
Carolyn De Swarte Gifford

U.S. Women in Struggle: A *Feminist Studies* Anthology *Edited by
Claire Goldberg Moses and Heidi Hartmann*

In a Generous Spirit: A First-Person Biography of Myra Page *Christina Looper Baker*

Mining Cultures: Men, Women, and Leisure in Butte, 1914–41 *Mary Murphy*

Gendered Strife and Confusion: The Political Culture of Reconstruction
   Laura F. Edwards

The Female Economy: The Millinery and Dressmaking Trades, 1860–1930
   Wendy Gamber

Mistresses and Slaves: Plantation Women in South Carolina, 1830–80   *Marli F. Weiner*

A Hard Fight for We: Women's Transition from Slavery to Freedom in South Carolina
   Leslie A. Schwalm

The Common Ground of Womanhood: Class, Gender, and Working Girls' Clubs,
   1884–1928   *Priscilla Murolo*

Purifying America: Women, Cultural Reform, and Pro-Censorship Activism, 1873–1933
   Alison M. Parker

Marching Together: Women of the Brotherhood of Sleeping Car Porters
   Melinda Chateauvert

Creating the New Woman: The Rise of Southern Women's Progressive Culture
   in Texas, 1893–1918   *Judith N. McArthur*

The Business of Charity: The Woman's Exchange Movement, 1832–1900
   Kathleen Waters Sander